D1118227

'Ethiopia demonstrates – as does this handbook for democrats – that democracy and development are indivisible.'
— **Hailemariam Desalegn**, former prime minister, Ethiopia

'Democracy is essential to governance, the rule of law and economic well-being. In Venezuela, we know to our cost what happens when democracy dies – we die with it. I urge all those concerned with the state of their nation to read *Democracy Works*, and act on its findings.'
— **María Corina Machado**, opposition leader, Venezuela

'We know the cost of failure of democracy in Zambia: a collapsing economy, disintegrating rule of law, a favouring of populist over productive policy, and social exclusion. *Democracy Works* persuades that fixing Africa requires nurturing, protecting and consolidating our democracies, a common interest of local citizens and the international community alike.'
— **Hakainde Hichilema**, presidential candidate, Zambia

'Much is made these days of Africa's buoyant prospects, of the dynamism to be found in the continent's youthful demographic profile and rapid urbanisation, especially when coupled with the embrace of new technologies. But this positive future is only possible if, as the authors vividly demonstrate here, African institutions are both democratic and effective.'
— **J. Peter Pham**, Atlantic Council, United States

'Democracy is key to Africa's success. It is the bedrock of competiveness. As *Democracy Works* shows, it demands good leaders and strong institutions.'
— **Saulos Chilima**, vice president, Malawi

'At a time when democratic values around the world are under threat, *Democracy Works* is a timely, clear and impressively researched analysis.'
— **Sarah Sands**, editor: BBC Today programme; former editor of *Sunday Telegraph* and *London Evening Standard*

'Democracy is not perfect, but it is the best system we have. In Tanzania we are seeing the cost of its failure all too clearly. This sober analysis reinforces the importance and need of democratic values for African countries to develop in a way that benefits their citizens.'

— **Zitto Kabwe**, leader of the Alliance for Change and Transparency, Tanzania

'Without growth, we have no jobs. Without democracy we lack the governance for growth. If you read one book this year on the benefits of democracy to Africa, make sure it's *Democracy Works*.'

— **Helen Zille**, premier: Western Cape, South Africa

'Politics matters to development – the more competitive the system, the better the prospects. *Democracy Works* will convert even the most hardened sceptics.'

—**Karin von Hippel**, director-general, Royal United Services Institute, London

DEMOCRACY WORKS

DEMOCRACY WORKS

Rewiring Politics to Africa's Advantage

Greg Mills
Olusegun Obasanjo
Jeffrey Herbst
Tendai Biti

Foreword by Ellen Johnson Sirleaf

HURST & COMPANY, LONDON

First published in the United Kingdom in 2019 by
C. Hurst & Co. (Publishers) Ltd.,
41 Great Russell Street, London, WC1B 3PL
© Greg Mills, Olusegun Obasanjo, Jeffrey Herbst, Tendai Biti, 2019
All rights reserved.

Printed in India

Distributed in the United States, Canada and Latin America by
Oxford University Press, 198 Madison Avenue, New York, NY 10016,
United States of America.

The right of Greg Mills, Olusegun Obasanjo, Jeffrey Herbst, and Tendai Biti to
be identifiedas the authors of this publication is asserted by them in accordance
with the Copyright, Designs and Patents Act, 1988.

A Cataloguing-in-Publication data record for this book
is available from the British Library.

ISBN 978-1-78738-145-2

This book is printed using paper from registered sustainable
and managed sources.

www.hurstpublishers.com

'One head alone is not enough to decide.'

— Ghanaian saying

Contents

Foreword

Liberia's transition from war to peace, stability and democracy after 2003 was a truly joint effort, involving multiple local and international actors working together.

Peace was possible through a combination of efforts led by the Economic Community of West African States with key support from the Nigerian and United States militaries. The United Nations Mission in Liberia was, from 11 September 2003, crucial in maintaining the Accra peace agreement. Internal groups, including the multi-faith Women of Liberia Mass Action for Peace, successfully pressured President Charles Taylor to attend peace talks.

Establishing democracy involved no less of a concerted effort. Looking back, I can see now that we could have done some things differently. We might have been tougher in trying to reduce the dependency of society on the government for income, and the systems of patronage that underpin this. Even today, some two-thirds of the national budget is spent on salaries, reducing the amounts needed for investment in key infrastructure. We could probably have worked differently, too, going beyond the establishment of institutions, in reducing corruption and deepening integrity in government.

It is difficult to determine an exact template for such transitions since each case is different. But there are some general rules that centre on the need to build institutions, laws and policies, and to change the policy and governance incentives away from public to private sector growth and employment. This demands getting the pain of reforms over with as early as possible, otherwise costly traits can become deeply ingrained.

All this requires strong leadership. There are both physical and moral components to this aspect. It involves tireless campaigning for your country and its best national interests. This requires leading from the front, setting an example, and never expecting others to do something you would not do yourself. It must be underpinned by moral courage, to do what is decent, honest and right. It requires sound judgement in making decisions informed by experience and advice, knowledge and understanding. And it necessitates making tough decisions. Leadership carries with it a duty to tell people when they are wrong, and not just to follow.

Individuals can make a difference. But success will ultimately depend on the strength and health of systems and institutions of government.

This book illustrates how the system of democracy is essential to the success of nations. This is not just for theoretical reasons, but for practical purposes. Democracy enables us to shine a light on corruption. It offers a peaceful remedy to alleviate pressures in society. It ensures that policies, like administrations, are more competitive, and thus deliver more to citizens. Democracy does indeed work for Africa.

Ellen Johnson Sirleaf
Former President of Liberia, 2006–18; Nobel Laureate, 2014
Member of The Brenthurst Foundation's Advisory Board
Monrovia, September 2018

Preface and Acknowledgements: Demography and Democracy

This book should be read in conjunction with *Making Africa Work*, which was published by The Brenthurst Foundation in 2018.

Making Africa Work outlines the biggest challenges that will face Africa's next generation: over the next three decades, Africa's population will double to nearly 2.5 billion people, which will make it the region with the highest number of young people globally. By then, more than half of all Africans will be living in cities. And this group of mostly young people will be connected through mobile devices. Properly harnessed and planned for, that book explained, this demographic shift can be an immensely positive force for change. It also illustrates how, without economic growth and jobs, population growth could prove a political and social catastrophe. *Making Africa Work* used both country and sectoral case studies to describe the challenges to prosperity in Africa, while identifying the strategies that have been successful in reducing poverty and increasing prosperity.

Making Africa Work highlights the link between democracy and development. This association is a key element in a prosperity agenda. Democracy has to go hand in hand with development; anything less is unsustainable. Democratic governments represent the interests of the general population, not just a connected elite. We argued that the bouts of stability that authoritarians can bring must be viewed sceptically, given the superior global economic performance and stability of democratic governments over the long term, in Africa as elsewhere. It is, in fact, democracies that can manage the changes that poor countries require far better than authoritarians.

Democracy is also invaluable for the basic freedoms it offers. This virtue is especially important given Africa's record of violence, human insecurity and state fragility.

Democracy Works, in turn, asks how we can learn to nurture, deepen and consolidate the democracies that are so necessary in Africa. It shows how democracies can be designed to address the particular political, economic and demographic challenges that Africa faces. Employing case studies of democratic transition inside and beyond Africa, it identifies a 'democratic playbook' that is necessary to meet the threats to free and fair elections. Additionally, the book argues that substantive democracy demands more than just regular polls. Democracy depends on the proper functioning of institutions, the rule of law and enshrined rights, including freedom of the press and checks on the executive.

Democracy Works is thus directed towards leaders and citizens who want to preserve, enhance and deepen their democratic structures and practices. It is meant to be a resource for members of civil society who are unsure of how to promote democracy in settings where leaders endure because they are able to manipulate the rules of the game for their own benefit. It aims to serve as a guide to all who want to enjoy the political *and* development benefits of democracy in what remains the world's poorest continent. Finally, it is for those donors and external actors who, especially after a number of ill-fated decisions, have to make critical decisions about the future of election observers and aid that promotes democracy and good governance.

* * *

Democracy Works is a product of a shared association through The Brenthurst Foundation. Established in 2005 by the Oppenheimer family, the bulk of the Foundation's efforts are spent working at the invitation of governments to strengthen Africa's economic performance. More information is available at https://www.thebrenthurstfoundation.org.

The Foundation's overall methodology, just like this book, revolves around collaboration across borders. In July 2018, the Konrad-Adenauer-Stiftung, the Foundation's long-time institutional partner, hosted a seminar attended by practitioners and scholars from around the world to review an early draft of this manuscript. Earlier, in 2017, it had hosted a meeting on devising a playbook for democratic elections in Africa. We are most grateful to the staff of the venue, the Villa la Collina in Italy, to Leila Jack and Henning Suhr for their organisational roles, and to the participants for making time available to lend their expertise. These events greatly enriched our findings. The Konrad-Adenauer-Stiftung also hosted two regional workshops in Tanzania and Tunisia in March and June 2018 respectively, which assisted in sharpening our understanding of the role of various local interest groups. Thanks go to Daniel El-Noshokaty, Holger Dix and Lukas Kupfernagel for their collaboration in this regard, and to Andrea Ostheimer for supporting this idea at its inception.

The result of more than 300 interviews across four continents, this book involved several complex study visits. Many people assisted to make this research agenda possible, helping to secure meetings and gladly offering their hospitality. Special thanks go to Maximilian Hedrich and Carlos Romero at the Konrad-Adenauer-Stiftung in Caracas; Lyal White in Chile; Luis Membreno in El Salvador; Tristan Pascall in Panama; Argentina's former finance minister, Domingo Cavallo; the high commissioner of India to South Africa, HE Ruchira Kamboj, and Ambassador Rajiv Bhatia in India; and Audrey Wang of the Taipei Liaison Office in South Africa. Eivind Fjeldstad and Mathilde Emilie Thue of the Norwegian-African Business Association arranged an important series of meetings in Oslo, as did Torben Brylle in Copenhagen, Ambassador Martin Slabber in Manila, and Barry Desker in Singapore. Thomas Vester and Daffyd Lewis assisted travel to Mauritius, Kenya and Tanzania, during which time a number of interviews were conducted, while the Polish Embassy in South Africa under Ambassador Andrzej Kanthak and Grazyna Koornhof organised an excellent study week in their country where we were warmly hosted by Patrycjusz Piechowski. Alex Vines kindly facilitated a trip to the Seychelles, along with Betrand Belle. Other interviews took place in Zimbabwe, Nigeria, Ethiopia, Somaliland, Liberia, Benin, Ghana, Guinea, Mali, Dubai, Mozambique, Lesotho, Morocco, Romania, Belgium, Mexico, Sri Lanka, Germany, South Korea, Niger, the United Kingdom and France. Jaco du Plessis was an invaluable 'fixer' during many of these trips, while Henry Sands and his team at Sabi Strategy offered important contacts and editorial backing.

A portion of the book was written up while Greg Mills was a visiting scholar at the Centre of African Studies at the University of Cambridge during June and July 2018. Christopher Clapham gladly and generously provided accommodation, sustenance and moral support for the duration, while Adam Branch and Victoria Jones were most welcoming at the Centre. Some of the case studies presented were published earlier in the *Daily Maverick*. Thanks go to its editor, Branko Brkic, for allowing their reproduction.

Our colleagues at The Brenthurst Foundation, Nchimunya 'Chipo' Hamukoma, Archimedes Muzenda and especially Nicola Doyle, were invaluable sources of reference material, while Ghairoon Hajad's role was essential in ensuring we ended up where we intended to go on the numerous study trips. Barney Campbell and Saul Musker proved tough but extremely helpful editors.

Finally, Nicky, Jonathan and Jennifer Oppenheimer have continuously and selflessly given their time and resources to the Foundation since its inception. In appreciation of her unwavering commitment to her adopted continent, this book is dedicated to the memory of Jennifer Ward Oppenheimer.

About the Authors

Greg Mills has directed the Johannesburg-based Brenthurst Foundation since its inception in 2005. He is the author of the best-selling books *Why Africa is Poor: And What Africans Can Do about It* (Penguin, 2010); with Jeffrey Herbst, *Africa's Third Liberation* (Penguin, 2012); and with Dickie Davis, Jeffrey Herbst and Olusegun Obasanjo, *Making Africa Work* (Tafelberg/Hurst, 2017). In 2008, he was deployed as strategy adviser to the president of Rwanda, has run strategic advisory groups in Malawi, Mozambique and Afghanistan, and has worked for heads of government in Ghana, Liberia, Lesotho, Kenya, Zambia and Zimbabwe. Mills holds a PhD from Lancaster University and an Honours degree in African Studies from the University of Cape Town. A member of the International Institute for Strategic Studies and Chatham House, and the Advisory Board of the Royal United Services Institute, in 2013 he was appointed to the African Development Bank's High-Level Panel on Fragile States. On the visiting faculty of the Royal College of Defence Studies, NATO's Higher Defence College and the South African National Defence College, he has also recently published *Why States Recover* (Picador Africa, 2014); and, with Jeffrey Herbst, *How South Africa Works* (Picador Africa, 2015).

Olusegun Obasanjo is the former president of Nigeria. He had a distinguished military career, including serving in the 1960 UN Peacekeeping

Mission to Congo and receiving the instrument of surrender on behalf of the Nigerian government from the opposing forces in the Nigerian Civil War in 1970. Having attended various educational institutions, including Abeokuta Baptist High School, the Indian Army School of Engineering and the Royal College of Defence Studies in London, he rose to the rank of general and became the Nigerian head of state after the assassination of the then military head of state in February 1976. He handed over to a democratically elected government in October 1979. Jailed for his pro-democracy views for three-and-a-half years until the death of General Sani Abacha in June 1998, on his release he was democratically elected president in 1999 and served two terms. With over 30 books in print covering a variety of topics, he pursues a passion for conflict resolution, mediation and development through a number of institutions, including the Olusegun Obasanjo Presidential Library in Abeokuta, Tana Forum and The Brenthurst Foundation.

Jeffrey Herbst is president of the American Jewish University based in Los Angeles. Previously, he was president and CEO of the Newseum in Washington, D.C. and president of Colgate University, a leading liberal arts college in the United States. Holding a PhD from Yale University, he has also served as provost and executive vice president for academic affairs at Miami University. Herbst started his career as a professor of politics and international affairs at Princeton University where he taught for 18 years. He is the author of *States and Power in Africa: Comparative Lessons in Authority and Control* (Princeton University Press, 2014) and several other books and articles. He has also taught at the universities of Zimbabwe, Ghana, Cape Town and the Western Cape. A member of the Council on Foreign Relations, and the Board of Freedom House, he has served on the Advisory Board of The Brenthurst Foundation since 2005.

Tendai Biti is the former finance minister of Zimbabwe's unity government (2009–13) and member of parliament. He served as the secretary general of the opposition Movement for Democratic Change (Renewal) team in contesting the 2018 presidential and parliamentary elections. In 1988 and 1989, during his studies at the University of Zimbabwe's law school, Biti was secretary general of the University of Zimbabwe's Student Representative Council, which led student protests against government censorship in academia. He became a partner of the law firm of Honey and Blanckenberg at the age of 26. He was detained without trial in 2008 and was arraigned, again, following the disputed 2018 election. In November 2013, he formed Tendai Biti Law, which specialises in international finance and domestic constitutional legal issues. He has been a visiting fellow at the Center for Global Development in Washington, D.C. and has testified before the US Senate Foreign Relations Committee.

Abbreviations

ANC	African National Congress
APC	All Progressives Congress
APRM	African Peer Review Mechanism
AU	African Union
CCM	Chama Cha Mapinduzi
CNE	National Electoral Commission
CPI	Corruption Perceptions Index
DPP	Democratic Progressive Party
DRC	Democratic Republic of Congo
ECOWAS	Economic Community of West African States
EPRDF	Ethiopian People's Revolutionary Democratic Front
EU	European Union
FRELIMO	Mozambique Liberation Front (Frente de Libertação de Moçambique)
GDP	gross domestic product
IMF	International Monetary Fund
INEC	Independent National Electoral Commission
IPS	Integrated Production System
KMT	Kuomintang
MDC	Movement for Democratic Change
MDM	Democratic Movement of Mozambique (Movimento Democrático de Moçambique)
MMD	Movement for Multi-Party Democracy
MPLA	Popular Movement for the Liberation of Angola (Movimento Popular de Libertação de Angola)

NDC	National Democratic Congress
NGO	non-governmental organisation
NPP	New Patriotic Party
OAU	Organisation of African Unity
PDC	Christian Democratic Party
PDP	People's Democratic Party
RENAMO	Mozambican National Resistance (Resistência Nacional Moçambicana)
RPF	Rwandan Patriotic Front
SADC	Southern African Development Community
SNM	Somali National Movement
SSS	State Security Service
STAE	Technical Secretariat for Electoral Administration
SWAPO	South West Africa People's Organisation
TPLF	Tigrayan People's Liberation Front
UK	United Kingdom
UN	United Nations
UNIP	United National Independence Party
UPND	United Party for National Development
UPRONA	Union for National Progress
US	United States
ZANU-PF	Zimbabwe African National Union-Patriotic Front
ZCTU	Zimbabwe Congress of Trade Unions

INTRODUCTION

The African Demand for Democracy

> A functioning, robust democracy requires a healthy, educated, partici-
> patory followership, and an educated, morally grounded leadership.
> — Chinua Achebe

A more positive future for African countries depends on their ability to make democracy work.[1] Strengthening Africa's democracies will improve the continent's development prospects. The alternative of authoritarian rule will not achieve long-term development. Across Africa, the record shows that the continent's 'big men' simply do not get things done as well or in as sustained a fashion as democrats. Fortunately, the available evidence suggests that Africans want democracy, contrary to international trends.

We define democracy as a system where there is universal adult suffrage, where voting is free and fair, the outcome of which reflects the people's choice, and there is a set of supporting institutions and freedoms. Democracy is invaluable for the basic freedoms it offers. This is especially important given Africa's record of violence, human insecurity and state fragility. The record also shows that the better the systems of democracy in Africa, the faster economic growth and more stable the society. While democracy of itself does not guarantee that good leaders are elected, it does provide the peaceful means to reject them next time around.

Making democracy work thus relies on much more than having free and fair elections. It depends on what happens between elections. It relies on the systems and institutions of government. It also hinges on what politicians want to do with the power they acquire beyond the power itself.

A less democratic world?

How Democracies Die; The People vs. Democracy: Why Our Freedom Is in Danger and How to Save It; How Democracy Ends; Can Democracy Survive Global Capitalism?; The Road to Unfreedom: Russia, Europe, America; Fascism: A Warning; Us vs. Them: The Failure of Globalism; Edge of Chaos: Why Democracy Is Failing to Deliver Economic Growth and How to Fix It; Anti-Pluralism: The Populist Threat to Liberal Democracy; It's Even Worse than You Think: What the Trump Administration Is Doing to America; How to Rig an Election ...[2] New book releases on the dystopian future of democracy have become common.

The heady days of the end of the Cold War seem a long time ago. When the Berlin Wall came down in November 1989, a new world seemed to beckon. In 1974, at the time of the fall of the dictatorship of Marcello Caetano in Portugal, there were only 41 democracies worldwide. By 1991, this had leapt to 76 of a total of 169 countries. By 2005, the number of electoral democracies had reached a high-water mark of 123 out of 192 countries worldwide.[3]

The fall of the Iron Curtain and the end of the Soviet Union were taken, in Francis Fukuyama's sensational words, to signal the 'end of history'. Many expected that liberal democracy would emerge as the final form of human government, putting an end to the dictatorships that had perpetrated horrific crimes against their own people for decades.[4] Sparked through popular dissent in the Eastern bloc, a fresh era beckoned – described by President George H.W. Bush as 'a new world order' – where, free from superpower interference and sponsorship, democracy would take root. By the late 1990s, the United States (US) government, for one, had set up democracy promotion programmes for more than a hundred countries. The example of the former Eastern bloc countries was fresh enough, it seemed, to encourage the promotion of democratic alternatives farther afield.

A quarter of a century on, enthusiasm for democracy seems to be declining, leading some to contend that the organising principle itself was in trouble. As Harvard's Yascha Mounk has argued:

> Citizens have long been disillusioned with politics; now they have grown restless, angry, even disdainful. Party systems have long seemed frozen; now, authoritarian populists are on the rise around the world, from America to Europe, and from Asia to Australia. Voters have long disliked particular parties, politicians, or governments; now, many of them have become fed up with liberal democracy itself.[5]

In the West, following the 2016 election of US President Donald Trump and other seismic political events such as the United Kingdom's (UK's) decision to leave the European Union (EU), democracy has suddenly been made to seem vulnerable to nationalistic populism and elections susceptible to digital and media malfeasance enabled by powerful interest groups.

The democratic trends worldwide are concerning. Autocratic China has become the world's second largest economy, without recourse to basic liberties or free elections. Russia's Vladimir Putin, Turkey's Recep Tayyip Erdoğan and the late Venezuelan leader Hugo Chávez have all developed playbooks for anti-democratic control. While they won power through elections, each quickly moved to undermine institutional constraints on executive power and ensure loyalty through the deployment of partisans to key positions, including the judiciary. In their model, the space for opposition parties and movements is constrained by controlling funding sources, while manipulating social media and buying up or censoring the news.[6] Here and elsewhere, including President Rodrigo Duterte's regime in the Philippines, such 'hybrid regimes', which combine elements of electoral democracy with autocratic governance, centre on strong, populist personalities and thrive on the absence of strong, functioning state institutions.[7]

As democracy enters an era of uncertainty in some parts of the world, authoritarians are, in fact, finding their international position more comfortable than in the past. As Freedom House put it in its 2018 report 'Freedom in the World': 'Democracy is under assault and in retreat around the globe, a crisis that has intensified as America's democratic standards erode at an accelerating pace.' The report found that 2017 was the 12th consecutive year of declines in global freedom. Some 71 countries suffered net declines in political rights and civil liberties in 2017, with only 35 registering gains.[8]

Strengthening democratisation in Africa amid a worldwide political recession will be difficult but is especially important. Should African countries, which account for roughly 25% of all states in the world, embrace freedom, the global picture will be profoundly altered.

Against the tide: The African demand for democracy

Yet, far from the West's weary cynicism about elections, whatever its imperfections and inadequacies, two-thirds of Africans polled in 36 African countries in 2014/15 by Afrobarometer responded that democracy is always preferable to any other type of regime.

Just 11% believed that a non-democratic regime can be better in some instances, while the balance said that 'it doesn't matter' what kind of regime their country had (12%) or that they 'don't know' (10%).[9] Democracy is not a Western imposition on African polities but the political system that the majority in the overwhelming number of countries support.

Most revealingly for the purpose of this study, in the Afrobarometer poll, on average 78% of Africans rejected presidential dictatorship and one-party rule and 73% opposed military rule as viable options for governing their countries.

Yet, as Figure 1 demonstrates, there are wide variations for support for democracy. In addition, Afrobarometer documents that after a decade of increasing support for democracy, demand for more freedom started to decrease in 2012. Why amid general support for democracy is there an

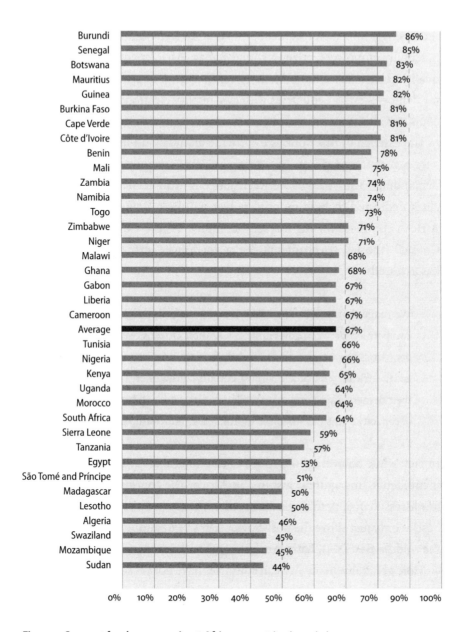

Figure 1: Support for democracy in 36 African countries (2014/15)

increasingly mixed picture? It appears that Africans value democracy when it actually empowers citizens. In particular, 'African countries with high-quality elections are more likely to register increases in popular demand for democracy than countries with low-quality elections'. Citizens in most countries also want more democracy than is available to them.[10]

The essence of this book is to provide analysis and lessons from countries across the world on how to make democracy work as Africans are demanding. The struggle between citizens who favour democracy and elites dedicated to holding onto power will be a defining issue in most African countries for the foreseeable future. As the National Intelligence Council (the US government's centre for longer-term strategic analysis) has assessed:

> We judge that Sub-Saharan Africa is entering a period of heightened competition between governments and their citizens over the nature of democratic governance that is likely to breed persistent volatility through 2022. African publics will almost certainly grow increasingly vocal in their demands for democracy, while African states will have mixed levels of capacity to insulate themselves from these bottom-up pressures.[11]

In fact, while on average one-third of elections across the globe are lost by incumbents, this figure is just 10% in Africa. The continent also has a very low assessed quality to its elections, which at 4.9 (on a scale where 10 is the best) is only just above the post-Soviet states (4.6) and Asia (4.8), but below the Middle East (5.4), Latin America (7.3) and Europe (8.9).[12]

More generally, many African countries have not yet solved fundamental issues of authority. For instance, the Fund for Peace lists six African countries (South Sudan, Somalia, Central African Republic, Sudan, Democratic Republic of Congo and Chad) among the ten most fragile in the world and another eight (Guinea, Nigeria, Zimbabwe, Ethiopia, Guinea-Bissau, Burundi, Eritrea and Niger) among the second ten most fragile.[13]

Identifying challenges to African democracy

Where basic institutions do not work, rule-based democracy is especially difficult. Young countries that suffer profound material deprivation have historically not been able to democratise.

These challenges have led some to advocate a slow transition to democracy, preferring instead coalition governments as a solution, especially in fragile circumstances, as will be seen in Chapter 8. There is also the belief across Africa, drawing superficially from the example of East Asian countries, that what poor countries need is an authoritarian who can make technocratic decisions for the benefit of the nation without the distractions of democracy. The appeal of the non-democratic 'developmental state' has been heightened by the well-publicised economic successes of Rwanda and Ethiopia, two countries that have notably emerged from disasters in the 1990s with political systems that are not free. Their actual record, which differs from the conventional wisdom in important ways, is examined in detail in Chapter 2.

The 'development first, democracy second' thesis supposedly epitomised by these states and others in Asia links with the view of Fukuyama that democratic institutions are only ever one component of political stability. According to this view, two other building blocks are required: a strong state and the rule of law. Fukuyama argues that it is necessary to get the sequence right. Without a strong state first, he believes that democracy will only amplify weakness since it is subjected to many competing and conflicting demands, eating away at its capacity to deliver and exercise authority. Yet, the paradox in this view is that without democracy, there is rarely a strong or legitimate state capable of reforming, of building capacity, or of respecting the will of the people. People who rule themselves have far greater opportunities to complain about governments they don't like, though the record of voting on the basis of economic performance in Africa rather than on the grounds of identity is patchy.[14]

When the prime minister of Malaysia, Mahathir Mohamad, observed in 1992 that 'authoritarian stability', as he termed it, has enabled prosperity, while democracy brought 'chaos and increased misery',[15] he could not have imagined the same system being responsible for returning him to power at the age of 92 in 2018.[16] Despite the recurrent enthusiasm for authoritarianism as a model to 'get things done', the sort of 'benign dictator' who is not corrupt but efficient, who maintains a paternalistic but admirable benevolence, almost never exists. The reality of such a model is, for the most part, quite different. Few of Africa's dictators have proved benign or developmentally astute. Most end their rule in chaos or violence, usually fatally so for the leadership. Before 1990, for example, sub-Saharan Africa had experienced 19 democratic elections, 14 undemocratic or contested elections and 77 incidents of undemocratic regime change. Seventeen heads of state had violent deaths in office or shortly after having been deposed in a coup.

The post-1990 reality of the continent is starkly different.

Since then, there have been significantly more elections. By 2016, there had been 118 democratic elections, 77 undemocratic or contested elections and 34 undemocratic regime changes. Eleven leaders suffered violent deaths in office. 'Democracies,' notes Kofi Annan, 'have far lower levels of internal violence than non-democracies. In an era when more than 90% of wars take place within, not between, states, the import of this finding for conflict prevention should be obvious.'[17] Democracy produces orderly changes of leadership. It enables people to be patient for their turn, rather than revert to a coup. Democracy, as now even Mahathir might admit, offers the opportunity for a peaceful reset.

Africa's third liberation

Africa's democracy project is thus central to what we have called in a previous work 'Africa's third liberation'.[18]

Starting in the late 1950s, the first uprising for freedom was the overthrow of the colonial powers, which happened faster and, with a few exceptions, in a more peaceful manner than was expected. The second such liberation was the escape, again overwhelmingly peaceful, from the authoritarian leaders who emerged in the 1960s and who helped to drive many countries' political and economic fortunes downward until the early 1990s. The third liberation comprises the debates that countries are having now about how to create economic and political systems that reflect the will of their people.

There has been an enormous amount of learning on how to promote democracy around the world. Accordingly, African countries do not have to start with a blank slate in developing more accountable systems of government. To be successful, leaders and citizens will have to design institutions that are aligned with their own countries' political, social and demographic realities, but they can do so armed with this scholarship and with examples of other countries around the world that have democratised in recent years. Therefore, in addition to the detailed fieldwork that forms the core of this book, we have conducted significant first-hand research in Latin America, East and South Asia and Central Europe to formulate advice and examples to be used by those engaged in the pursuit of freedom, democracy and progress across the continent.

This book is organised into three parts. In Part One, we discuss the state of African democracy. We first examine the possible virtues of democratic rule by reviewing cases where attention to popular preferences and the establishment of countervailing institutions have allowed for constructive economic policy and development. Chapter 2 then discusses why authoritarian rule is unlikely to have similar long-term returns, even though there may be cases where economic policy has been helpful in the short term. Finally, Chapter 3 analyses overall trends in African democracy.

Part Two of the book analyses the challenges to constructing African democracy in different transitional circumstances.[19] We rely on Freedom House's classification of 'free', 'partly free', and 'not free' states for two reasons.[20] First, they are comprehensive. No other system of rankings extends so far back in history, allowing us to summarise the continent's performance since the 1970s, or includes so many countries. Freedom House's work is also well known in Africa, including among African leaders, as opposed to more recent constructs that have appeared in academic journals, allowing our analysis and conclusions to be easily conveyed to the audiences we seek to engage.[21]

Chapter 4 examines the challenges of sustaining democracy in countries rated 'free' and that already enjoy a wide range of political rights, including free and fair elections, competitive politics and the protection of minority rights. Chapter 5 analyses countries in the 'partly free' grouping and how they can break out of the political stagnation that has resulted in at most only partial protection of political and civil rights. Finally, Chapter 6 discusses how those countries that are rated 'not free' can begin to change their political systems that have very restricted or no political rights, and 'are ruled by one-party or military dictatorships, religious hierarchies, or autocrats'.

Part Three examines two critical sets of issues. Chapter 7 discusses how elections can be made more free and fair. While we consistently argue that elections are not the end of democracy, countries cannot reap the rewards of democratic forms if the formal contests for political power are not credible. Chapter 8 reviews the role of outsiders in promoting democratic consolidation in Africa, a particularly fraught question given the emerging conflicts between African and non-African countries as well as the divisions among those who seek to influence events from beyond the continent's borders.

In the final section, the Conclusion makes recommendations for what government leaders, oppositions, civil society and external powers can do to promote democratic consolidation. While at the end of the day, the decisions of African leaders will be most consequential, we consistently argue that promoting an open political system is so complicated and fraught that there are roles for a great many actors in the ongoing African dramas.

* * *

No liberation is easy. The process inevitably involves the overthrow of old elites and entrenched systems of power, neither of which will change willingly. Yet, we are optimistic that in many African countries citizens will find a way to create political systems and vindicate those who previously fought to end colonial rule from Europe, then to end military rule, and now to end rule by the authoritarians whose power has enriched only themselves. The search for democracy remains a continuous work in progress. It is not a destination, but a journey.

We hope that this contribution will help with what we believe will be one of the great global questions of the twenty-first century: how Africans, who have been ruled for so long by others – be they foreigners or isolated elites – finally become fully empowered to design their own futures and to satisfy the needs and aspirations of every citizen.

Part One

THE STATE OF
AFRICAN DEMOCRACY

1

Why Democracy Works

Given our current politics, there is no option except pursuing multi-party democracy supported by strong institutions that respect human rights and rule of law.

— Prime Minister Abiy Ahmed, Ethiopia, July 2018

Chapter takeaways

- The coming doubling of Africa's population offers extraordinary opportunities and existential challenges.

- Currently, most African countries will not achieve the necessary growth to exploit the youth bulge because their governance records are not good enough to foster sustained development.

- Democracies are generally better governed and can offer significant economic benefits to citizens when institutions function well and politicians adhere to democratic norms.

- Democracies generally have lower levels of corruption and better judicial systems.

- Democracy has the potential to self-correct because of its institutions.

At 17h30 on 25 November 1981, Lieutenant Colonel 'Mad' Mike Hoare and a group of 43 mostly South African and Zimbabwean mercenaries flew into Seychelles International Airport on the island of Mahé in a chartered Royal Swazi Airways plane. Disguised as holidaying rugby players bearing gifts from a charitable beer drinking club, Ye Ancient Order of Froth-Blowers, used as a cover for a large group of mostly fit, young (all-white) men arriving on an island with fragile politics, their plan was to link up with a nine-strong advance party and take over the government on behalf of the former president, South African ally and full-time playboy James Mancham. They would do so in copybook *Dogs of War* fashion, by seizing the radio station, police station and the army camp to the south of the airport at Pointe La Rue.

A Second World War veteran, Hoare had plied his trade as a mercenary during various phases of the Congo civil war. In 1977, supporters of Prime Minister France-Albert René launched an armed coup in the Seychelles using Tanzanian troops while Mancham was at a Commonwealth summit in London. A socialist one-party state had been established after elections in 1979, nationalising businesses, seizing land, instituting a national youth brigade, and doing away with a free press and private schooling. In the process, René had made powerful enemies.

The wild scheme had been hatched between Mancham, a lawyer who became president upon Seychelles' independence from Britain in June 1976, those Seychellois dispossessed by René's nationalisations, and the apartheid South African government. Mancham had been 'enthusiastically wooed' by the disgraced former South African information secretary, Eschel Rhoodie, as a politically useful ally.[1]

The coup ended in ignominious failure when airport security discovered an AK47 in the false bottom of the bag of one mercenary. 'The airport security chief rushed outside and shouted an order that our waiting buses were not to depart,' recalled Stan Standish-White, then a 19-year-old Rhodesian SAS veteran. 'This precipitated immediate frenzied action among the team as each man tried to unite himself with his weapon, many of which were already on the roof-racks of the buses. I leapt up alongside an amazed porter and started hurling his neatly packed bags to the ground again. It was like one of those time warp situations. A bunch of gaudily dressed holidaymakers frantically assembling weapons of war while the civvies stood gaping, paralysed with shock and indecision.'[2]

The mercenaries eventually commandeered an Air India aircraft to fly them back to South Africa where they were arrested, tried and served sentences of various duration and severity. Yet, without the South African mercenaries' involvement, the coup would probably not have raised much of a glance at the time, given the volume of coups on the continent overall. It gained notoriety more because it was unsuccessful and less because, just like René's original putsch, it was unconstitutional.

The likelihood today of another successful mercenary-led coup in Africa in the genre of Bob Denard of the Comoros, the psychopathic self-styled 'Colonel' Callan in Angola, or the Seychelles misadventure, is negligible. Only the exceptionally stupid, arrogant or out of touch would even contemplate such an action. The misadventure in Equatorial Guinea in 2004 plotted by the hapless Simon Mann and Mark Thatcher, among others, is a case in point. Mercenaries aside, however, the African coup habit has not been broken completely. Since 2000, there have been not less than 32 attempted and 12 successful coups.[3]

The 1981 coup was not the last of political and military instability in the Seychelles. In August 1982, soldiers mutinied against conditions in the service. Having seized the radio station, they were overcome by Tanzanian troops, again requested by René. In 1992, a prominent local business person, Conrad Greslé, was arrested for his part in another coup plot, this time allegedly sponsored by the US Central Intelligence Agency.

René was elected unopposed in perfunctory 'elections' in 1983 and 1987. Then in 1991, in line with the winds of change of the time, he announced a return to a multi-party system of government. Among the returning exiles was the former president, James Mancham, who would (briefly and unsuccessfully) revive his Democratic Party. Illustrating how much political tensions on the island had lessened, he died peacefully at his home on Mahé in 2017. Elections held in 1993, 1998 and 2001 were all won by René, better known to his government and party colleagues as 'the Boss' or 'Ti France'.

René retired in April 2004, passing the baton to his vice president, James Michel, who in turn handed over to his deputy, Danny Faure, in 2016. Faure, born to Seychellois parents in the Ugandan town of Kilembe, studied political science in Cuba before starting his career in government at the age of 22. Appointed as minister of education in 1998, he went on to serve as minister of finance, during which time Seychelles carried out a series of International Monetary Fund (IMF)-advised reforms, before becoming vice president in July 2010.

Faure says that René's coup and the subsequent one-party state need to be viewed within the context of 'the geopolitics of the time. The ruling party considered itself a liberation movement. It believed that the only way to have transformation was through the establishment of a constitution that gave full power to the president, where there was fusion between the party and state.' He says that René himself believes that 'mistakes were made in the area of the economy, especially around the nationalisation of land, based as it was on the philosophy of the time that you needed to have both capital and land'. He admits that 'we imposed the state in everything, but lacked the right people with the right competencies'.[4]

As the politics have matured, the economy has grown steadily to the point where the 95 000 Seychellois enjoy the highest per capita income in Africa. This achievement is largely due to a steady increase in tourism, from 250 000 visitors in 2010 to 350 000 in 2017. The investment in an international airport in 1971, aimed at reducing the dependence of the fragile economy on fishing and copra harvesting, has paid spectacular dividends. Today the tourism industry accounts for 28% of gross domestic product (GDP), employs 75% of the workforce and brings in $400 million, or three-quarters of foreign exchange earnings.

The Seychelles possesses a remarkable international tourism brand. But its geography and natural beauty do not of themselves ensure the country's success. To its south, the Indian Ocean archipelago of Comoros has lurched from its own mercenary history through instability and economic crisis. Like the Seychelles, it is a melting pot of cultures; yet its politics and economy have routinely melted down, the difference between the two a $16 000 to $1 000 per capita economy. Better policy choices have been at the heart of the Seychelles' success.

One consequence of increasing liberalisation in the Seychelles has been much tougher political opposition. While the ruling People's Party (or Parti Lepep in Seychellois Creole) might have controlled every government since 1977, victory by the opposition Seychelles Democratic Alliance (LDS) in National Assembly elections in 2016 means that consensus now has to be sought as a matter of course. 'The role of the opposition,' admits President Faure, 'is to increase the level of scrutiny in the management of government and its financial affairs.' Still, concerns remain about corruption and lack of transparency, the treatment of migrant workers, especially in the free trade zone, and lengthy pretrial detention. Freedom House assesses the Seychelles as 'partly free'.[5]

'Africa,' says President Faure, 'has a history of coups, out of a belief that the only people strong enough to make economic progress were the military. But times have changed. We need to pay respect to creating and empowering institutions to give them capacity to do their job properly. Strong institutions protect the welfare of people, and enable economic prosperity. While we had popular participation before,' he observes, 'even in the one-party state, democracy has strengthened our stability. It has reinforced social cohesion by giving a voice to civil society and the media which previously was not there.'

Or, as the tourism minister, Didier Dogley, sums up, 'Democracy is very important to us, especially among that young population that has been educated in Europe and is used to these standards and values. Today we live in a different Seychelles to 1977. It is not the same Seychelles, and it is not the same world.'

* * *

Democracy is important in and of itself. No other political system developed in human history has allowed for the sustained expression and enjoyment of rights that all deserve. Functioning democracies do not kill their own people in significant numbers, or allow them to die from famine, or work to keep them from communicating with the rest of the world. Democracy is a particularly important issue in Africa because the continent has been governed for so long by those who have sought to prevent mass political participation and freedom of association, both in the colonial period and much of the post-independence era. Indeed, most African countries now hold multi-party elections on a regular basis, albeit of varying quality.[6] Today, even most authoritarians in Africa are all too ready to trumpet their devotion to democracy in grandiose speeches, even while they stifle it by their actions. The authoritarians' empty rhetorical commitment to democracy suggests that it has persuasive normative power, as leaders feel compelled to perform their allegiance to it even if only as a facade.

Regardless, there are voices across the continent who look at Rwanda, Ethiopia and certain East Asian nations – countries with authoritarian leaders that have performed well economically in recent years – and argue that a strong 'developmental state' with a severe leader who can supposedly make technocratic decisions without political influence is the better system. There is a long-held assumption that a developmental state cannot be democratic, and that democracy must follow economic development instead.

In this chapter, we first review Africa's governance and economic challenges and then explain why we believe that democracy will promote growth. In Chapter 2, we argue, on the basis of new fieldwork, that the lessons of Rwanda and Ethiopia and of East Asia have not been understood correctly.

The African governance and economic challenge

Merely reducing the chronic poverty that African countries face today is a challenge that places high demands on government and necessitates very effective political institutions. In addition, over the next 35 years, African countries will also be faced with an extraordinary demographic challenge. Most countries will double their population by 2050 and there is almost nothing that can be done to change this demographic reality. The continent's population is expected to more than double to 2.6 billion by 2050 and account for 57% of the world's growth in people.[7]

Africa's population growth will cause most countries to become younger, a trend that will occur at the same time that the rest of the world ages. As *The Economist* noted, 'Africans will make up a bigger and bigger share of the world's young people: by 2100, they will account for 48% of those aged 14 and under.'[8]

Or, put differently, the world's ten youngest countries will be in Africa.[9]

If properly planned for, Africa's population increase and the resulting large number of young people present an enormous opportunity and asset. Young people are tremendous sources of entrepreneurship, energy and willingness to innovate as new technologies emerge. If young people are able to participate in their economies, being the world's youngest continent would be a great advantage. The World Bank has estimated that the demographic dividend alone could generate 11% to 15% GDP growth between 2011 and 2030.

However, reaping the demographic dividend will be extremely challenging. China only managed to provide for its large and once impoverished population by growing its economy at 12% annually for 30 years. And the sheer scale is daunting. The IMF has estimated that, in order to maximise their booming population dividend, African countries will need to produce, on aggregate, an average of 18 million high-productivity jobs per year until 2035. The IMF also notes that over this period, policies are required to gradually transition jobs from the informal sector, which accounts for

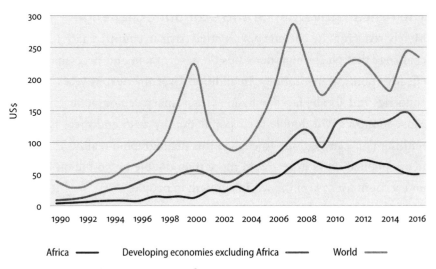

Africa ▬▬ Developing economies excluding Africa ▬▬ World ▬▬

Figure 1.1: Foreign direct investment inflows per capita, 1999–2016

about 90% of the 400 million jobs in low-income sub-Saharan African countries, to the formal sector.[10] To do so, the continent will have to radically change its current record of investment attraction.

To date, Africa's job creation has not kept up with existing birth rates. The *African Economic Outlook 2015*, for example, reported that only 7% of the continental population aged 15 to 24 in low-income countries had a 'decent' job. In Africa's middle-income countries, this figure increased marginally, to 10%.[11]

Increasing economic growth will demand creating the space for the private sector to operate, and the opportunities through which it can thrive. The African Development Bank observed that 'the private sector is Africa's primary engine of growth. It generates 70% of Africa's output, two-thirds of its investment and 90% of employment. Creating private-sector jobs is the most effective and sustainable strategy for lifting more Africans out of poverty.' The Bank also notes that 'Africa continues to perform poorly on standard governance indicators, scoring 30% lower than the Asian average and 60% lower than industrialised countries'. This helps to explain why

Africa performs so badly in attracting foreign direct investment, and thus driving diversified economic growth, as Figure 1.1 illustrates, compared to other developing markets. Foreign direct investment flows to Africa were just $59 billion in 2016, according to the United Nations (UN) Conference on Trade and Development, of the $1.75 trillion made worldwide, or 3.4% of foreign direct investment for 16% of the world's population.[12]

If leaders are not successful in reforming their economies, their countries will face great peril. The risks stemming from large numbers of digitally connected young people concentrated in urban areas without jobs are high, as was clearly demonstrated in the early 2010s by the Arab Spring. Young people who are pessimistic about their economic futures are unlikely to sit idly by waiting for change. They will demand it.

Democracy, good governance and economic growth

Democracy has a better long-term record in promoting economic growth. While a few authoritarians have accumulated some good years of growth in a small number of countries, there are many examples across Africa where those not held accountable to their citizens have made decisions that were directed at enriching the elite rather than elevating the masses.

Figure 1.2 illustrates the economic performance of the three Freedom House categories of countries over the last quarter-century. It shows that the freer the politics, the better the economic performance. It also indicates that democracies are more diversified and less dependent on one commodity for their development.[13] As the prices of commodities have gone down, democracies have been less negatively affected, given their comparatively diversified nature. And, finally, it shows that the real advantage, in terms of stability and prosperity, comes in the achievement of free status.

When they work well, democratic regimes improve accountability through elections where leaders are required to demonstrate what they

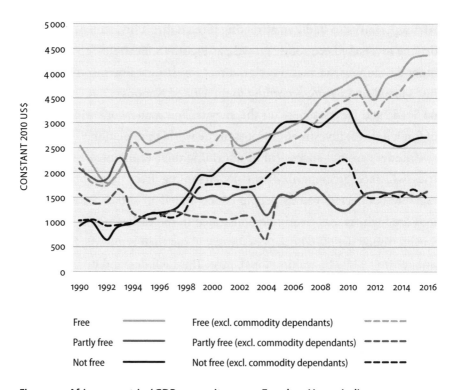

Figure 1.2: African countries' GDP per capita across Freedom House indicators

have delivered to voters in order to be returned to power. Timothy Besley and Torsten Persson, for example, have argued that democracy is important in creating institutions that serve common rather than narrow clientelistic interests.[14] Freer regimes also offer the possibility of testing philosophies in a competitive political market. Finally, one of the potential strengths of democratic systems is their flexibility and pragmatism. They enable consensus to be implemented and institutions to work, and corrections to be made, if necessary, in the regimes themselves.

To explore the empirical association between democracy and good governance, it is important first to describe the general political condition of each country. Since the early 1970s, Freedom House has classified countries as 'free', 'partly free' or 'not free', based on a combination of scores evaluating political rights and civil liberties. In its 2018 survey based on data from 2017, Freedom House found ten African countries to be 'free', 22 to be 'partly free' and another 22 to be 'not free'. Table 1.1 shows how each country is classified by Freedom House:[15]

Free	Partly free		Not free	
Benin	Burkina Faso	Mali	Algeria	Eritrea
Botswana	Comoros	Morocco	Angola	Ethiopia
Cape Verde	Côte d'Ivoire	Mozambique	Burundi	Gabon
Ghana	The Gambia	Niger	Cameroon	Libya
Mauritius	Guinea	Nigeria	Central African Republic	Mauritania
Namibia	Guinea-Bissau	Seychelles	Chad	Rwanda
São Tomé and Principe	Kenya	Sierra Leone	Congo (Brazzaville)	Somalia
Senegal	Lesotho	Tanzania	Congo (Kinshasa)	South Sudan
South Africa	Liberia	Togo	Djibouti	Sudan
Tunisia	Madagascar	Uganda	Egypt	Swaziland
	Malawi	Zambia	Equatorial Guinea	Zimbabwe

Table 1.1: Freedom House evaluation of ten African countries, 2017 data

We have compared the Freedom House categorisation of African countries with the judgements made by the Heritage Foundation's Index of Economic Freedom. The index is particularly persuasive because it measures 12 different aspects of how governments manage the economy grouped in four general areas: rule of law, government size, regulatory efficiency and open markets.[16] It also covers almost all African countries (only Libya, South Sudan and Somalia are not evaluated because of lack of data), an important consideration for our analysis.

This metric of economic governance has been shown to be strongly linked with the economic performance that is critical to Africa's future. As the authors of the Index of Economic Freedom note:

> There is a robust relationship between improvements in economic freedom and levels of economic growth per capita. Whether long-term (20 years), medium-term (10 years), or short-term (five years), the relationship between positive changes in economic freedom and rates of economic growth is consistent. Improvements in economic freedom are a vital determinant of rates of economic expansion that will effectively reduce poverty.[17]

Nations that have political systems that are judged 'freer' by Freedom House do better on these consequential measures of economic governance. The highest-ranking African country in the index is Mauritius, coming in at 21st (between Chile and Malaysia). The next highest-ranking African countries are Botswana (35), Rwanda (39) and South Africa (77). Of these four African countries, three are considered 'free' by Freedom House, while only Rwanda is 'not free'. It is particularly striking that the two countries – Botswana and Mauritius – with the highest degree of economic freedom have also been the democracies with the longest duration in Africa. Both countries have transformed their economies since independence in the 1960s when they were poor, even by the standards of colonial Africa, and when very few predicted that they would become the best performers on the continent in the next 50 years.

At the other end of the index, the lowest-ranking African countries (out of a total of 180 nations) are the Republic of Congo (Brazzaville) at 177, Eritrea (176), Equatorial Guinea (175) and Zimbabwe (174). All four are rated as 'not free' by Freedom House.

Looking systematically, it becomes clear that there is a correlation between political freedom and economic governance. Figure 1.3 portrays the average Index of Economic Freedom score (upon which the rankings are based) for each of the Freedom House classifications.[18]

Countries ranked 'free' are significantly better governed than those that are 'partly free' and do better than those that are 'not free'. Put another way,

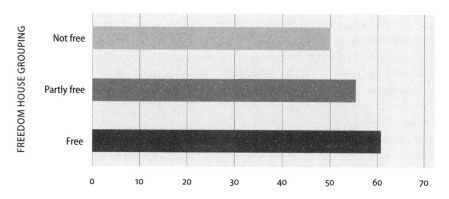

Figure 1.3: Index of Economic Freedom average

the 'free' countries have an index score that equates to Honduras, ranked number 94. The 'partly free' countries are scored most closely to Mongolia, Senegal and Papua New Guinea, which are ranked between 124th and 126th. The 'not free' countries have a score similar to Niger, which is ranked 160th.

The 'free' country scores may not seem impressive on a global scale, but that simply indicates how great the African governance challenge is. The overall ratings for Africa as a continent are similar to Pakistan, which is rated 131st.

To confirm the validity of the Index of Economic Freedom scores, we repeated the analysis using Transparency International's 2017 Corruption Perceptions Index (CPI) metrics. Transparency International's annual survey of corruption is widely read and, while no index of corruption can claim complete accuracy, the work that the organisation has done over many years has been highly influential. The CPI is also used in the Index of Economic Freedom but it is only one of many sources used in that aggregate.[19]

Again, the countries rated as 'free' by Freedom House are perceived as less corrupt than those that are 'partly free', which, in turn, are perceived as less corrupt than those that are 'not free'. If the 'free' category were a country, they would be equivalent to Malaysia, which is ranked 66th (out of 180)

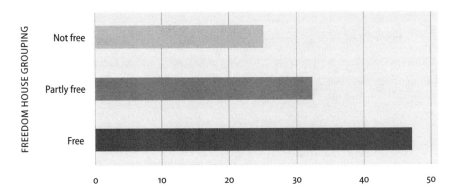

Figure 1.4: Average Transparency International score

in the world on the CPI. The 'partly free' countries would be equivalent to Ecuador, which is ranked 120th. The 'not free' countries as a grouping would be equivalent to Mozambique, which is ranked 157th. While it is true that even the 'free' countries' score is not impressive, this again reflects the poor African average overall. On aggregate, African countries get a score of 32, which is, as with the index, equivalent to Pakistan (rated 123rd in the world).

One of the primary reasons for the better economic performance of democracies is, in fact, the ability of popularly elected regimes to self-correct against corruption, an important consideration given how fraud and outright theft have hindered African economic performance. For instance, in Panama, rated 'free' by Freedom House, President Ricardo Martinelli promised to promote free trade, establish a metro, reform health care and complete the canal expansion project started by his predecessor. He did all this, but in the process was accused of using public money for illegal surveillance and of financial crimes, taking bribes and giving illegal pardons. In 2018, he was extradited from the US to face trial on these charges in Panama. Similarly, in El Salvador, also rated as 'free' (although it is also ranked 'most dangerous'),[20] the first president, Mauricio Funes, from the former FMLN (Farabundo Martí National Liberation Front) guerrilla movement, in power from 2009 until 2014, was found guilty of illegal enrichment. By then, Nicaragua had granted him political asylum. His presidential predecessor, Tony Saca, was arrested in October 2016, accused along with others in his administration of siphoning off $246 million of public money. Saca's predecessor Francisco 'Paca' Flores Pérez was accused (but never convicted) of having diverted $15 million in funding from the Taiwan government. Freedom allows these cases to be brought to light by a critical public.

Our work is also consistent with others who have found that democracies perform better. Analysis by Takaaki Masaki and Nicolas van de Walle substantiated the link between democracy and growth.[21] In scrutinising 43 (out of 49) countries in sub-Saharan Africa for the period 1982 to 2012, they found 'strong evidence that democracy is positively associated with economic growth', and that this 'democratic advantage' is more pronounced for those African countries that have been democratic for longer periods of time.

Similarly, Joseph Siegle has demonstrated that since the end of the Cold War, only nine out of 85 autocracies worldwide have realised sustained economic growth. Moreover, 48 of these autocracies had at least one episode of disastrous economic experience (defined as an annual contraction in per capita GDP of at least 10%) during this period.[22]

There is a link, too, between democratic and more broadly determined 'development' performance in this regard. Of the top 51 countries in the UN Human Development Index[23] – i.e., those classified as having 'very high human development' – 41 are deemed as 'free'; four (Hong Kong,[24] Kuwait, Montenegro and Singapore) as 'partly free'; and six (Bahrain, Brunei, Qatar, Russia, Saudi Arabia and United Arab Emirates) as 'not free'.

One frequently cited critique of this argument, highlighted by Jason Seawright, is that the association between democracy and development actually runs in the reverse direction.[25] In other words, that development causes democracy in the long run, and must therefore come first. This is often used as a justification for authoritarian rulers who claim that their country must 'grow now and democratise later'. The difficulty in resolving this controversy is that cross-national correlations, which merely compare outcomes in democratic versus non-democratic countries, cannot reveal which way the causation runs.

Accordingly, we have conducted detailed case studies of particular countries to explore the actual mechanisms by which democracy creates development. It is clear from a close examination of these cases that democracy brings about development by specific means: through curtailing corruption and increasing accountability, preventing the risk of expropriation and abuse of power, and increasing competition, which allows for leadership rotation and policy innovation.

We first turn to Mauritius, one of Africa's exemplary cases – rated 'free' by Freedom House in every year since 1988 – which demonstrates the powerful political and economic benefits of an institutionalised democracy.

Mauritius: An exemplary case of democracy and growth

The success of Mauritius is often ignored today because it has been such a high performer for so long that its achievements seem preordained. In fact, there was nothing automatic about the success that Mauritius has garnered. The reason it is relatively rich today is due to the decision very early on, unlike the vast majority of African countries, to opt for not only the form of democracy but the practice of its politics, which tends to soften the hard edges of conflict.

Mauritius is at the top of the charts when it comes to African governance, not surprisingly given its democratic record. Its average score in the World Bank's Doing Business indicators is 77.54, ranking it 25th worldwide, compared to the sub-Saharan average of 50.43, or the score of its Indian Ocean neighbour Madagascar in 162nd position at 47.67. The next highest sub-Saharan African country, Rwanda, is in the 41st slot. Kenya is

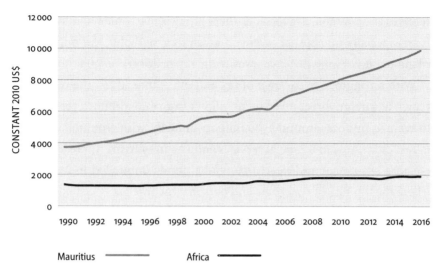

Figure 1.5: Africa and Mauritius: GDP per capita comparison

at 80th, South Africa 81st and Botswana 82nd. Similarly, on the Ibrahim Index of African Governance, defined as the provision of political, social and economic public goods, Mauritius again tops the African rankings, scoring 81.4 in 2017. Seychelles is second with 73.4, and Botswana completes the top three with a score of 72.7.

Mauritius' relative wealth is a reflection of its excellent governance record over a long period of time along with its liberal financial system. It has a GDP per capita of $9 630, well above the sub-Saharan African average ($1 464), and that of Madagascar ($401) and South Africa and Botswana ($5 284 and $6 924). Only in this key regard does it rank below Seychelles where, with a population of just 95 000, it is over $15 000. The average life expectancy of Mauritians in 1960 was 58; now it is 74, whereas sub-Saharan Africa has gone from 40 to 59 over the same period.

From a low-income economy based on agriculture, principally sugar cane, Mauritius has progressed quickly, diversifying through textiles, apparel and tourism into offshore financial and technology sectors. The number of tourists has doubled in this century alone. Mauritius now receives as many tourists today as there are citizens, some 1.3 million. This is an especially notable achievement given its geography. Not only is it an island but it is a long distance away from any major travel hub.

With an aggressive package of tax and other incentives, the island has grown its foreign direct investment inflows from $1.6 million a year in 1970 to average, by 2018, around $500 million annually, with around half of this in real estate, 16% in financial services and 13% in tourism. There are 21 500 offshore businesses and nearly 930 global funds domiciled in Mauritius, where the top rate of corporate and personal income tax is just 15%.

Yet, in the early 1960s, analysts gave the island little hope of progress, given its geographic isolation, rapid population growth and a fraught colonial history. Mauritius surprised even close observers because they did not appreciate how the early turn to democracy would help the island nation grow. In particular, political freedom has fostered a developed legal system and code that have made the foreign investment climate in Mauritius one of the best in the region, along with other strong institutions. However, Mauritians have greatly benefited from this system as well. Some 90% of entrepreneurs in the Export Processing Zones and in the manufacturing sector are Mauritian nationals.

Mauritius has also taken what it can from the past and used its heritage to create a civil polity.

On the quayside of the new waterfront in Port Louis is a statue of Sir Seewoosagur Ramgoolam, viewed as the father of the nation and known by his nickname Chacha (literally, 'uncle'), who led the independence movement. Facing him, across the road, is a statue of the ambitiously named Bertrand-François Mahé de La Bourdonnais, a central figure during the French colonial period between 1721 and 1810. This juxtaposition is not surprising since Mauritian politicians are at pains to point out the importance of racial inclusion in their society, especially of the tiny (perhaps 1%) French minority, which continues to wield a disproportionate economic influence.

Ramgoolam was the first prime minister of a coalition government of the Labour Party and the Parti Mauricien Social Démocrate. In 1969, the opposition Mauritian Militant Movement, led by Paul Bérenger, was founded. As Bérenger notes, 'we were very, very radical – sometimes called the Mauritian Marxist Movement and even,' he smiles, 'the Mauritian Military Movement'. He was among the Mauritian Militant Movement leaders held, as he refers to this period, 'in political detention' for a year in 1971 after strikes, which led to an outbreak of violence.[26]

Yet by 1982, Bérenger was in a coalition government serving variously as deputy prime minister, minister of finance and foreign minister, and was prime minister from 2003 to 2005, the first white to serve as head of government of a post-independence African country.

Speaking from his study in Vacoas piled high with government documents, Bérenger says that Mauritius was 'supposed to fail rather than succeed. Things in our history and at independence were indicative of trouble ahead. Many in the private sector were against independence, and 44% of the population voted against it in a referendum. There was violence in the run-up and immediately afterwards, and elections were postponed in 1969. It was,' he recalls, 'the Wild West of politics' at the time.

However, Mauritius did not go the way of many African countries for several reasons. First, he notes, 'the Labour Party, which, too, was very radical, did not go ahead and nationalise industry, even though some saw this as a betrayal, including my own party. If we had done this we might have ended up as another Zimbabwe.' The result was a clear division of responsibility between what the state saw as its role and that of the private sector. Second, reflects Bérenger, 'personalities were also important. The old man, Sir Seewoosagur Ramgoolam, was very special. We fought like mad, but got on very well.'

And third, 'democracy has undoubtedly also played an essential part in Mauritius' success, along with the constitution, which is very strong on fundamental freedoms, separation of power and protection of private property. We have an exemplary electoral set-up, with an independent electoral commissioner with the security and tenure of a judge, with their own staff, and an electoral commission chosen by the president after wide consultation.'

All this does not mean, he notes, that Mauritius is without other problems, including 'corruption and abuses of power – though compared to other countries in Africa, we are better'. The democratic system also allows, he admits, accountability, policy innovation and self-correction. In fact, in 2018, President Ameenah Gurib-Fakim was forced to resign over accusations that she had misused credit cards provided by a private charity. This was an extremely rare instance where charges of corruption toppled a head of state in Africa, even though the actual sums of money involved were trivial compared to the amount routinely diverted by many other leaders across the continent.

Mauritius' vice president, Barlen Vyapoory, 'definitely agrees' that the island's 'economic success is related to our democratic success', maintaining that 'democracy is like, as Churchill said, the worst system of government apart from all the others. We have believed in the process of democracy as the best option, and we have worked towards making everyone feel secure, through welfare and through accommodating each ethnic group's aspirations.'

'Democracy,' he notes, 'has to work hand in hand with education to be a bottom-up process. This has enabled us to capitalise on our strengths. And it has ensured political stability and security, and institutional development, which has played in our favour.'

Of course, the vast majority of countries in Africa were not born democratic and did not begin their economic transformation so early in their history. Instead, most followed a more tortuous path that usually included retrograde movements due to poor policies. One of the virtues of democratic governments is that they offer the potential to halt and reverse decline as the voters' voice is heard and institutions react to dysfunctional practices.

A powerful example of self-correction is offered by South Africa, which suffered enormously from 'state capture' under Jacob Zuma, but whose institutions were able to wrest power from strong vested interests. South Africa demonstrates, in particular, that while democracies can suffer from corruption, they have avenues to resolve dysfunctional politics that are not open to authoritarian regimes.

South Africa: Self-correcting democracy

South Africa was part of the post-Cold War world turn from dictatorships to democracies between 1990 and 2005. Yet, by the end of 2017 it was faltering. A generation on from the end of apartheid, with the country marching towards its fifth election, it appeared to be democratic only in name since the capture of the state by a cabal was seemingly nearly complete.

South Africa's dramatic downward spiral began with the election of Jacob Zuma as president in 2009. Zuma had had 783 criminal charges pending and had been dismissed as deputy president in 2005 by President Thabo Mbeki due to concerns that he was corrupt.

Eight years after achieving ultimate power, Zuma's plans for state capture had seemingly succeeded. A master of manoeuvre, deception and control, he substantially eroded the integrity of state institutions through political appointments and with the help of his friends. As befitted a KGB-trained head of the intelligence department of the African National Congress (ANC) in exile, he quickly captured key aspects of the security sector, extending its control into the heart of parliament and its tentacles into public life.

Enemies were fabricated, deflecting attention from the process of state capture. The targets shifted from 'counter-revolutionary' forces, who were then succeeded by 'white monopoly capitalists', a convenient political caricature of powerful white industrialists and interests seeking apparently to keep black South Africans from benefiting from and taking part in the mainstream economy.[27] In response, new, more radical legislation was promulgated around mining, black indigenisation and land reform.

While such slogans offered the pretext for accelerated radical economic transformation, they were the guise for making significant money through public procurement and to distribute public funds to the faithful. By 2016, the state itself revealed that 40% of its R600 billion budget in goods and services was being lost to fraud and inflated expenditure. Perhaps as much as R100 billion was funnelled directly into corrupt purposes.[28] These findings were announced amid increasing concerns about the budget, with lower tax collection, higher tax rates, and greater and more expensive borrowing on international markets.

In 2014, at the start of Zuma's second term, the public protector reported on the upgrades at the president's private residence at Nkandla.[29] The report found that President Zuma was required to pay back a reasonable portion of the money spent installing non-security upgrades at his residence. A cattle *kraal*, chicken run, swimming pool, visitors' centre and amphitheatre were built at public expense at Nkandla, justified as a security upgrade. On appeal, the full bench of the Constitutional Court found in March 2016 that the president should pay back the money. It also found that the National Assembly's resolution exonerating the president from liability was inconsistent with the constitution and unlawful, and that the president had failed to 'uphold, defend and respect' the constitution. In September 2016, six months later, it was confirmed that President Zuma paid back the R7.8 million he owed for these upgrades.

These judgments were initially ignored by Zuma and he seemed unaware of the humiliation. He appeared similarly nonplussed, amused even, at the fisticuffs that erupted in parliament during the State of the Nation address in February 2015, and routinely thereafter.

While the president may have been immune to the courts and parliament, the markets were more sensitive. An important moment was the appointment of Des van Rooyen as finance minister for four days in December 2015, which wiped R500 billion ($33 billion) off South African assets, including R95 billion ($6.3 billion) off the value of the state pension plan alone as the rand plunged to record lows. Zuma claimed, 'Des Rooyen is my comrade, MK [Umkhonto we Sizwe – the ANC's military wing] for that matter, he's a trained finance and economic comrade and more qualified than any minister I have ever appointed in the finance issue.'[30] Still, the president eventually backtracked, replacing Van Rooyen with Pravin Gordhan, a respected former finance minister. The rand staged a partial recovery.

Despite the president's protestations, Van Rooyen was a frequent visitor to the Saxonwold, Johannesburg, home of the notorious Gupta family, who enjoyed a close relationship with the president and his family. The Guptas had remained firmly anchored to Zuma when he had been 'released' from his position in July 2005. The family moved from computers into mining and media with Zuma's accession to the presidency, establishing the *New Age* newspaper and ANN7 television channel in 2010. Government contracts for transport and coal fed their burgeoning empire, drawing in international names including McKinsey,[31] EOH, SAP, and Bain & Co., along with Bell Pottinger, the now-defunct London-based public relations firm.

Zuma's regime was described privately by some government ministers as a 'mafia', one that was poisoning South Africa's politics and economy. The extent of the rot was indicated by the takeover of the Waterkloof Air Force base outside Pretoria in April 2013 for the guests to be flown to the wedding of the Gupta brothers' niece.

Van Rooyen's costly appointment seemed to have occurred simply because of President Zuma's frustration with the Treasury's reluctance to endorse a trillion rand nuclear power station deal with Russia, for which it was alleged large kickbacks were to be paid.[32] The deputy finance minister, Mcebisi Jonas, had been appointed in the expectation that he was a pliant figure.[33] However, when he turned out to be the opposite, it was decided that his boss, Nhlanhla Nene, had to be shifted to make way for

Van Rooyen, the 'weekend special' as he became known on account of the duration of his finance ministerial tenure.

Jonas publicly confirmed in March 2016 that he had been offered Nene's post by the Gupta family in exchange for R600 million.[34] Spurious charges were brought against Jonas' boss, Minister Gordhan, both as a means of soaking up his time and energy and of tarnishing his good name. Then, in October 2016, Gordhan revealed in a court affidavit that R6.8 billion (then $490 million) in payments made by the Gupta brothers and companies they controlled had been reported to authorities as suspicious since 2012.[35]

Another important moment was the November 2016 report of the public protector into state capture. In 355 pages, Advocate Thuli Madonsela and her team outlined just how much control the Gupta family had over South Africa's resources and the state itself.[36] It was little surprise when President Zuma, as well as two ministers implicated in the report, went to court to stop its release. The report offered proof that the president sanctioned the use of state companies for personal enrichment.

There was also a legion of courageous civil society activists, including Sipho Pityana who launched into Zuma at the August 2016 funeral of ANC stalwart Makhenkesi Stofile, and in so doing instigated a campaign to 'Save SA' from President Zuma, whom he called the 'champion of corruption'.[37] In response, the government went out of its way to condemn non-governmental organisations (NGOs) who, in the words of Zuma's state security minister, David Mahlobo, were working 'to destabilise the state'. As he put it, 'there are those who are used as NGOs, but they are not. They are just security agents that are being used for covert operations.'[38]

Despite the accusations, the president rode out the storm. In the months immediately following the report's release, at least three ministers challenged him in the inner sanctum of the ANC, the 100-strong National Executive Committee, though he was able to retain power.[39] Then, in March 2017, Zuma fired the two ministers in the Treasury who had been the greatest thorns in his side, Gordhan and his deputy, Jonas. They themselves only heard of this on the television news, and the president did not speak to them about it before or after.

South Africa seemed desperate. The economy was dipping into recession. Investors were turning their backs. Public services were faltering. State capture seemed nearly complete, with just the courts and constitution to go.

However, the public was not all fooled. Zuma had paid a heavy price at the polls, especially in the August 2016 local government elections, losing control of three major cities – Tshwane, Port Elizabeth and Johannesburg – to the official opposition, the Democratic Alliance. At the same time, some public figures and investigative reporters and writers found their voice in bravely working to expose state capture.[40]

Zuma's fortunes started to unravel with the release of hundreds of thousands of emails from the Guptas in May 2017. Brought to light by the Centre for Investigative Journalism, amaBhungane, in collaboration with the *Daily Maverick*, the emails showed the extent of the Gupta family's control over cabinet ministers, state-owned companies and the South African Revenue Service and their involvement in government contracts. It was no longer possible to deny the details of state capture, or its agents.

Next, Zuma's candidate for the December 2018 ANC elective conference, his former wife and once head of the African Union Commission, Nkosazana Dlamini-Zuma, lost to his arch-rival Deputy President Cyril Ramaphosa by a margin of just 179 votes in over 5 700. Within two months, Zuma was out of a job and Ramaphosa had become president, promising 'ethical behaviour and ethical leadership' in signalling a break with the Zuma era's years of economic decline and rampant corruption.[41]

Zuma was evicted ultimately because enough of his own party turned against him. But the ANC acted only when it became abundantly clear that it was risking a calamitous showing at the polls in 2019 in the face of mounting civil society pressure through media investigations and revelations, and by the courts holding firm. It was the full democratic package that worked to exert pressure on the party. There were some extremely brave individuals in the public sector – notably Madonsela, Gordhan and Jonas – who acted as role models around which civil society could mobilise.

But they were all able to operate because at South Africa's core was a commitment to constitutional democracy. As Helen Zille, the long-time leader of South Africa's liberal opposition and premier of the Western Cape, reminds us: '[Jacob Zuma] was evicted because democracy is about checks and balances on power. The opposition does not get the credit for this, but without the role of parliament and these checks and balances, those who claim the credit among civil society or even in the ANC itself would not have the space in which to operate.'[42]

The greatest asset in the struggle against state capture was possibly President Zuma himself. The irony is that Zuma's actions, instead of driving the country towards populist authoritarianism, energised civil society and provoked public support for constitutionalism, the courts and the rule of law. As Anthony Butler noted at the time, 'one day the country may look back on this President [Zuma] as democracy's accidental saviour'.[43]

On the other side of the world, Chile demonstrates that even a powerful ruler without policy or personal dysfunctions cannot by himself (or herself) deliver economic success. While General Augusto Pinochet was celebrated as an enlightened despot, Chile has actually boomed in the post-coup, democratic era.

Chile: The democrats are the real successes

Chile's economic growth since the 1980s has been nothing short of remarkable, particularly during the 1990s when it averaged an annual rate of over 7%. In 1972, it was recorded to have the second-worst economy in Latin America, inflation had reached 500%, and there were frequent strikes and widespread nationalisation. Price controls and high tariffs were pervasive, with the state controlling two-thirds of economic output. Yet, from poverty levels of 50% and a per capita GDP of just $730 in 1975, real income per person has increased to over $13 000 in four decades.

Today, poverty in Chile is just 11%. Whereas there were 300 000 students in higher education in 1992, today the figure is 1.5 million. Two-thirds of children are educated in high-quality private schools. Life expectancy is 79 years, higher than the US. It has the highest Human Development Index ranking in Latin America (38/188 countries), ranks 26/180 on Transparency International's Corruption Perceptions Index (second behind Uruguay in the region),[44] and scores 'free' on the Freedom House rankings.[45]

Some authoritarians are likely to attribute Chile's success to the military government of Pinochet, who overthrew Salvador Allende's leftist government and stayed in power for 17 years until 1990. While the military regime was bloodier than most, with 3 000 killed, it was also better able to manage the economy than most of its Latin American counterparts. The shock treatment it provided was excessive, but it stopped the inflationary, statist chaos of the Allende period.

Chile's true success, however, was built on three pillars.[46]

The first was the institution of free market economic reforms in the mid-1980s. The second pillar, economic transformation, relied on a massive increase in domestic copper production. Copper, of which Chile supplies nearly one-third of the world's annual consumption, accounts for two-thirds of the country's export revenue.[47] The transformation of this sector over a quarter of a century has been spectacular. In 1990, the private sector accounted for less than one-quarter of Chilean copper mining output. By the end of the 2000s, the state mining company CODELCO (Corporación Nacional del Cobre de Chile) was producing more than twice as much copper as it had done 20 years before; yet the private sector was responsible for two-thirds of the annual national output of six million tonnes. In 1970, Chile produced the same amount of copper as Zambia; four decades later it produced eight times more. Foreign investment was facilitated by low and stable taxes and non-discriminatory treatment of foreign and local companies. Chilean tax laws provided for a 'contract' between the investor and the state of Chile, the establishment of free trade zones, the introduction of policies guaranteeing the remittance of profits and capital, free choice as to the percentage of foreign ownership and non-discrimination with local investors, and tariff liberalisation.

By 2011, foreign capital totalling almost $82 billion had been invested in the mining industry, more than half of all foreign capital since 1974.[48] Byzantine labour policies were unwound through a series of measures aimed at decentralising collective bargaining, improving transparency in union voting and allowing greater choice in union membership. Reform of the pension system in 1980 allowed workers to opt out of the government-run pension system and instead put the formerly mandatory payroll tax (10% of wages) in a privately managed Personal Retirement Account.

Third, despite the pervasive mythology of the authoritarian growth thesis, economic prosperity really took off with democratisation in the 1990s. As the veteran economist Ricardo Ffrench-Davis reminds us, the growth occurred because 'you have to negotiate with the other side in a democracy. You cannot be a dictatorship of just one view.' Difficult decisions lay behind the country's impressive political, social and economic progress, though as the former president, Eduardo Frei, notes, 'If you are not achieving unity in your decisions, you cannot solve the problems of the country.'[49]

Frei's successor as president, Ricardo Lagos, noted the critical importance of changing leadership empowered by voters: 'It [extending terms in office] might be good for President Xi, but it's bad for China. You need to have a renewal of leadership. Every generation will have different views and will come with their "epic" moment. In our case it was to defeat Pinochet. I know,' says the former president, 'what the experience was in Singapore with Lee Kuan Yew. I understand what some are also saying in Africa. But you have to understand as a leader that all the accruements of power you enjoy are because you represent the state, and it is not because of you. Five or ten years is enough, no more than that, otherwise it is going to be a tremendous mistake and a problem especially for the younger generations.'

Chile's experience also speaks of the importance of policy stability, which can, somewhat paradoxically, be ensured by democracy. 'We have enjoyed the sort of continuity we have never had before in our history,' states Frei, 'the same coalition in power for 20 years. And all finance ministers were there for the whole period of government.'

Conclusion: Democracy and prosperity

Africans want democracy when it works, and democracy can, as Mauritius demonstrates, provide significant economic benefits to citizens when institutions function well and politicians hew to democratic norms.

Democracies also have a built-in self-corrective capacity, as South Africa shows in enabling the transition from Jacob Zuma's costly misrule to the government of Cyril Ramaphosa. This transition illustrates the importance of having a full range of functioning and well-resourced institutions – parliament, the public protector, the attorney general and the courts. Chile also illustrates how a country can change its political path with overwhelmingly positive results from a system that promises order through military rule to one that delivers through democracy – and not just authoritarians committed to democracy.

Yet, there still is great scepticism about democracy because of vague hopes that other systems can do better, the costs of continued party competition in the run-up to elections, and the significant self-interest on the part of rulers. We next turn to an evaluation of the nominally successful cases of Rwanda and Ethiopia, along with the example of Singapore, often held up by African leaders as a model, to show why these really should not be considered as persuasive alternatives to the aspiration of Africans to have both democracy and development.

2

The Authoritarian Myth

Oppression is not an alternative to poverty. Nor is development an alternative to freedom. Poverty and oppression go hand in hand, while true development means freedom from both.

— Kofi Annan

Chapter takeaways

- Rwanda's record since the 1994 genocide is impressive. However, its authoritarian-led development is made possible by a set of circumstances not found in other African countries.

- Ethiopia's nascent democratic reforms, despite its growth record with an authoritarian government, suggest that even its substantial economic successes are no substitute for greater freedom.

- Singapore's development is due to more than just Lee Kuan Yew. While visionary leadership is an essential prerequisite, success demands having a group of people with a commitment to development and the capacity to argue how to bring it about.

- Those who argue that authoritarian rule is worth the sacrifice of freedoms that Africans value have not proved their case.

The view of Maputo is today dominated by the 137-metre concrete towers of the three-kilometre bridge linking the Mozambican capital with Catembe on the other side of the port's estuary, making it the longest suspension bridge in Africa. Designed by a German firm, the $725 million project is being constructed by the China Roads and Bridges Corporation, the 8 000 tonnes of steel supplied by Chinese steelmaker Angang Steel Co.

From building bridges and airports, railways in Kenya and roads in rural Ethiopia to running mines in the Congo, China has radically changed the African economic landscape this century. Trade between Africa and China has grown at around 20% annually since 2000 from $10 billion in 2000 to $190 billion by 2017, nearly three times as much as the US, and investment has grown to $40 billion, just behind the UK ($56 billion), US ($58 billion) and France ($49 billion).[1] China lent some $125 billion to Africa between 2000 and 2016, and pledged a further $60 billion at the 2018 Forum on China-Africa Co-operation.[2] The number of Chinese firms working in Africa has increased to 10 000, and the number of Chinese workers and business people has risen from virtually zero in 1990 to somewhere between 250 000 and two million 20 years later, the discrepancy due to the undocumented status of many migrants. It is estimated that 12% of Africa's industrial production, or $500 billion annually – nearly half of Africa's internationally contracted construction market – is carried out by Chinese firms.[3]

China's demand for resources has also driven up commodity prices. China was responsible for over 30% of the increase in global demand for crude oil in the 2000s, 64% of the increased global demand for copper, 70% of demand for aluminium and 82% for zinc. By 2008, China had 7 000 steel factories, double the number in 2002.[4]

This progress reflects China's own economic transformation and the demand of its increasing middle class for housing, cars and consumer goods. The superlatives are hard to beat. 'The most powerful man in the world' read The Economist's cover in October 2017, in reference to China's President Xi Jinping.[5] Its economic growth, which touched 13% between 2000 and 2008, has been primarily responsible for a dramatic fall in the number of people worldwide living in poverty (defined as less than $1.90 a day), which dropped by nearly 1.1 billion between 1990 and 2013, even

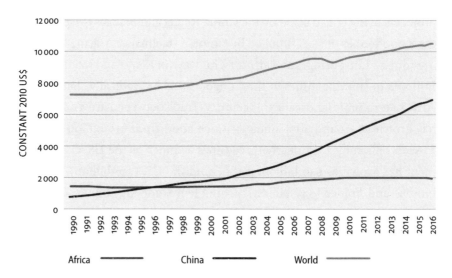

Figure 2.1: Growth and per capita wealth: China, Africa and the world

as the world's total population expanded by nearly 1.9 billion over this time. Today, as a result of China's transformation, over half of the world's poorest now live in sub-Saharan Africa.

Instead of reforming along liberal lines as some predicted would occur as it raised living standards and incomes, China has advanced a different worldview, centred on massive state-led initiatives such as the Belt and Road Initiative, an aid, trade and infrastructure scheme through which China would elevate itself to global pre-eminence in three decades. Far from domestic political liberalisation, in March 2018, the Chinese National People's Congress removed term limits for the president and vice president and Xi was reappointed by the Chinese legislature as president. This gambit runs counter not only to Western, liberal democratic concepts, but those of China itself. Deng Xiaoping's reforms did not only guide China towards a market economy, but mandated retirement age at 70.

For those Africans tending towards autocracy, the Chinese model is enticing, one of economic growth without serious political competition.

The same can be said for those businesses that might prefer not to have to negotiate the vagaries, inertia and checks and balances of African parliamentary systems.

However, the prospects of simply transplanting the Chinese model to Africa seem far-fetched. China is a country with over one billion people and has been a state, in one form or another, for centuries. The Chinese Communist Party has a degree of control over society, organisation in the countryside, and ability to draw upon security and technological resources to suppress the population that are without equal in Africa. More than a million Communist Party officials have been disciplined for corrupt practices in recent years,[6] and thousands executed annually. Moreover, there is little evidence that most citizens in most countries, with their commitments to democracy documented in the Introduction, would stomach the Chinese means of ensuring rules-based development, such as the forced movement of millions of people or even the drastic methods to end corruption, often without due process. Respect for human rights is at the forefront of African public debate, even if they are often ignored by governments in practice.

In sum, it is questionable whether the Chinese authoritarian development experience offers a model for African government. For one, much of Africa has already attempted an authoritarian path, which has been overwhelmingly rejected by its citizens, and which failed to deliver. Critically, there is also much more to the Chinese model than just economic liberalisation *sans* economic reform. It involved significant and ongoing bureaucratic reforms to ensure efficiency and accountability. As Yuen Yuen Ang cautions: '[F]or other authoritarian governments keen to emulate China, their leaders should not pick up the wrong lessons. China's economic success is not proof that relying on top-down commands and suppressing bottom-up initiative work. In fact, it's the exact opposite: the disastrous decades under Mao proved that this kind of leadership fails.'[7]

* * *

49

The nuanced question that China raises is not if its model can simply be copied by Africans. Rather, the fundamental issue is if its example has changed the nature of the debate in Africa about the benefits of more locally produced authoritarianism. In this chapter, we take a granular look at how Rwanda and Ethiopia, seemingly successful authoritarian states in Africa, have really worked in practice. We also focus on the experience of Singapore, perhaps the most influential example in the debate over regime type and economic development, given its famous nominally authoritarian leader and sustained growth, diversification and development success.

The longing for a political silver bullet

Development is difficult. Almost every African country has had its share of disappointments. Long before China became an economic success, it was tempting for African leaders to dismiss institutionalised political competition as wasteful and costly for their poor states, and as an impediment to action. This was one of the foundations of the movement towards *de jure* one-party states that quickly swept many African countries after independence in the 1960s. The movement's ideological champion was Tanzania's Julius Nyerere who famously said that democracy was 'an over-sophisticated pastime which we in Africa cannot afford'.[8] Kenneth Kaunda argued, when establishing Zambia's 'one-party participatory democracy' in 1973, that it would allow for a focus on human development and at the same time defend the country against possible foreign interference. 'Having attained independence, the people, through their party,' said the Zambian president, 'have proclaimed one-party participatory democracy as the only political system that could safeguard it.'[9]

Of course, there have always been those authoritarians who simply wanted to monopolise power and therefore associated their unquestioned rule with the country's well-being. Few African countries have gone as far as Burundi, which elevated President Pierre Nkurunziza to the rank of 'supreme eternal leader', a title that certainly has at least one error. Even though he subsequently announced he would not stand in the 2020 election, Nkurunziza's consolidation of power reflects the ambitions of many leaders, even as they stage an elaborate show of elections.[10]

Our discussions with numerous African leaders suggest that, while they have hardly ignored China's example, the lessons from a country with over a billion people are of only limited relevance. More important has been the recent example of Rwanda. Over a span of only a few months, three African heads of state or government told us without prompting how much they had been impressed by Rwanda. The country has, as discussed below, had a high growth rate and has reduced poverty markedly since the genocide in 1994.

Rwanda's president, Paul Kagame, has become the most prominent African sceptic of the relationship between democracy and development. 'Genuine democracy,' he has remarked, 'can never be equated to election cycles.' The emphasis, he has said, on such 'cycles' is often at the expense of sustainable socio-economic development. 'Those who disagree with or criticise our development and governance choices,' he said in 2013, 'do not provide any suitable or better alternatives. All they do is repeat abstract concepts like freedom and democracy as if doing that alone would improve the human condition. Yet for us, the evidence of results from our choices is the most significant thing.'[11]

Rwanda: Replicable across Africa?

It is indisputable that Rwanda has made dramatic progress in its development and security since 1994.

In April 1994, when South Africa emerged from apartheid to enjoy the warmth of global acclaim after its first democratic election, Rwanda descended into genocide. Rwandans slaughtered one another in a cauldron of tribal-political violence, pitting Hutu against Tutsi, radical against moderate, village against village, neighbour against neighbour, friend against friend, and even, at its horrific climax in 'mixed' marriages, husbands against wives and parents against children. A 30 000-strong Hutu Interahamwe ('those who attack together') militia affiliated with the dominant political party spearheaded the attacks and fed hate ideology that denigrated the Tutsi as *inyenzi* – 'cockroaches'. The violence was carefully planned and implemented by a cabal of ethnic Hutu extremist elites in the context of civil war, with the intention of eliminating political opponents in naming an ethnic 'other' in the Tutsi. Not only were more than 800 000 killed in this premeditated onslaught, but the 100 days of slaughter left more than 300 000 orphans and two million refugees, among them the remnants of the Génocidaires who fled mostly to Zaire (as the Democratic Republic of Congo was then known) and Tanzania.[12]

Rwanda became, over 100 days, 'hell in a small place', an unadulterated illustration of the cost of getting things radically wrong, of playing the exclusive politics of racial identity at the expense of national unity, liberty and security. As the Genocide Memorial Centre in Kigali reminds, 'The country smelt of the stench of death … Rwanda was dead.' It was the consequence, the memorial contends, of 'a highly centralised, repressive state with a single party system', propelled into terrible action by an economic slump coming from the fall of the global coffee price in the mid-1980s.

Little wonder then that Kagame, *de facto* Rwandan president since the Rwandan Patriotic Army he led took power from the fleeing interim government in July 1994, does not permit politicians to mobilise on ethnic grounds.[13] The official line is that there are no Tutsis or Hutus, only Rwandans. This political philosophy assists the access to power of the minority Tutsi, of course, like Kagame, but there is a wider and more practical dimension to this diktat, an imperative to foster a sense of encompassing nationalism subsuming ethnic differences, thus preventing the genocide from ever reoccurring. Officials cite the pre-colonial history in this regard,[14] when Rwanda supposedly shared 'one language and one culture and the same race ... like any society ... defined by wealth, economic activity and political power', where the term 'Tutsi' referred to richer cattle owners, 'Hutu' to subsistence farmers, and 'Twa' to the poorer class, dependent on casual labour and hunting for survival.

As the Rwandan high commissioner to South Africa, Vincent Karega, notes: 'We come from a divided, bipolar country with extreme poverty, coupled with ignorance and a lack of education. To get to democracy, we have to address the fundamentals of unity, access to education and information, increasing income, and building institutions.' While he does not discount the emergence of a 'fully fledged, Western democracy', he adds, this ambition 'will always have to be adjusted to context'.[15]

'We believe,' Karega says, 'that democracy should not be intermediated, by NGOs for example, but rather should go down to the grassroots, to the village level, to youth and other organisations to hear their views. We don't want to gamble,' he reflects, 'as we have seen the costs of failure, and have experienced the fear. So we prefer to talk less about democracy than to talk about governance, about eliminating corruption, increasing economic chance, and providing opportunity at the lowest possible levels to tell government their views.'

Kagame and the ruling Rwandan Patriotic Front (RPF) hold the view that tribal ties will become irrelevant if there is enough prosperity to go around. Instead of rival ideologies that threaten mass violence, Kagame's Rwanda offers tightly controlled development infused by Rwandan characteristics: the concept of *Umuganda* ('coming together in common purpose to achieve an outcome'), for example, whereby communities work together on the last Saturday of every month to conduct shared projects; or the ideas of *Imihigo* ('to deliver') and *Guhiganwa* ('to compete among one another') around which local authorities are empowered; or the better known concept of local justice, *Gacaca* ('a bed of soft green grass'), which enabled a local truth and reconciliation process.

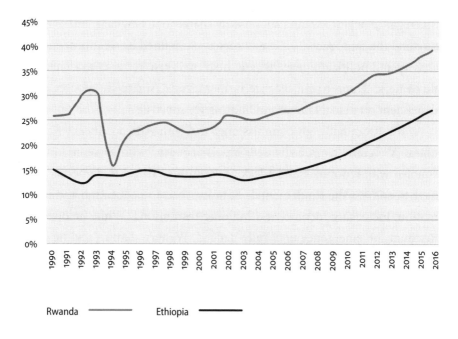

Rwanda ⸺ Ethiopia ▬▬▬

Figure 2.2: Rwandan and Ethiopian per capita income as percentage of African average

A quarter of a century on from its terrible trauma, Rwanda is an exceptional African story, due to economic growth rates that enabled some of its 12 million citizens to escape the dire poverty of the early 1990s.[16] For example, between 2005 and 2016, Rwandan income per capita grew at an annual rate of 5.2%, second in Africa only to Ethiopia. Literacy has increased from 60% in 1994 to 70% two decades later, while child mortality has been halved and primary school attendance has trebled. The poverty headcount ratio using the national poverty line fell from 78% in 1995 to 45% in 2010/11 according to the World Bank.[17]

While Rwanda remains poor, indeed much poorer than the African average, like Ethiopia, its wealth has risen faster elsewhere across Africa, as Figure 2.2 illustrates, all the more impressively so given the inheritance from the genocide.

There is much to admire and attempt to replicate, especially given

Rwanda's traumatic history.

Rwanda is immediately accessible to foreigners, which explains their admiration at a personal level. The country's national airline works efficiently and Rwanda offers all travellers visa-free or visa-on-arrival access, which is remarkable in Africa.[18] The capital is clean with safe streets and traffic police who do not seek bribes. The country is adjudged the ninth safest country in the world by the World Economic Forum (behind Finland, United Arab Emirates, Iceland, Oman, Hong Kong, Singapore, Norway and Switzerland), which is all the more noteworthy given the history.[19]

Rwanda is also a standard-bearer for women, who make up the majority in parliament, at 64% the highest proportion in the world. It ranks fifth overall (behind only Iceland, Finland, Norway and Sweden) in the World Economic Forum's gender equality rankings. At 86%, Rwanda has one of the highest rates of female labour force participation worldwide, compared to 56% in the US, for example. As the World Economic Forum noted in 2017, 'Not only are participation rates high, but the wage gap is narrower – in Rwanda, women earn 88 cents for every dollar men do; in the US, it is just 74 cents.'[20]

Decisions in government are increasingly data-driven, and implemented. Rwanda is well organised, despite the president's occasional frustrations. Cabinet ministers are held publicly accountable for targets. In 2018, for example, at the annual government retreat, Kagame took senior officials to task over their inability to work together to the benefit of the country.[21] The Rwanda Development Board actively and efficiently woos and processes investors.[22]

Rwanda has used its scant resources exceptionally well. The World Bank's Ease of Doing Business statistics put Rwanda as the second most competitive economy in Africa, after Mauritius (25th), and, at 41st in the world, way above others like Costa Rica (61st), Morocco (69th), Botswana (81st) and South Africa (82nd).[23]

It has had to overcome its landlocked geography, sometimes cited as an insurmountable obstacle to African development, by focusing on removing trade barriers in East Africa. Rwanda has also coped with its status as continental Africa's most densely populated country (at 440 people per square kilometre, compared to the sub-Saharan average of ten times less, and a world average of 57 per square kilometre). Instead, it has turned this density to its advantage in rolling out infrastructure.

Rwanda's leadership is compellingly focused and tough-minded, though Kagame's outspokenness is sometimes a lightning rod for international criticism.[24] For him 'development is a marathon that must be run at a sprint'.[25] He has managed to be critical of aid and clamp down on internal critics, while maintaining the support of donors, an impressive juggling act. External assistance has averaged at 45% of government revenue since the genocide, justified by donors in spite of the authoritarian politics and on the basis of Rwanda's record of delivery.

The country also has an impressive record in using technology to its advantage, for example in the delivery of blood supplies through drones,[26] in introducing electronic cargo tracking, and in funding for start-ups. It has led in Africa in using laptop technology in schools.[27] In 2018, Rwanda was ranked third in Africa in science, technology and innovation by the African Capacity Building Foundation.[28]

There are other positive lessons to admire and from which other African nations might learn. Kagame has assiduously cultivated a following among international personalities as a means of support and external diplomatic 'protection'. As a regular user of Twitter, Kagame has noted, 'We used communication and information warfare better than anyone. We have found a new way of doing things.'[29] His list of international admirers includes influential figures such as former British prime ministers Tony Blair and David Cameron, former president Bill Clinton (who described the Rwandan as 'one of the greatest leaders of our time'), former British international development secretary Clare Short (who oversaw the increase in her country's aid in the 1990s) and Andrew Mitchell (whose official memos emphasise that 'Rwanda is an excellent development model and delivers results'),[30] along with Howard Schultz, CEO of Starbucks, who was persuaded to invest there, and Howard Buffett, the son of Warren Buffett.[31] They have been willing to stake their reputations on Kagame, whatever his obvious democratic shortcomings, at least by Western standards. Buffett went so far as to say in a 2016 World Economic Forum session chaired by Blair that 'the bottom line is that if we didn't think President Kagame was going to be here another seven years, we wouldn't even consider what we are trying to do'.[32] Together Blair and Buffett called on the donors to 'Stand with Rwanda' in the face of threats from Western governments to cut aid on account of Kigali's role in the Congo in 2013.[33]

African leaders cannot fail to be impressed that Kagame has managed to be such a favourite of donors and powerful figures while changing the constitution so that he could remain in power for decades and maintaining a rhetorical independence and criticism of donor intentions at the same time.[34]

But there are aspects that African leaders would do well to avoid, not least since they might eventually trip up Rwanda.

While Kagame notches up economic successes and scores international acclaim, his regime's iron fist is seldom hidden and the political space greatly constrained. Rwanda has been ranked as 'not free' politically every year since the RPF's liberation of the country in 1994. Kagame was, for example, re-elected for a third seven-year term as president in August 2017 with an unbelievable 98.79% of the vote.

Rwanda performs similarly poorly in terms of media freedoms, placing it 159th out of 180 on the Reporters Without Borders' Press Freedom Index.

Kagame cannot, as *The Economist* concludes, rule a country on fear forever.[35] The newspaper noted that 'a land ruled by fear can never be happy or secure'. This critique points out that the only robust, independent institution in Rwanda is the RPF, which is accused of 'rampant' cronyism. 'Having the ruling party, rather than the state, exert such control,' *The Economist* notes, 'is trebly worrying. It is an invitation to rent-seeking. It is a deterrent to private investment at a time when growth is slowing and debts are rising. And it virtually guarantees that no other party can compete with the RPF.'[36]

Rwanda's tough approach towards its critics has come at some cost to its regional relations, too, notably with South Africa. In 2014, just weeks after the murder of his former top spy Patrick Karegeya in a South African luxury hotel, Kagame warned that dissidents 'will pay the price wherever they are' and that 'We don't seek permission to defend our country'.[37] This threat came on the back of several plots on the life of the Pretoria-based dissident Rwandan general, Faustin Kayumba Nyamwasa.[38] Such violence has caused some foreign investors to worry about the security of their stakes.

Rwandan hypersensitivity towards external criticism, while understandable given the history and the imperative for stability and the overall attentiveness to perceptions of external meddling, risks alienating an otherwise well-inclined and influential audience. At Kagame's swearing-in ceremony in 2017, he said of international critics that 'attacks on our character only make us stronger'.[39] And Rwandan officials appear to be unable or unwilling to tolerate any external appraisal and much less criticism of the regime, an intimidation tactic that reflects badly on their democratic credentials. For example, Clare Akamanzi, the otherwise exceptional CEO of the Rwanda Development Board, referred to the BBC's John Humphrys as 'either ill-informed or unintelligent' and 'biased' for questioning Rwanda's sponsorship of Arsenal Football Club despite its receiving international aid, and Kagame's rule.[40]

Finally, there is a set of unique circumstances present in Rwanda that suggests that both its model, and the role of a Kagame-like figure, would not be similarly successful elsewhere in Africa. As a very densely populated nation, Rwanda has always been much easier to rule than other African countries, whose people are generally distributed over a comparatively vast hinterland. Indeed, Rwanda has a long history of relatively strong pre-colonial state rule compared to other African countries. In a fundamental way, the genocide in 1994 was the best example of a powerful (although profoundly misguided) state that was able to mobilise a vast constituency at short notice to do things – killing neighbours, friends, spouses – that most people would have found unimaginable. Rwanda, unlike most other African countries, had a tradition of a strong, capable state long before Kagame. He has simply put state power to better use.

At the same time, the history of genocide has enabled authoritarian rule in a specific way. Kagame justifies his rule because of the horrors that happened only a few years before and it is reasonable to believe that Rwandans of all backgrounds will do almost anything to avoid even the possibility of a repetition of the violent past. Other African governments simply do not have the same ability to argue that it is their rule or else disaster. Of course, as time passes and an ever-greater percentage of Rwandans have no personal memory of their national tragedy, Kagame's argument that his way is the only method to prevent the horrors of the past will become less and less credible.

Without increasing media openness and greater political inclusion and competition, there is a risk that eventually Kagame, or his successors, may go the way of Yugoslavia's Josip Broz Tito, another leader whose authoritarian rule was said to be essential to holding an ethnically diverse country together. There is little left of the marshal's legacy today as his country was torn apart little more than a decade after he died and is now divided into seven ethnically defined nations.

This begs a critical question for Rwanda under Kagame: is authoritarianism necessary for its continued success? Somewhat ironically, the need to loosen control is recognised by Kagame himself. He once remarked that if he was unable to find a successor by 2017, 'it means that I have not created capacity for a post-me Rwanda. I see this as a personal failure.'[41]

Ethiopia: Demography and democratic yearnings

'I work seven days a week,' says Prime Minister Abiy Ahmed Ali from Menelik Palace, his official headquarters in the centre of Addis Ababa, 'for $300 a month. I am not getting rich, but I am not corrupted. I have a modest office,' he indicates down the red-carpeted hallway, making the point.[42]

'But I am interested in making change.'

Abiy swept in as prime minister in April 2018, upsetting the established Tigrayan-dominated political order, which had effectively ruled Ethiopia since the fall of Mengistu Haile Mariam's Marxist-Leninist regime in May 1991. Abiy's predecessor, Hailemariam Desalegn,[43] had resigned in February 2018 because of what he personally described as his 'failure to progress reforms'.

Both Hailemariam and Abiy share the view that democracy is key to Africa because of the need to meet seismic demographic changes. As Hailemariam put it: 'Democracy is an existential issue for Ethiopia. There is no option but multi-partyism.'[44]

Both cite the pressures created by having 70% of Ethiopia's population under the age of 30. 'The median age [in Ethiopia] is falling to between 16 to 18,' notes Hailemariam. 'Unless we have a truly democratic state, we will not be able to provide for them.' Not only should the government 'appreciate the frustration young people have', he says, but it has to acknowledge that there 'is no extra choice that authoritarian regimes give us over democracies in meeting these challenges'.[45]

Ethiopia is a much bigger and more complex country than Rwanda – or, for that matter, Singapore, to be discussed below. It is, alongside Rwanda, one of the two great African economic growth successes over the past 15 years. However, despite the legitimacy that its high economic growth record might be thought to garner, Ethiopia has been racked by political demands for more openness. The dramatic changes brought by Prime Minister Abiy in 2018 repudiated the authoritarian economic model that was previously seen as an important aspect of Ethiopia's positive development story.

Understanding what has happened in one of Africa's largest and most complex countries is therefore critical to assessing the role of democracy in development, and the leadership challenges and obligations involved.

Ethiopia had long been synonymous with poverty and man-made disaster. After Emperor Haile Selassie was overthrown in 1974 by Mengistu's Soviet-backed dictatorship, the country descended into chaos, best known for mass killings and the starvation brought on by the government's retrograde economic policies. After Mengistu was overthrown by the Ethiopian People's Revolutionary Democratic Front (EPRDF), Meles Zenawi became prime minister and ruled until his death in 2012. Even though the fighters of the Tigrayan People's Liberation Front (TPLF) had led the war against Mengistu, Meles recognised that Tigrayans, just 6–7% of the population, could not rule without the support of others. The EPRDF therefore includes the TPLF along with three other parties, the Oromo People's Democratic Organisation, the Amhara National Democratic Movement and the Southern Ethiopian People's Democratic Movement. Each party has 45 seats in the EPRDF, a structure that grants the Tigrayans disproportionately more power than they possess in population terms alone.

After several years of consolidation to combat the chaos of the civil war and an extraordinarily wasteful war with Eritrea in 1998, Ethiopia began a dramatic and impressive growth trajectory. Its annual economic growth rate averaged 10.5% from 2005 to 2016, better than that of China or India during the 2000s. This record is particularly impressive given the scale of its challenge: landlocked, with a population of over 100 million people (making it Africa's second most populous nation after Nigeria), which is increasing at 2.5% per annum, and required to exercise governance over 1.1 million square kilometres.

In 2005, Ethiopia's annual foreign direct investment inflow was $200 million, equivalent to 3.6% of GDP, similar to Chinese inflow ratios during the 1990s. It then increased tenfold.[46] Between 2010 and 2016, for example, the stock of foreign direct investment increased by $11 billion.[47] Ethiopia's development progress can be seen visibly, not only in the capital, Addis Ababa, and other major towns, but through the road network and into the countryside, contrasting markedly with the histories of famine and conflict for which the country had been notorious.

Ethiopia's high rate of economic growth has been cited to extol the virtues of strong leadership and a 'developmental state'. During the first visit by a sitting US president to the country in July 2015, President Barack Obama commended Ethiopia's progress in development while controversially describing the government as 'democratically elected'.[48] Earlier, on his death in August 2012, Meles was praised by America's UN ambassador, Susan Rice, as leaving 'behind an indelible legacy of major contributions to Ethiopia, Africa, and the world'. Former British Prime Minister Gordon Brown described his demise as 'a tragedy for the Ethiopian people'. Brown's successor David Cameron recalled him as an 'inspirational spokesman for Africa', while Bill Gates tweeted that he was 'a visionary leader who brought real benefits to Ethiopia's poor'. In the *New York Times*, Abdul Mohammed and Alex de Waal declared that Meles' passing 'deprives Ethiopia – and Africa as a whole – of an exceptional leader'.[49]

Given its guerrilla-struggle origins, it was not surprising that the EPRDF under Meles traditionally adopted a far-left, 'command' economic model, with the state at the centre. This has morphed into a 'developmental state' narrative, but still one in which there is little space for the private sector, especially foreigners, to operate. Banks are state-owned and there is, for example, no stock exchange, simply because there are no shares and stocks to trade. The private sector, which is supposed to be driving the productive side of the economy, has been frozen out by the power of the state, both through competition from state-sponsored or state-owned enterprises, and by a squeeze on investment capital created by the government's need to extract resources for its infrastructure plans.

Then, in 2014, things started to fall apart. Demonstrations in the Oromia and Amhara regions, home to the two biggest ethnic groups in the country, had their roots in economic conditions and political restrictions. Protests erupted in Oromia, which makes up one-third of the population, after a master plan was unveiled to expand the boundaries of the capital, Addis Ababa, with local farmers fearing their lands would be confiscated. Shortly thereafter, the Amhara people, who comprise nearly 27 million, launched protests in their region.[50] 'Our reforms,' Hailemariam notes, 'had been going too slowly to save the country from ethnic disintegration.'

While Freedom House had considered the political system 'partly free' in 1995, reflecting the advent of multi-party elections, it regressed to 'not free' in 2010 as the government clamped down on political opposition, in which hundreds died. In the words of one cabinet minister (who preferred not to be personally identified), 'by December [2017] it was not even certain that we could continue as a nation so great was the crisis. There was a total disconnect,' he said, 'between the population and the ruling party,' of which he is a member. 'By resigning,' he argued, 'Hailemariam made himself part of the solution.'[51]

The former prime minister warns that reform 'is a chicken and egg issue. If there is no growth, democracy is less likely and vice versa. Without full citizen support and engagement, you cannot achieve the growth without which you will fail. We thus need to ensure a truly participatory process, otherwise the effects of growth will not reach everyone. And doing so is important as this engagement helps them to become productive, to be economically active, and value-creating.'[52]

'Before my resignation,' observes Hailemariam, 'we had a 17-day discussion among the party. I presented a paper there on deep renewal, which I said should be our motto as we are lagging behind on democratisation, judicial reform, in respecting human rights, in fighting corruption and embezzlement. We needed to discuss these issues openly.'

Hailemariam was replaced as prime minister in April 2018 by Abiy, just 41, who also became chairperson of the ruling EPRDF and the rebranded Oromo Democratic Party. It was the first time an Oromo, the majority ethnic group in Ethiopia, had led the country. Abiy moved quickly, releasing political prisoners, taking steps to normalise relations with neighbouring Eritrea, against which it had fought a costly war at the turn of the century, and launched reforms in the economy through the sale of stakes in state-owned enterprises.

Strikingly, in June 2018, Abiy criticised the behaviour of the country's security and intelligence services, saying that they tortured and wrongfully arrested people.[53] When asked in parliament why people accused of terror-ism offences were among the thousands recently released from prison, he responded by saying that 'terrorism includes using force unconstitution-ally to stay in power'. Earlier, he had sacked the country's intelligence and military chiefs. 'Does the constitution say anyone who was sentenced by a court can be tortured, put in a dark room? It doesn't,' he noted. 'Torturing, putting people in dark rooms, is our act of terrorism,' he said to members of parliament.

Abiy's message was clear: the authoritarian political and closed econom-ic model of his predecessors required a thorough overhaul.

'Most politicians,' he says, 'know how to describe democracy, but they couldn't deliver it. It is because it's a borrowed concept, and they couldn't apply it. It's for the same reason that the TPLF struggled when talking about labour policy, or about communism. These are imported ideas.

'We have been talking about democracy for 20 years, yet there have been huge human rights violations. The party holds 100% of seats in parliament, yet it talks about democracy.' In the same vein, he says, 'The government talks about an agrarian society, yet only 12 million people work in this sec-tor.' Even though he is critical of the impact of social media on Ethiopia's youth and their values, 'You can't talk about democracy and block blog-gers and jam the voices of our society,' he says, taking a dig at the previous government's regular clampdowns on Facebook and other social media outlets. 'Why,' he asks, 'did we not automate the election process if we held democracy to be so valuable?' He also asks why Ethiopia's leaders never made it their job to visit the whole country, 'to understand our culture, language, society and demography. I am the first who has been to more than half of all cities in the country.'

For Abiy, democracy is thus not an abstract, imported concept, but rather 'one that is important because inclusiveness and coexistence is critical in Ethiopia due to differences in terms of tribalism and religion, and the virtually feudal system of land ownership that prevailed in the past. We must not,' he adds, 'just give the concept [of democracy] expression, but practical purpose,' whether this is to 'increase yields in agriculture or reduce very high levels of unemployment'.

The constitution, he says, 'cannot just give rights, but it has to work in practice'.

This goes to the nature of the election of the prime minister too. 'Eighty people in the council of the EPRDF made me prime minister, even though there are 100 million Ethiopians. We need to open up the leadership to direct elections, otherwise the system of governance is incompatible with democracy.'

And there is, he says, 'a need for the rule of law, otherwise the term democracy is just blah-blah, just jargon'. Yet, some of 'Africa's old leaders, who have been there many years,' he says, singling out Uganda's Yoweri Museveni and Sudan's Omar al-Bashir, 'would like to teach us about the concept of democracy [in countries] where there are no elections and no second opinions.'

The pace of change in Ethiopia, a donor darling even while it had governments that did not respect human rights niceties, should give outside actors pause for thought. Aid continued to flow regardless of the nature of the regime, since success was defined in technical rather than political metrics, and by the strategic interests, too, of the donors. Yet, Abiy is charitable towards the donors in this regard, even though he thinks some should spend their money better and in a more focused fashion.

'If you asked the youth on the streets, they wouldn't know that the United

States gives us $1.3 billion a year.' Rather than spreading this 'around NGOs' it could 'go on big projects – for irrigation,' he suggests, 'or building a university. It is not the donor's agenda to be critical of the political system, but to pursue a development agenda. But the donors could,' he admits, 'teach governments in other ways, for example by improving the conditions in prisons, which would have sent a message.'

Until now, Abiy argues, government in Addis Ababa was 'about tribe, family and party, exclusive and not inclusive, and interested in power to the neglect of others'. To get this right, you have to lead by example. 'The maximum time I will stay in office is two terms. If you don't do that, you cannot consider yourself a democrat. The EPRDF also needs to give up power to other groups, beyond the party. If you are a leader who thinks that you are the alpha and omega of everything, you are gone, irrelevant. Rather, if there are people with better ideas, younger people or people in business, from outside government, then we need to be open to them. That is why I have, for example, opened up my circle of economic advisers.'

The message: despite its growth record with an authoritarian government, Ethiopia's nascent democratic reforms suggest that even its substantial economic successes are no substitute for greater freedom.

More than authoritarian: The Singapore story

Perhaps no country has had a greater impact on development thinking than Singapore. When Lee Kuan Yew started as the leader of independent Singapore in 1965, the country was a fragile, poor backwater. Born amid crisis arising from the separation of the Malay Federation and confrontation with Indonesia, the city-state was riven with racial, ethnic and religious fault lines. Its infrastructure was geared to colonial purposes, including the dockyards. Two-thirds of its 1.6 million people lived in overcrowded slums, most without water-borne sewerage, and many without employment, on an island of just 580 square kilometres. It was far from inevitable that Singapore would ever be rich. Independence was a tough time, reflected S.R. Nathan, the sixth president of Singapore, who served nearly a dozen years before retiring from his post in 2011: 'We had our backs to the wall.' Nathan noted in an interview in 2013: 'We had no money, no skills and no resources. But we had a group of leaders with a common purpose and a common vision.'[54]

Fifty years later, Singapore's GDP per capita stood at nearly $54 000 – 100 times more than at independence and nearly 20% greater than that of the UK, its former colonial power. Over the same period, per capita incomes in sub-Saharan Africa increased from $165 to just under $1 500.

Yet, back in 1968, it was Singapore that looked to Africa for lessons on growing its economy. That year, recalled Kenya's former prime minister, Raila Odinga, 'a team of Singaporeans came to Kenya to learn our lessons, since we were then a more developed country than they were'. Nearly four decades later, Odinga reflected: 'I took a study trip to Singapore with six ministers. That was the latest in many trips taken by the Kenyan government, about which no report was ever written, and where the participants kept everything to themselves. I said that this trip had to be different, that we had to translate our findings into actions. On our return, I asked for a plan of action from each minister learning from Singapore, since there was no point in reinventing the wheel. Each minister was tasked to prepare their action plan against our Vision 2030 … But after I left government [in 2013],' he depressingly observed in 2016, 'nothing further happened.'[55]

Singapore offers an excellent learning opportunity to understand Africa's growth puzzle from an East Asian perspective.

While Singapore, like others in the region – including South Korea, China, Indonesia and Taiwan – has developed under a system of rigid political control, the image of Lee Kuan Yew as the technocratic authoritarian lacks sufficient nuance. Singapore's economic development involved much more than one person and fundamentally relied on the establishment of robust institutions with strong and honest leadership and commitment.

Although Lee presented the articulate public face and adroitly managed the politics and personalities, his was a formidable team. Lee's memoirs are testimony to how highly he regarded the opinion of his colleagues and how often there were differences of outlook within government on key issues.[56] His government, and those of his successors, involved top-quality peers, not just one enlightened leader. Lee took advantage of this talent by encouraging debate. Goh Chok Tong, Singapore's second prime minister, said that 'Lee taught us always to allow us to be challenged by others. To do this we needed to create an opposition within our own party.' When 'we could sense that people wanted to have genuine opposition voices we experimented by having non-constituency members of parliament'.

Goh cites a large number of fierce debates within government. Also contrary to the authoritarian thesis, Goh argues that there is a 'need to ensure that there are good leaders who can follow you' – what he terms 'key man risk'. He continues, 'Mr Lee would talk to us about what would happen if he fell under a bus or if he was on an army plane that might crash.' He notes that 'we could talk about key man risk as we had leaders who were not corrupt, and could leave politics, as no one had any hold on you.'

Singapore's deputy prime minister, Tharman Shanmugaratnam, notes that in the early days, there was inevitable concern for democracy's 'guard rails'. Especially concerning were matters to do with race and religion, particularly in light of the ethnic composition of Singapore and the failed union with Malaysia. But politics and the inevitable 'progress to more fair play' have to be matched by efficiencies in civil service delivery and, at its foundation, education.[57] 'Education is our most important economic and social strategy,' he says. 'From the early days the paradox was that we depoliticised the substance of education yet we took a great political interest in creating an ethos of performance and autonomy in so doing.' Singapore 'moved educators around continuously as an organising principle to enable the spread of success and isolation of failure', and, from the 1990s, instituted a performance-based pay system. This ethos stems, he argues, from Singapore's political system, where 'incumbents are only at an advantage if they deliver to their constituency. The People's Action Party is not entitled to rule Singapore; it depends on how we deliver.'

There are many other aspects of Singapore's economic success that have been similarly overlooked by advocates for autocracy. These include bureaucratic responsiveness, attractive policy for business investment, low-wage industries, high productivity, investment in infrastructure, raised agriculture outputs as an initial spur to growth and an overwhelming focus on competitiveness.

Certain African governments like to cite Singapore as an example in order to continue to support their own parastatals and 'partystatals' (companies owned or run by ruling parties), both routinely notorious for crowding out private sector competition to the advantage of narrow financial and patronage interests. Again, such lessons are wide of the mark. An example of how to do this differently is Temasek Holdings, a government-owned, $200-billion Singapore investment company. Despite its statist origins, Temasek's strategy and role are based on commercial rather than political rationale. This avoids the intellectual suffocation and bureaucratic inertia of nationalised entities and creates a powerful investment vehicle for Singapore.

In Goh's view, 'authoritarianism is not essential for success. Rather than a sign of authoritarianism, or a lack of democracy,' he says that 'having one party in power [since independence] is a consequence of being able to deliver.'

Sylvia Lim, chairperson of the opposition Workers' Party in Singapore, characterises the political system as 'authoritarian'. However, she, too, admits that the presence of the same ruling party for more than five decades 'is evidence of people's satisfaction. The standard of living rose under Lee Kuan Yew and his cohort. People had also not forgotten that Singapore was a very dangerous place in the 1940s and 1950s.' She cites her own father who had served in the police force. 'We never knew if he would return each day alive.' As 'Singaporeans place a high premium on safety and security, people preferred to give up many things to achieve this'.

Lim says that, despite changes to the system, the authoritarian tendencies are still there – 'about 70 or 75% of what they once were. But there are features of democracy, not least that I am walking around today as an elected opposition politician.' Then again, she adds, 'while our relationships are quite cordial and professional, because the ruling party is so dominant, they don't really need our support'.

And the opposition faces, she says, many challenges. 'The civil service has only known one party for 60 years. The concept of neutrality is not there most of the time.' It is also very challenging to match the ruling party from the point of view of resources, she states, especially in human terms, given the need for joint multi-seat election tickets, which she argues need to be scrapped.

'It is a fake choice between democracy,' she argues, 'and continued economic success.' To the contrary, 'democracy is imperative where you need creativity. You cannot simply compartmentalise efficiency only in terms of the technological field, but it is required also in political institutions that enable this. My studies in law made me realise that politicians covered each other, and the system did not check this.'

Freedom House rates Singapore as 'partly free' and no one argues that it is a democracy. However, its government worked, notably during its formative economic period, in a manner radically different from the caricatures that have developed in Africa to justify authoritarian rule. Lee developed a government that saw its role as an enabler of private enterprise rather than as a supreme economic allocator. Government may not have had much turnover due to elections but a highly competent leadership group were developed, irrespective of race or religion, that was conscious that it would need to develop successors. Finally, and perhaps most importantly, legitimacy was secured by the success that the country had in delivering growth and development. Leaders understood that without this performance legitimacy, they would not be able to continue to rule. They were thus held accountable to the population.

Conclusion: The poor evidence for authoritarianism

Defenders of authoritarian rule have to answer a profound question: is there enough evidence that their preferred regime type delivers economic benefits that enable them to sacrifice democratic freedoms that African majorities across the continent prefer?

Rwanda has delivered important development and governance results. But the circumstances of its performance arising out of a genocide make it unique. The Ethiopians themselves do not see the authoritarian model as sustainable or providing any options that a democratic system cannot. Rather, Ethiopia's leaders argue that failure to democratise has presented an existential crisis, threatening security and prosperity. And the Singapore story is much more nuanced than simply a 'big man success story', in that the success of its transitions rested less on authoritarianism than sound policy and implementation. To the contrary, competition around ideas has been a central component of its ongoing success.

There are other important examples, where authoritarianism is the wrong lesson of reform. For example, from a per capita income of just $80 in 1962, poorer than the sub-Saharan African average at the time, South Korea achieved an average economic growth rate from 1965 to 1990 of 9.9%, the highest in the world. Today, its per capita income is $30 000, and a number of its companies are global market leaders, including Hyundai, Samsung and LG. A focus on early authoritarianism under President Park Chung-hee as the reason for Korea's rapid growth and transformation obscures the complex incentivisation schemes and tough deliberate choices made in the process.[58] This involved, at its heart, the strategic reorientation from protectionism to export-led growth and the rapid refocusing of society on competitiveness.

Similarly, there is evidence to suggest that the growth of the Philippines' economy – long considered the 'sick man of Asia' – has been held back by autocratic tendencies, rent-seeking and a lack of transparency permitted, most notably, during the regime of Ferdinand Marcos (1965–86). While democracy has brought higher growth, especially during the twenty-first century, this has once more been threatened by the authoritarian tendencies of President Rodrigo Duterte, elected in 2016. By October 2018, it is estimated that more than 12 000 people had died in his drug war, many of them victims of summary execution by the police.[59]

Overall, there is too little evidence to rely on the authoritarian model to deliver the growth that Africa needs but, as Chapter 1 notes, significant evidence that democracy in the long term can deliver more for citizens.

3

The State of Democracy in Africa

I went to Madiba and said to him: 'South Africa needs you to stand a second term.' He replied to me: 'Olu, where in the world do you have a man of 80 running the affairs of his country? My answer to you is: No.'

— Nelson Mandela to Olusegun Obasanjo, 1999

Chapter takeaways

■ In 1980, only three African countries were considered as 'free' democracies.

■ From the 1960s through to the end of the 1980s, African politics was often turbulent; coups were more likely than elections to cause leadership transitions.

■ Since the 1980s, there has been a rapid growth in African multi-party systems of government, with measurements of freedom peaking in 2005.

■ Freedom has in significant ways stagnated since the last decade with the 'partly free' category losing ground to the 'not free', after many years when it was ahead.

■ The number of countries in the 'free' category (ten) has remained nearly constant for the last ten years. At the same time, there are very few countries that deteriorate once they achieve this status.

■ Freedom of the press, working parliaments, effective judiciaries, human rights and transparency – the stuff of democracy beyond the process of elections – are relatively uncommon in Africa.

■ There is little correlation between structural conditions in countries and the degree of freedom except that the number of 'free' countries is relatively small. However, not all small countries are 'free'.

'Before 2011,' claimed Hatem Ben Salem, Tunisia's minister of education in 2017, 'we had a strong state. You can call it authoritarian, or even a dictatorship, but governance and public administration were efficient. At the end of each day we had results in Tunisia, measured in terms of the economy, agricultural output and so on. At the same time, there was no possibility of the freedom of speech. Also, the efficient state that we had could not last as it was built around one person. In our case, the institutions were built around the authority of the president.'

However, the Tunisian state was neither efficient nor responsive enough to meet the population's demands. On 17 December 2010, Mohamed Bouazizi, a poor flower seller from Sidi Bouzid, a city in the centre of the country, set himself alight[1] after a run-in with police over his alleged refusal to pay a bribe.[2] His death two weeks later triggered anger and protests, leading to the toppling of long-time President Zine el-Abidine Ben Ali, the first leader to go in what became known as the Arab Spring.[3]

Reminiscent of events in the Soviet bloc of states in Eastern Europe's 1989 'Autumn of Nations', Ben Ali fled to Saudi Arabia on 14 January 2011 in the face of mounting protests. Within the month, Egyptian President Hosni Mubarak had resigned as the '25 January' movement occupied Cairo's Tahrir Square and protestors fought battles with the army and police. Muammar Gaddafi was overthrown in Libya on 23 August 2011 and killed near Sirte on 20 October. In Yemen, President Ali Abdullah Saleh signed a power transfer deal in exchange for immunity from prosecution. The Syrian civil war conflict was sparked in the southern city of Daraa in March 2011 after the arrest and torture of teenagers who had painted anti-government slogans on a school wall. By 2018, it had claimed nearly half a million lives.[4] After all the tumult, only Tunisia came out on the other side as a free country in Freedom House's parlance and has retained the top ranking since 2014. In fact, as noted below, it is one of the few African countries to make substantial political progress this decade.

Differences between Carthage and the area around Massicault illustrate one driver of contemporary political change and economic challenges in Tunisia. While Carthage, once the centre of ancient civilisations and conquest, is now an upper-class suburb with large homes, tennis clubs and classy restaurants, Massicault, just 30 kilometres outside the city, is a relatively deprived, largely agricultural place, whose people live a meagre existence. 'A lack of regional development', observes Jalloul Ayed, a former minister of finance and 2014 prime ministerial candidate, is one of the reasons why the Arab Spring occurred, as 'there was no strategy to develop the regions of the country, and very little infrastructure to ensure [development] was evenly spread. This is why,' he says, 'all revolutions in Tunisia have been triggered from the interior of the country.'

The underlying tensions that ejected Ben Ali so quickly, and which had been building for some time in Tunisia as elsewhere across the region, have proved much more difficult and complex to resolve, reflecting years of inadequate governance and policy. Ben Ali had been re-elected president in 1989, 1994, 1999 (nominally his peak popularity when he won with a hardly credible 99.4% of the vote), 2004 and 2009. Changes to the constitution allowed him to run for re-election on the last two occasions. A lack of opposition permitted corruption to become entrenched.

While unemployment was officially 14%, in reality it was twice as much, with a widening chasm between the affluent coast and deprived interior. These tensions were exacerbated by population growth. As the population surged from four million in 1960 to just under 11 million in 2010, youth unemployment steadily rose too. As a result, the IMF has estimated that Arab economies like Tunisia must grow at a rate of at least 6.5% annually to keep up with population increases, two percentage points higher than the average growth rate during the decade of the 2000s.[5]

After eight years, the promise and ambiguities of democratisation in Tunisia are clear. In intensive conversations with representatives of the media, civil society and political parties in 2018, we found no one who thought that the democracy that Tunisia had established could be reversed.

They readily admitted to challenges, including an economy that has not been transformed, to weaknesses in the media due to a lack of professionalism and technological change, and to the threat of Islamist parties funded from the outside. However, none of these were considered existential challenges to the political settlement reached after 2010. This is a considerable achievement given its non-democratic history and the instability and chaos that reign in its neighbourhood.

The major challenge to Tunisia is the economy. The economic trends, notably the inability to provide jobs, which contextualised the revolution, have not diminished. Tunisia, not surprisingly, has had multiple governments since the uprising, and that has done little to assuage investors, who previously saw it as a safe harbour. The government's wage bill has increased dramatically as the pressure to provide some kind of employment intensifies. Finally, in a point agreed by most, economic management has trailed the political transition. In particular, the democratisation of the top of the state has not been mirrored by changes in those who manage the economy for the government, the 'deep state'. The same civil servants who managed and, ultimately, profited from the rentier state previously are still in place because it is hard to dislodge them and because politics has been so turbulent that there has not yet been time to develop an economic vision for the new Tunisia. By and large, the political parties that compete for power do not do so on the basis of economic platforms.

The economic challenges facing Tunisia are not in doubt. The unemployment problem was acknowledged by everyone we spoke to across the political spectrum. However, no one could describe a political alignment that would allow a future leader to take the bold steps necessary for economic transformation. Policy steps that would increase unemployment, however necessary in the short term, are extremely difficult to imagine. As a result, no respondents could say when Tunisia would turn the economic corner.

The donors have been extremely supportive of Tunisia given that it is a democratic 'lighthouse' for the entire region. However, they acknowledge the paradox that their financial and political support for democracy provides little impetus for economic change. Tunisia has missed many of the targets the donors set and the money keeps flowing because no one wants to destabilise the Arab world's only democracy. As a result, the economic challenges are allowed to fester.

The economic challenges Tunisia faces have been acknowledged by President Beji Caid Essebsi. 'We have developed in terms of our democracy. But now we need economic advancement. Demography is the main issue, not just in terms of the absolute numbers, but in terms of the education we offer them. At our independence in 1956,' says Essebsi, who was sworn in as president on 31 December 2014 at the age of 88, 'the main challenge was to provide education. Now it is to give a job to those who have a diploma.'

Tunisia represents the great hope that politics can be transformed in African countries. However, it also illustrates that in the post-heroic phase of transitions, there is a great deal of mundane work to do to make politics live up to the hopes of the people who overthrew the previous regime. At the same time, in a continent of great demographic change, democracies must wrestle with severe economic problems. Free countries may be better equipped to deal with these issues but real leadership is required with new ideas and a willingness to implement, irrespective of the short-term costs.

* * *

Democracy, for all the reasons described in the previous two chapters, has been a central concern for Africa since the winds of independence swept across the continent in the 1950s. However, the early democratic structures of the newly independent countries, which were little more than copies of colonial models, quickly collapsed, so that most of the continent, with a few notable exceptions, was ruled by one-party authoritarians or soldiers until the late 1980s. Then, coinciding with the fall of the Berlin Wall, the implosion in the early 1990s of a number of one-party states was quickly followed by multi-party elections, notably the first democratic elections in South Africa in 1994. Democracy re-emerged as a powerful force in Africa.

However, there is a sense today that democracy has stagnated on the continent. Elections continue to be held, but in a large number of countries there is scepticism that voting will lead to real change. Unlike in the early 1990s, authoritarian leaders have become adept at manipulating elections and playing the international observers who claim to monitor the results. Elections occur as scheduled but many of the supporting institutions of democracy – including a free press, legislatures that debate and courts that enforce rights – are weak or missing. Consequently, the democratic-inspired policies and practices that would provide an economic dividend are missing.

Africa's early democratic failures

Each nation's political evolution is unique. However, in Africa from the mid-1960s, by which time most countries had achieved independence, to 1989, democratic progress was relatively slow. Between 1970 and 1994, only Botswana, Mauritius and the Gambia had routine multi-party elections. The first peaceful transfer of power in Africa occurred in 1982 when Mauritian Prime Minister Sir Seewoosagur Ramgoolam was defeated by Anerood Jugnauth and promptly left office.

Emblematic of African democratic failure in the first generation after independence was the presence of coups as the driver of leadership change rather than elections. Instead, African countries have experienced more than 250 military coups, successful or otherwise, since 1960.[6] Civilian control of the military, a fundamental requirement of democracy because the people's will must be paramount, was missing.

Most coups took place in West Africa, and of these twice as many in Francophone as Anglophone Africa. The majority of coups had their

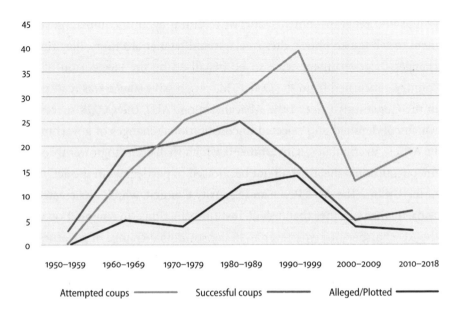

Figure 3.1: Coups d'état in Africa, 1950–2018

origins in ethnic and other fault lines, along with economic collapse and the belief of the military that it could do a better job than its civilian counterparts. The prevalence of coups in West Africa seems to be due to the greater number of states in that region, together with the impact of regional contagion, and the inability of the Economic Community of West African States (ECOWAS), whose composition was dominated by military heads of state at its formation in 1975, to promote regional democratic norms.[7]

The coup habit slowed with the end of the Cold War and subsequent drying up of external assistance to authoritarians. The temptation for soldiers to interfere in politics was also diminished by the adoption by the Organisation of African Unity (OAU) of the Lomé Declaration in 2000, which established a framework for a continental response to unconstitutional changes of government. Lomé defined four such 'unconstitutional changes' to a democratically elected government: i) a military coup; ii) an intervention by mercenaries; iii) a seizure of power by armed dissident groups and rebel movements; and iv) a refusal by an incumbent government to relinquish power after free, fair and regular elections. Illegitimate changes in government were to be penalised by the suspension of the country concerned from the OAU. This progressive stance was reaffirmed in the Constitutive Act of the African Union (AU), the OAU's successor, which condemned and rejected unconstitutional changes of government. Its Article 30 stipulates, 'Governments which shall come to power through unconstitutional means shall not be allowed to participate in the activities of the Union.' The AU's Peace and Security Council, which was created in 2003, further specifies that it shall 'institute sanctions [in conjunction with the AU chairperson] whenever an unconstitutional change of government takes place in a member state, as provided for in the Lomé Declaration'.

The Lomé Declaration and subsequent acts and announcements represented a profound shift in official African approaches to changes in leadership. From the 1960s to the 1980s, the OAU recognised as the legitimate government whoever had physical control of the capital. It therefore welcomed many military officers and authoritarians to its summits and gave them a platform for continental pronouncements. The low point may have been 1975 when Idi Amin became chair of the OAU. The evolution to a stance where coups (or other types of violent overthrow) against a democratically elected government are now considered illegitimate is a profound shift and shows that the popular African sentiment for democracy discussed in Chapter 1 and elite thinking in the region's most important organisation are moving in parallel.

Of course, the AU is hardly perfect. To date, it has only opposed the overthrow of democratically elected governments. It still has nothing to say about authoritarians who continue to rule their country through sham elections or, in the extreme case of Eritrea, no elections whatsoever. That Robert Mugabe chaired the AU in 2015 suggests that at the level of Africa's international organisations, the embrace of democracy is not complete.

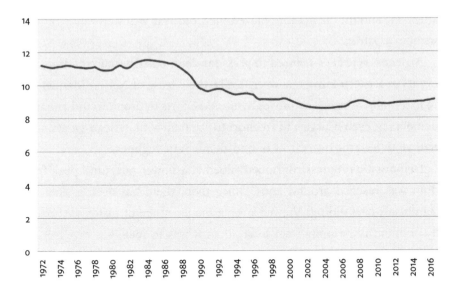

Figure 3.2: The evolution of African freedom, 1972–2017

The complex pattern of democracy since 1989

Figure 3.2 portrays the course of freedom in Africa by combining Freedom House scores for political rights and civil liberties. In the Freedom House rubric, one is the best for each score and seven is the worst. Thus, for the two scores combined, two is the best and fourteen is the worst.[8]

As can be seen from Figure 3.2, the 1970s and 1980s were a stagnant time for democracy in Africa. There followed a sudden burst of freedom in the late 1980s and early 1990s as some weak regimes (for example, Benin, Malawi, Mali and Zambia) that were bankrupted by poor economic policies fell as soon as democratic protests occurred, even though the demonstrations themselves did not amount to a large percentage of the population.

Other regimes (such as Ethiopia, Liberia, Somalia and Zaire, as it was then known) lost power after the Berlin Wall fell. Their viability was based not on their domestic legitimacy but on their strategic value to one or other great power. However, the calculus of Washington and Moscow changed

81

after 1989 and the clients who played the Cold War well were suddenly left without a patron.

Africans were also inspired to press for democracy because of dramatic events in Eastern Europe and, critically, the release of Nelson Mandela in 1990. Finally, Western countries instituted efforts to promote and enhance democracy, even if largely in an effort to catch up with African events rather than to lead the overthrow of non-democratic regimes.

Democratic progress continued, albeit at a slower rate, until peak freedom was reached around 2005. Since then, there has been a slow but significant backsliding. Viewed over a longer range of history, Africa as a continent is certainly freer today than it was in 1988, but many of the legitimate hopes of democratisers have been dashed.

There are multiple forces propelling this stagnation in Africa's democratic performance. Perhaps most importantly, democratisation is a complex process that, at its most fundamental level, requires elites to give up power willingly. It is also difficult to construct the institutions – including parliament, the courts and a free press – that are vital to checking leaders' power in a democracy. It took many decades, sometimes centuries, for Western countries to construct these institutions. Given the sharp swing of the pendulum towards freedom in the early 1990s, it was also only natural that some African experiments would fail and that there would be a movement backwards.

Elites have also learnt how to stay in power. There were a considerable number of transitions in the early 1990s, in part because many leaders were surprised by the speed of events and thought that if they held multi-party elections they would win. They only realised their lack of popularity when the voters came out. Since then, leaders who pay attention to what happens to their neighbours and to the statements of Western governments have become smarter and learnt how to steal elections and suppress opposition by carefully seeking out the international community's red lines without quite crossing them. For instance, leaders who are aware that Westerners closely monitor actual balloting have learnt that the best way to steal an election is either months before by suppressing the opposition as they mobilise voters or during the actual process of counting, and then daring observers to disqualify the election and risk 'instability'. Opposition leader Raila Odinga describes how he perceived foreign observers in Kenya's August 2017 election, a vote that was declared free and fair by outsiders but was subsequently nullified by the courts: 'By their conduct on 8 August they [foreign observers] were a disgrace to Kenya and, by extension, to Africa and its democracies. These missions have become a ritual – a holiday, staying in nice hotels, sending some locals out into the field, and in the end saying that, although there was some violence and some irregularities occurred, by and large the elections reflected the will of the people.'[9]

There have also been, in recent years, several 'constitutional coups', whereby leaders consolidate their power and erode democratic institutions by means of elections. In 1998, for instance, Sam Nujoma, Namibia's founding president, introduced a bill allowing him to serve a third term despite a constitutionally mandated two-term limit.[10] Zambia and Malawi followed suit in 2001 and 2003 respectively, though the incumbents, Frederick Chiluba and Bakili Muluzi, failed to secure their return. Referenda changed the constitutions in Chad, Guinea and Niger. Uganda's Yoweri Museveni combined the scrapping of term limits with the promise of a return to multi-party democracy in 2005.[11] Ironically, in 1986, when Museveni first took power in Uganda, he railed against those who stayed in power forever; he was, however, still in office in 2018. In December 2015, the Rwandan constitution was changed by a referendum with a majority of 89.3%, allowing Paul Kagame to run for an additional seven-year term and then two further five-year terms, by which time he would have served 40 years in office. In answer to the question 'Why pursue a third term?' – asked by his colleague, former UK Prime Minister Tony Blair in 2016 – Kagame responded that he was only respecting the wish of the Rwandan people. 'I didn't ask for this thing,' Kagame said. 'But they kept saying, no, we want you to stay.'[12]

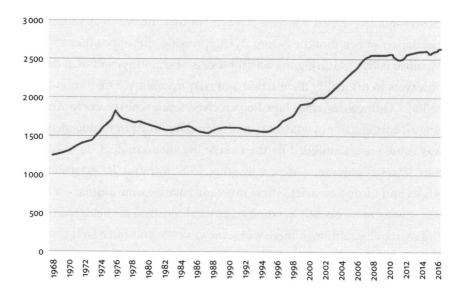

Figure 3.3: African GDP per capita (constant 2010 US$)

As the former Kenyan anti-corruption czar John Githongo has detailed, during the 1990s, 48 new constitutions were drafted in Africa. Of these, 33 included term limits for heads of state, most of which were two five-year terms. But by 2015, in at least 24 of the 33 countries with term limits, attempts were made to remove them – half of them successful, as was the case in Uganda, Rwanda and Burundi.[13] Some leaders, such as Museveni, have also been able to blunt Western pressure for democratisation by co-operating on issues important to the US and Europe such as counter-terrorism in Somalia. Chapter 7 analyses in depth the dilemmas that Western and other countries face when trying to promote democracy in Africa.

The 'supercycle' of high commodity prices that lasted roughly between 2000 and 2014 due to high and increasing demand for commodities from China also helped authoritarians in the short term. African countries grew (continental per capita income increased from $1 918 in constant 2010 US dollars in 2000 to $2 592 in 2014),[14] not because of improvements in governance but simply because the prices of what they were already producing

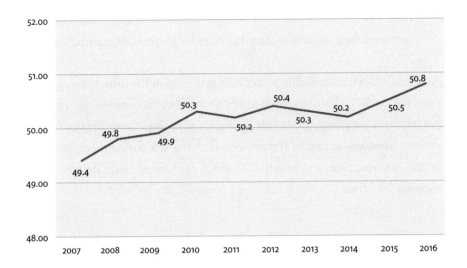

Figure 3.4: Ibrahim Index of African Governance score, 2007–16

from beneath the ground improved. As a result, leaders had a windfall profit to pay their security forces and supporters and to grow patron-client networks that could be counted on to dampen democratic movements.

Actual governance improvement during the 15 years of relatively high growth was not impressive, hardly a surprise given this deceptive driver of higher economic activity. As Figure 3.4 illustrates, the Ibrahim Index of African Governance confirms the slow and slowing pace of improvement over the last decade.

While overall governance has improved over the last decade at an average yearly rate of +0.16, in the last five years (2012–16) the pace of progress has slowed down, improving only at an average yearly rate of +0.10.[15] Or as the World Economic Forum observes:

> On average, sub-Saharan Africa's competitiveness has not changed significantly over the past decade: while a little ground was gained between 2011 and 2015, it has been partially lost again over the past two years.

85

Only four countries (Ethiopia, Senegal, Tanzania, and Uganda) have improved their performance for five consecutive years since 2010.[16]

As a result, once commodity prices began to cool in the mid-2010s, growth rates fell back.[17] The more limited ability of governments to pay off supporters and suppress opposition groups, including those pressuring for greater freedom, is one of the reasons that the US government, as noted in the Introduction, forecast that conflict over democratic demands will increase in Africa.

Actual democratisation

There was a sudden initial burst of countries that entered into the 'free' category, from two in 1988 to nine in 1998. However, in the next 20 years, the number of countries rated as 'free' increased by only one. There appears to be a glass ceiling at the high end of the 'partly free' category that few countries have been able to break since the crescendo of freedom in the mid-2000s.

The real movement in African democratisation has, not surprisingly, been from the 'not free' to the 'partly free' category. In 1988, 34 countries were considered 'not free' and only 15 were judged 'partly free'. Two decades later, in 2008, the number of 'partly free' countries outnumbered the 'not free' by 24 to 19.

By disaggregating the Freedom House scores, it becomes more apparent what has happened across the continent, as is evident in Figure 3.5.[18]

Given how difficult it is to democratise, it is hardly a surprise that most of the political liberalisation in Africa was from truly authoritarian regimes to a more ambiguous condition that was freer but did not constitute full democracy. In these ambiguous political settings, elections are usually held on schedule, although of highly variable quality; a free press is allowed in theory, although some journalists are still oppressed; and there is some

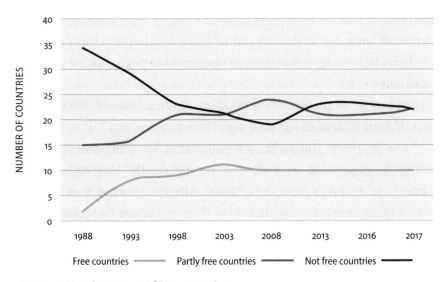

Figure 3.5: Freedom across African countries

institutional development although many citizens are still concerned that the rules of the game are not fair.

Since the mid-2000s, the dynamics of the backsliding documented in Figure 3.1 are clear. While the number of 'free' countries has stagnated for 15 years, the 'not free' category is growing again. In 2017, the number of countries 'not free' equalled the 'partly free'. This means that, in effect, not much has changed in the last 15 years. Indeed, of the countries coded as 'not free' in 2010, all but two had the same rating seven years later.

Democracy between elections

Elections are, of course, critical to democracy. Without robust electoral campaigns that determine who will control high office, leaders cannot be held accountable. However, elections are a necessary but insufficient condition for true democracy. Other institutions must also function well in order for democracies to perform the critical work of holding leaders accountable to populations. As hard as it is to conduct meaningful elections, it may be even more difficult to build these other institutions that must work day in and day out to guarantee freedom. It is outside of elections that the record of African countries has been, not surprisingly, especially poor.

Freedom of the press is one of the most significant non-electoral indicators of African democratic progress. There is not a long history of press freedom in Africa. During the colonial period, few independent African outlets for expression were allowed. Throughout the long authoritarian period that ended in 1989, independent African countries were likely to have a single newspaper, one television channel and one radio station controlled by the ruling party.

Information flows are greater today in Africa because of the rise of the internet, but true press freedom remains rare. In Freedom House's separate report 'Freedom of the Press',[19] only three small African countries, all islands, are rated as having a free press in 2016: Cape Verde (population 540 000), Mauritius (1.3 million) and São Tomé (200 000). That there is not one country on the African continent that is rated as having a free press is striking. In contrast, 27 countries are judged to have a partly free press and 24 a not-free press.

In addition, there has been a deterioration in press freedom over the last ten years. For instance, in Freedom House's evaluation of press freedom in 2008, it found that there were seven African countries that had a free press: the three island nations and Ghana, Mali, Namibia and South Africa. The latter four lost that designation in the subsequent ten years. The number of countries with an unfree press in 2017 (24) was only two less than ten years before.

Parliaments are often considered to be central to the effectiveness of democracies. Here again in Africa, democracy's prospects run up against the youth of political systems, their relatively brief democratic experience, and basic resource constraints. African leaders are also often loath to contemplate the development of another branch of government with important powers. In their survey of African legislatures, Robert Rotberg and Jennifer Erin Salahub report:

> Many African parliaments attempt to carry out those responsibilities conscientiously, and to the best of their too often circumscribed ability. The political culture of each country may constrain parliamentarians from holding a head of state or a head of government to account. Lack of experience (the turnover rate in African legislatures is high), lack of knowledge, lack of time (African legislatures are in session only periodically), lack of funding (some legislatures cannot afford to pay for legitimate member expenses), and lack of basic logistical support all make it harder for African than for European parliamentarians to oversee executive actions.[20]

The courts, another institution central to democracy, are also weak in many African states. Strong judicial systems are exceptionally difficult to establish given that they require not only a government that will obey judicial verdicts but an entire infrastructure of judges, lawyers and associations that work effectively on a day-to-day basis. In the colonial period, there was exceptionally limited redress for Africans and building the courts was certainly not a priority for the immediate post-independence governments. Indeed, even nominal democrats can be suspicious of powerful, independent judiciaries because they are, by definition, an uncontrollable base of power. While there have been some shining moments for judges in Africa – notably the nullification of the Kenyan elections by the Kenyan Supreme Court in 2017 and some heroic actions by judges who tried to stop some of Robert Mugabe's early abuses of power in Zimbabwe – courts have generally proved to be weak in Africa.

Hard as it is to evaluate democracy, judging the effectiveness of courts is even harder. The Heritage Foundation's Index of Economic Freedom does provide a sub-category measuring 'judicial effectiveness' that includes

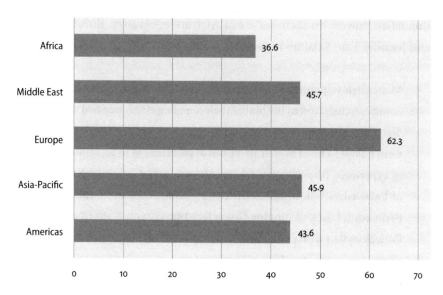

Figure 3.6: Judicial effectiveness score

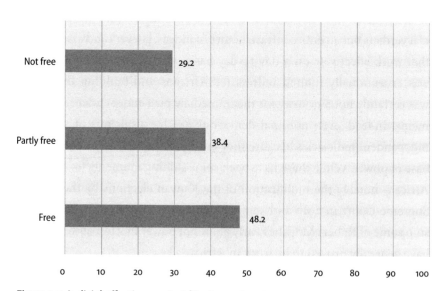

Figure 3.7: Judicial effectiveness in Africa by regime type, 2018

measurements of independence of the courts, the quality of the process and the likelihood of obtaining favourable court decisions.[21] As Figure 3.6 shows, Africa has, by some measure, the weakest judicial systems in the world.[22] And as Figure 3.7 illustrates, the weaker the democracy, the worse the system.

Democratic design

As important as the current state of particular institutions is the process of designing the forms of democracy across the AU's diverse membership. We do not believe that there is something called 'African Democracy' any more than there is a political system that could be termed 'European Democracy'.

As Arendt Lijphart has long noted, democracies can take many different forms.[23] For instance, the UK and Switzerland have radically different political systems: they differ by type of voting (first past the post versus proportional representation), degree of federalism (low versus high), the use of referendum (seldom versus often), the salient division represented by parties (class versus region and language), whether they have a written constitution (the UK does not while Switzerland's is detailed) and several other dimensions. Yet, both are healthy democracies. African countries will similarly have to develop political systems that are appropriate for their particular historical, sociological, economic and political circumstances. As long as they meet the definition of democracy that we described in the Introduction (universal adult suffrage, voting is free and fair, the outcome of which reflects the people's choice, and there is a set of supporting institutions and freedoms), their citizens will benefit. Indeed, the important question is less the particular choices that African countries make regarding democratic design than if they are actively attempting to change their institutions to align with their political, social and demographic circumstances.

There have been some important trends in African democratic architecture that are of note and indicate that countries in the region are capable of the necessary constitutional engineering. Perhaps one of the most notable innovations has been the requirement in Nigeria that a presidential candidate must win at least 25% of the vote in two-thirds of the country's 36 states. This has encouraged the formation of 'split tickets' so that parties can develop at least some pan-ethnic support. It is therefore probably impossible that Nigeria would ever again have a party with a name similar to the 'Northern People's Congress', which supplied Nigeria's first prime minister, Sir Abubakar Tafawa Balewa, in the 1960s.

Another important development has been the incorporation of traditional leaders into formal political systems. While hardly unique to Africa (the House of Lords is an obvious analogue), the creation of bodies like the National House of Traditional Leaders in South Africa to advise the president on matters related to customary law is an attempt to recognise the legitimacy of rulers who are important to many citizens, especially in the rural areas. Similar bodies are found in Botswana (Ntlo ya Dikgosi, formerly the House of Chiefs), Ghana (National House of Chiefs) and Zimbabwe (Zimbabwe Council of Chiefs).[24] While it is obviously problematic to attempt to bring leaders who are at their heart non-democratic into political systems that seek to treat everyone equally, these institutional innovations reflect a reality in each country that legitimacy often resides outside of the formal political system.

Finally, there has been a trend towards executive presidents in Africa. For instance, many Anglophone countries at independence had prime ministers and a titular head of state (usually the British monarch). The Anglophones have changed systems with many migrating to executive presidencies. Ghana, Kenya, Tanzania, Uganda, Zambia and Zimbabwe are among those who over time moved to an executive president. The motivations vary, no doubt, from country to country but certainly reflect the belief that poor countries need a powerful chief executive and also the personal motivations of those who control the process of state design.

Overall, there have been important democratic innovations in Africa. However, the pace and scope of reform are not sufficient at the moment to ensure that countries have the institutional architecture they need to withstand all of the threats to democracy. Indeed, precisely because democratisation is so difficult and failure not unexpected, African countries will continue to have to experiment with new and different democratic forms.

That there is no easy template for democracy makes the task confronting Africans who want to move towards freedom even more difficult. But this reality should add to the urgency to begin this journey now.

National trajectories

The fate of democracy and freedom at the continental level is important to understand. However, the individual stories of Africa's countries inevitably vary. Perhaps the most important meta-trend in Africa is the increased differentiation between countries over the last 50 years, a trend that is only likely to become starker in the future. Thus, Ghana has developed a political culture where incumbents transfer power peacefully when they have lost the vote, while Burundi, the Democratic Republic of Congo (DRC) and Somalia, among others, struggle just to sustain basic institutions and hold peaceful elections in the first place.

Of the ten countries considered 'free' by Freedom House in 2018, many have had a high level of democratic performance for all or almost all of the period since 1989. The long-standing 'free' countries include Benin, Botswana, Cape Verde, Ghana, Mauritius, Namibia, São Tomé and South Africa. Of those, Botswana, Mauritius, Namibia and South Africa have all been free more or less since independence or, in the case of South Africa, since the African National Congress (ANC) won the first non-racial elections in 1994. Benin underwent an early transition in 1991 to free when the authoritarian Mathieu Kérékou was forced by widespread protests to call an election, which he lost to Nicéphore Soglo. There have been several changes in the party in power since then, including a return of Kérékou, who won an election in 2001, but the country has continued to be free in what has been one of the more impressive democratic performances in Africa. Ghana only became 'free' in 2000 when Jerry Rawlings stepped aside after a long period of rule as, first, a soldier, and, later, a civilian.

Interestingly, several of the countries that are rated 'free' have yet to have elections that lead to a transfer of power, the signal moment of a democracy and a true test of its strength. Despite free and fair elections, Botswana has been ruled since independence in 1966 by the Botswana Democratic Party, originally founded by Sir Seretse Khama. The South West African People's Organisation (SWAPO) in Namibia (since 1990) and the ANC in South Africa (since 1994) have also both been returned to power each time voters have gone to the polls. They are both classic liberation parties but have a more democratic orientation than other groupings that engaged in armed struggle, including the Zimbabwe African National Union (ZANU) in Zimbabwe, FRELIMO (Mozambique Liberation Front) in Mozambique, and the MPLA (Popular Movement for the Liberation of Angola) in Angola. Especially in the case of Botswana, the incumbent party has gained a certain amount of performance legitimacy due to that country's excellent economic performance, to some degree copying Singapore's political trajectory.

Very few countries have joined the 'free' category in recent years. In fact, only Senegal and Tunisia have emerged as full-fledged democratisers since 2012. The North African country is an important case because it had a long history of alternating between 'partly free' and 'not free' until the upheaval in December 2010 detailed above. Senegal has had a more varied history, alternating between 'partly free' and 'free' since 1989. However, the elections in 2012, when challenger Macky Sall defeated the incumbent Abdoulaye Wade (running for a controversial third term), were a turning point that consolidated important democratic tendencies.

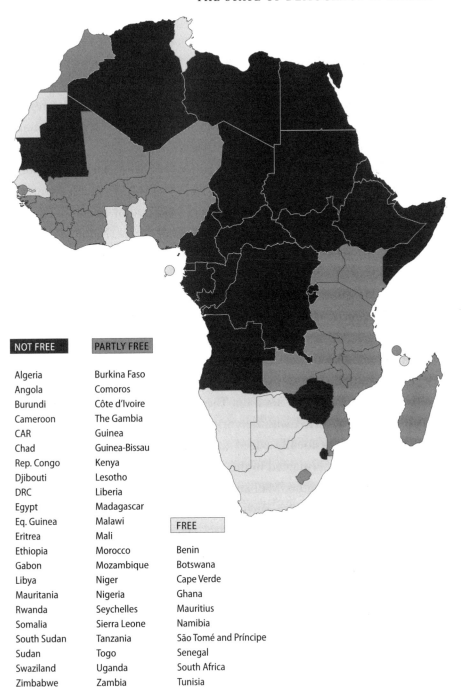

NOT FREE

Algeria
Angola
Burundi
Cameroon
CAR
Chad
Rep. Congo
Djibouti
DRC
Egypt
Eq. Guinea
Eritrea
Ethiopia
Gabon
Libya
Mauritania
Rwanda
Somalia
South Sudan
Sudan
Swaziland
Zimbabwe

PARTLY FREE

Burkina Faso
Comoros
Côte d'Ivoire
The Gambia
Guinea
Guinea-Bissau
Kenya
Lesotho
Liberia
Madagascar
Malawi
Mali
Morocco
Mozambique
Niger
Nigeria
Seychelles
Sierra Leone
Tanzania
Togo
Uganda
Zambia

FREE

Benin
Botswana
Cape Verde
Ghana
Mauritius
Namibia
São Tomé and Príncipe
Senegal
South Africa
Tunisia

There are a limited number of commonalities among those that are 'free'. Most are small with only South Africa (55 million people) and Ghana (27 million) having relatively large populations. Only South Africa and Namibia are large by geographic standards. Southern Africa is well represented (Botswana, Namibia, South Africa and, depending on classification, Mauritius) as is West Africa (Benin, Ghana, Senegal and, again depending on classification, Cape Verde and São Tomé), while there is only one from North Africa (Tunisia) and none from East Africa. These countries have a varied colonial history, having been colonised by England, France, Portugal (Cape Verde and São Tomé) and South Africa (Namibia), so it is hard to make generalisations about the importance of their colonial experience for this classification.

Some 22 countries, fully 41% of all of Africa, are in the ambiguous category of 'partly free'. Of these, as many as 15 (Burkina Faso, Comoros, Guinea-Bissau, Kenya, Madagascar, Malawi, Morocco, Mozambique, Niger, Nigeria, Seychelles, Sierra Leone, Tanzania and Zambia) seem to be perpetually stuck in this category, unable to transition to 'free' despite not showing obvious deterioration. These are countries, as Chapter 5 discusses, that have flirted with democracy, sometimes held consequential elections, and occasionally edged towards authoritarianism, but nonetheless have finally remained in the messy middle. Other countries (Côte d'Ivoire, Guinea, Lesotho, Mali and Togo) have moved in and out of the 'partly free' category. Some, such as Mali (discussed in Chapter 4), were briefly 'free' and then reverted. Similarly, Lesotho, after a number of years of being considered 'free', reverted to 'partly free' after an aborted military coup forced then Prime Minister Tom Thabane to flee to South Africa for three days in 2015.

Perhaps inevitably for a category that is defined by what a country is not – neither 'free' nor 'not free' – and that contains a large number of countries, there are no common identifiable characteristics of the 'partly free'. They have had varied colonial histories, are located in all regions of the continent, and differ in size and other measures.

Of the African countries that have performed the worst in terms of democracy, there are a significant number that have maintained the same authoritarian regime type for decades. Some 13 countries (Algeria, Angola, Cameroon, Chad, DRC, Egypt, Equatorial Guinea, Eritrea, Libya, Rwanda, Somalia, South Sudan, Sudan and Swaziland) have received a rating of 'not free' perpetually or almost every year since 1989. Of course, even within what should be considered the hardcore of the 'not free' category, there is variation. Some, like Angola, have had one-party (the MPLA) and essentially one-leader (Eduardo dos Santos, who came to power in 1979 and left in September 2017) rule for the entire period. Similarly, Idriss Déby has continuously ruled Chad in an authoritarian manner since he overthrew Hissène Habré in 1990. Teodoro Obiang has led Equatorial Guinea with impunity since 1979 when he ousted his uncle Francisco Macías Nguema from power. And Paul Biya has also headed Cameroon continuously since succeeding Ahmadou Ahidjo in 1982.

Other authoritarian countries have shown less leadership continuity. For instance, after a period of being considered 'partly free', Algeria has been 'not free' since the military intervened in 1992 to cancel elections that were seen as likely to lead to rule by the Islamic Salvation Front. The DRC has experienced multiple leaders, including Mobutu Sese Seko until 1997 when the country was Zaire, then Laurent-Désiré Kabila and, after Kabila was assassinated in 2001, his son Joseph. Rwanda has always been 'not free' in the period despite a calamitous history that included rule by the Hutu until the genocide in 1994 and the subsequent rise to power of the Tutsi-dominated Rwandan Patriotic Front of Paul Kagame. Egypt was also more or less continuously 'not free' during the rule of Hosni Mubarak until he was overthrown in 2011. But this has continued through the chaos that eventually led to the election of Mohamed Morsi and the Muslim Brotherhood in 2012 and, after the coup in 2013, the installation of the authoritarian Abdel Fattah el-Sisi the following year.

There are also few commonalities among these hardcore authoritarians. Some are large in people or land (DRC, Egypt, Algeria) or quite small (Equatorial Guinea, Eritrea, Rwanda, Swaziland). Egypt, Sudan, South Sudan and Swaziland were colonised by the English, while the rest were subjugated by the Belgians, French, Italians and Portuguese. Regimes that have been consistently authoritarian can be found in every region of Africa except for East Africa, unless South Sudan is assigned to this area.

Another sub-group in the 'not free' category consists of countries that at some point made a clear break with their 'not free' past but failed to consolidate those gains and eventually returned to the lowest ranking for combined political and civil rights. Countries in this category include Burundi, Central African Republic, Republic of Congo, Djibouti, Ethiopia, Gabon, the Gambia, Mauritania, Uganda and Zimbabwe. It is their collective failures that are responsible in good part for the backsliding of the overall African scores during the last ten years.

Population and democracy

The only consistent characteristic that stands out is the relatively small size and homogeneity of many of the 'free' countries and the fact that Africa's giants by population (DRC, Egypt, Ethiopia, Nigeria) or by land mass (Algeria) have not democratised. In fact, all of the large countries by population or land size are 'not free' except for Nigeria, which is categorised as 'partly free'.

When we alter Figure 3.8 on the continental trajectory of freedom by weighting each country's score by population (for example, Nigeria accounts for 15% of the continental average instead of 1/54th if measured as just another African country), the line documenting African freedom has the same shape but there are some notable differences.

Most importantly, Africa, once population is taken into account, is marginally less free than a simple averaging of country scores across

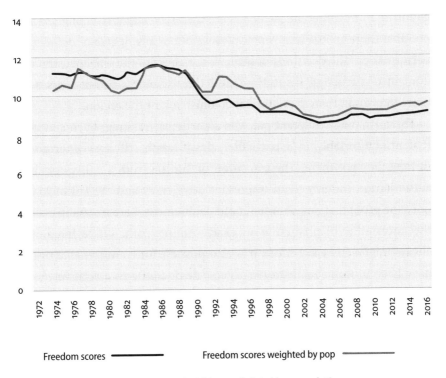

Freedom scores ━━━━━━   Freedom scores weighted by pop ┅┅┅┅┅

Figure 3.8: Political freedom scores in Africa, weighted by population

the continent suggests. Small size appears to be helpful in democratisation because it is easier to govern societies where the number of people is limited. However, there are enough small countries that are persistently in the 'not free' category (including Equatorial Guinea, Eritrea, South Sudan, Swaziland) or that have tried democratisation and failed (Burundi, Djibouti, the Gambia) to dispel the notion that small size automatically leads to greater freedom.

Conclusion: No path is guaranteed

Several lessons stand out from this country-level analysis.

There do not appear to be many structural barriers to democracy. The countries in the different categories are themselves diverse enough to suggest that there is little that is preordained about any degree of democratic performance. The decisions of leaders, the views of the citizenry, the wisdom in constructing institutions and the usefulness of outsiders seem more important than the nature of colonisation or the region.

There are many different paths to a particular ranking. Even countries that fit comfortably in a particular classification still vary enormously in how they got there. The transition of Tunisia from a 'fairly standard' authoritarian country to an important democracy and the fall of Mali – once the proof that any country could democratise – are instructive about the uncertainty of predicting an exact country path. While freedom is always fragile and can be lost, it is also possible for countries that to date have had authoritarian histories to still democratise in a relatively short period of time. The weakness of almost all institutions in almost all African countries means that no path is guaranteed.

The next three chapters delve into each grouping of countries – 'free', 'partly free' and 'not free' – to discuss the particular political dynamics of why and when authoritarian elites do and do not give up power. The chapters provide not only an analytic framework but also in-depth case studies of African countries and those outside of the continent. We hope that this combination of analysis and case studies provides some 'ground truth' for government and civil society leaders who are struggling in the quest for democracy.

We, therefore, first turn to the countries that have been most successful in instituting democratic practices to understand their key lessons, and one – Mali – that is a notable failure.

Part Two

POLITICAL TRANSITIONS

4

The Challenges of Sustaining Democracy

For all countries and provinces which enjoy complete freedom, make ... most rapid progress.

— Niccolò Machiavelli, *Discourses on Livy*

Chapter takeaways

- Of the 54 African countries measured by Freedom House, only 16 are considered to be 'free' for even one year since 1988. Of the 16 ever to be 'free', ten were 'free' in 2017.

- The history of African democratic transitions contradicts the notion that the advent of democracy demands certain levels of development.

- The most successful democracies in Africa are those that were 'born free', that is the democratic forces were able to control decolonisation or transition from the old order (such as South Africa) and set the rules of the game.

- Social media is a double-edged sword. It can be used to challenge the authoritarians' hold on information but is also a vector for those who want to disrupt elections.

- For those countries not 'born free', the transitions are much more problematic. In already independent countries, transitions occur not because of elite pacts, but because the old order has simply collapsed.

Outside the control room of the 1 000-megawatt Akosombo Dam on the Volta River, about 100 kilometres from the capital Accra, are two bronze plaques. The older one marks the formal inauguration of the Volta River project by Osagyefo Dr Kwame Nkrumah, president of the Republic of Ghana, on 22 January 1966. The second was unveiled on 21 December 1972 by Colonel Ignatius Kutu Acheampong, 'Head of State and Chairman of the National Redemption Council', on the official commissioning of the expansion programme and completion of the hydro-electric works.

The Akosombo project became a centrepiece of President Nkrumah's plans for Ghana. In creating the largest man-made lake (Lake Volta) worldwide and by supplying 60% of its output to the aluminium smelter at Tema, it was to spur the country's industrialisation. Early on, however, there was controversy around the linking of funding for the Tema smelter by American investors to the supply of electricity, resulting in accusations of neo-colonialism, and a tilt in Ghana's foreign relations towards the Soviet bloc.

Seven years after Ghana's independence in March 1957, Nkrumah declared a one-party state under the ruling Convention People's Party. Then, just a month after he unveiled the plaque at Akosombo, he was topped in 'Operation Cold Chop', a military coup that put into power the National Liberation Council. This set the stage for serial coup-making. Between Ghana's independence and the second military coup staged by Flight-Lieutenant Jeremiah John Rawlings on New Year's Eve in 1981, there were no less than eight successive governments in Ghana – five military and three civilian – five of which were overthrown by violence and not through the ballot box. These events had common roots, including economic collapse, threats to the military's prestige, perks and power, and the centralisation of power in the presidency.

Though most coups routinely mark an end to democracy rather than the beginnings of a transition to democracy, following the military-civilian transition in the 1990s Ghana became something of a model of how to transit from a military regime to democratic rule. During the decade, it was also one of Africa's steady performing and reforming states, this status being recognised by both international financial institutions and Western governments.[1] Then, after two elections following its last coup in 1981, Ghana managed the critical test of a transition to democracy in the form of a change of regimes at the ballot box with the 2000 elections, which took John Kufuor into Flagstaff House as president in early 2001.[2]

In the process, from 1981 Ghana steadily moved away from a government that came to power by means of a military coup towards a government that is not only elected but also increasingly subject to the constraints of greater public accountability. By 2017, Ghana had three turnovers of party political regimes at the polls: from Rawlings' National Democratic Congress (NDC) to Kufuor's New Patriotic Party (NPP) in 2001; from the NPP to the NDC's John Atta Mills in 2009; and from John Mahama (NDC) to the NPP's Nana Akufo-Addo in 2017. It has been rated 'free' by Freedom House every year since 2000.

Former President Kufuor says that external factors played a key part in both sparking democratic change in Ghana and keeping it on track. 'Not much,' he says, 'happened in the 1980s. The key moment was the fall of the Berlin Wall in 1989, the collapse of the Soviet Union, and the end of the bipolar world, which created the move to constitutionalism in 1992.'[3] But he notes that 'while Rawlings transformed himself in the process, the spots of the leopard did not go simply by him falling into the water'. The new constitution in 1992, which provided for a presidential tenure limited to two terms, threatened to create, in Kufuor's words, only 'the certification of the dictatorship' if Rawlings chose not to adhere to its provisions. Kufuor's NPP boycotted parliament after the 1992 election 'on account of election fraud'. In the 1996 event, which Kufuor himself contested, 'even though the electoral commission deliberated on the results for five days, we did not even have a penknife to threaten them, and thus had to accept their decision'. The stage was thus set for the 2000 event when Rawlings had to step down or renege on his agreement to two terms. 'It would have been too glaring,' says Kufuor, 'for him to go back on his constitutional commitment. It was also public knowledge that some ambassadors, including the British, worked closely with the electoral commission to ensure that there was no electoral hanky-panky.'

What makes reform processes like Ghana's stick – and how does this shape up to the experience elsewhere?

* * *

Although continental democratic performance has been poor and since the mid-2000s there have been signs of backward movement, some African countries have managed to institutionalise their democratic practices. The number of countries that have developed a consistent track record of being 'free', as noted in Chapter 3, is limited, but their accomplishments are significant given how difficult it is to construct a democracy from scratch. The lessons from those that achieved a high degree of democracy are important for the continent, especially in light of the democratic hopes of so many citizens in dozens of countries. We argue that prospects for sustained democracy are actually relatively good if leaders can navigate the initial crisis that brought them to power and then begin to construct institutions that will govern political competition in the future.

In this chapter, we examine how Benin and Zambia have struggled to consolidate their democracies and Mali has been such a disappointing failure.

The select club of free countries

Of the 54 UN member states in Africa identified by Freedom House, only 16 have been considered to be 'free' for even one year since 1988. Breaking into the club of free nations is obviously exceptionally difficult. However,

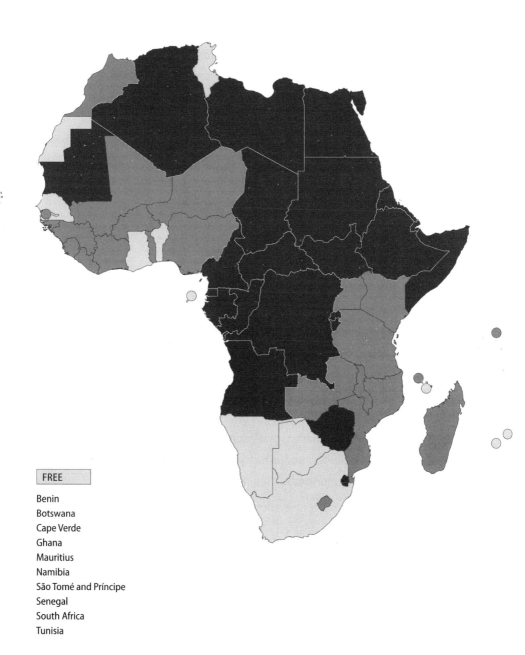

FREE

Benin
Botswana
Cape Verde
Ghana
Mauritius
Namibia
São Tomé and Príncipe
Senegal
South Africa
Tunisia

it is equally interesting that of the 16 ever to be 'free', ten were 'free' in 2017. Only six countries have been considered 'free' at some point between 1988 and 2016, but subsequently lost that designation. Of the 'free' countries today, Botswana and Mauritius are long-standing members, having been classified 'free' from 1988 through 2017. Namibia and South Africa have been 'free' since, respectively, independence in 1990 and the birth of the non-racial order in 1994. In a sense, these four are 'born free'.

Other 'free' countries have shown similarly remarkable stability. Benin (since 1991), Cape Verde (1991), Ghana (2000), São Tomé (1991) and Tunisia (2014) have all been 'free' since the overthrow of their respective authoritarian states until today without interruption.

Only a relatively small number of countries have had interludes when they were considered 'free' and then deteriorated. As noted previously, Mali is probably the most dramatic example, having been 'free' from 1992 to 1993 and again for a long stretch from 1995 to 2011 before the democratic system fell apart. There is no other case in Africa that parallels Mali's democratic lapse after 16 years of being 'free' and only a few that experienced shorter bouts of freedom and then failure. Senegal has had a more complex trajectory than most, having been considered 'free' from 2002 to 2007 and then continuously from 2012 onwards. Three other countries have had significant democratic stretches: the Gambia (1988 to 1993), Lesotho (2002 to 2008 and then 2012 to 2014) and Malawi (1994 to 1998). The other interludes were much shorter, including Sierra Leone for one year (2012) and Zambia for two (1991 to 1992).

The challenges to democratisation

Democratisation is difficult, and it appears to be particularly challenging for countries to 'get over the hump' to be recognised as 'free' polities for more than four to five years. There is a relatively high failure rate during the initial period. Once free institutions have survived for five years or so, the chances of sustaining democracy over the long term appear to improve markedly.

A sustained period of freedom gives leaders the opportunity to establish institutions that will continue the democracy and cause opponents to at least begin to believe that everyone will follow the rules of the game. The political struggles among elites become less severe because the losers begin to recognise that they can participate in political competition and democratic governance, and that change can occur from outside by the electorate. A democratic political culture, and accompanying public expectations, are allowed to develop.

We agree with former US Secretary of State Condoleezza Rice that 'leaders in aspiring democracies are faced with all kinds of pressures, but their overarching goal should be to strengthen their country's democratic institutions. The only way to do that is to work within the institutions and respect their rules.'[4] Similarly, it seems reasonable that democracy can inaugurate a virtuous cycle of stability: 'In the long term, countries that ultimately gain the political, societal, and cultural attributes of fully fledged democracies are likely to evolve into stable states. Autocratic systems, by contrast, tend to be more brittle and prone to severe forms of instability such as state failure.'[5]

The initial challenges facing democratic regimes are so significant because they involve basic issues of order and finance.

Most societies in the world remain 'limited access orders', which are characterised by personalised economic relationships, the dominance of a small elite, and high barriers to forming or joining private organisations. Few countries have made the successful transition to an 'open access order', in which economic exchange is impersonal and regulated by the rule of law, individuals have no special status based on their identity or political connections, and membership of political and economic organisations is open. Douglass North, John Joseph Wallis and Barry Weingast have argued that for societies to transition from limited to open access orders, intra-elite reforms must first take place to create the rule of law (and institutions to support it) within the elite itself, before these are extended to the rest of the population.[6] In this way, democracy and freedom are gradually expanded to apply first to certain groups, and then to everyone. Daron Acemoglu and James Robinson, however, disagree. They contend instead that elites will only give up power when they realise that they have no other option and the costs of repression are considered too high. These processes, they argue, depend on the strength of civil society, the structure of domestic political institutions, the nature of political and economic crises, the level of economic inequality, the economic structure, and the nature and extent of the country's global links.[7] This seems to be more typical of many African contexts, such as the transition to democracy in South Africa. In many cases, though, political change occurs through violence rather than gradual reform or negotiated agreements. In these instances, democracy must be built out of the ashes of conflict, destruction and intense social divisions, which is an altogether more difficult task.[8]

How do these regimes change?

Most of the transitions in Africa are not carried out in a planned manner. They differ radically from the orderly transition that Taiwan (discussed in Chapter 6), for instance, experienced where elite pacts moved the country towards democracy, arguably ahead of civil society. In Africa, regime changes seldom happen because income levels reach a certain level: the democracy follows development argument.

Democratisation is not driven by the middle class in Africa. The African Development Bank notes that the number of 'middle-class' Africans was just 13% of the population in 2011, some 120 million people, excluding those who 'float' between various categories, while more than 60% remains poor.[9] Most African countries were not rich at the moment of transition to multi-party rule, which generally occurred in the 1990s. The (weighted) average per capita income (in constant US$) was just $1 252. Figure 4.1 illustrates the average income moment at which transitions between 'not

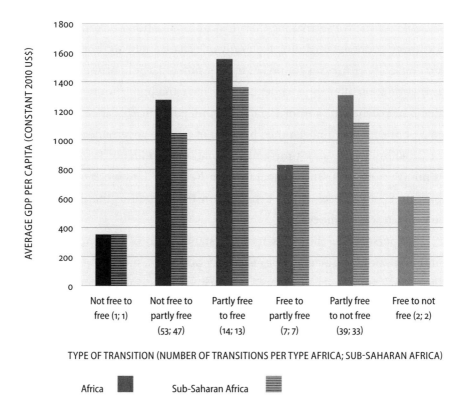

Figure 4.1: GDP per capita at 'moment of transition' in Africa, 1988–2016

free', 'partly free' and 'free' occurred in Africa. While the countries making the transition to greater freedom are marginally wealthier, they are scarcely above the continental average.[10] Interestingly, the average income in those countries transitioning from 'free' to 'partly free' is $1 304. Democracy cannot be said to be only a 'middle-class' concern since that income stratum is far from dominant across the continent.

In African countries, democratic forces usually win out when the old order collapses. Countries have, therefore, been particularly successful when democratic forces were able to control the transition from the old order, as the ANC did at the end of apartheid or SWAPO did at the moment of independence in Namibia. These democrats were able to set

111

the rules of the game, making their institutionalisation of freedom easier. However, countries obviously have only one chance at being 'born free'. The vast majority of African countries, having suffered a bout of authoritarianism at or soon after independence, only have the opportunity to reignite democracy when the authoritarian post-independence order collapses due to a poor economy undermined by years of terrible governance, the death or disability of the long-time authoritarian or a sudden price shock that diminishes exports. The democrats then have the hard work of not only picking up the pieces but of actually constructing all of the institutions associated with democracy.

This perspective allows us to understand some of the opportunities and limitations of social media. The early optimism, much of it fuelled by Facebook's supposed role in the Arab Spring, that social media would be a boon to democrats and the enemy of authoritarians, was clearly incorrect. Many African governments have learnt to exploit, monitor and, at critical moments, turn off social media to promote their own ends. At the same time, however, the possibilities that Facebook, Twitter and now encrypted messaging offer to beleaguered activists, who otherwise find it difficult to organise, should not be discounted. Yet, as the National Intelligence Council notes, social media is 'a double-edged sword', stating: 'We assess that the application of existing and developing communication technologies will enable publics to press governments more effectively while also improving regimes' capacity to crack down on opponents.'[11]

The use of social media overall highlights the divides between Africa's young populations and elderly leaders. The average age of African political leadership is 62,[12] more than three times the overall average of the youngest inhabitants of the continent. It also corresponds to the shift in concentrations to urban areas. City dwellers can physically threaten the state more directly than peasants, by using technology to catalyse mass movements, a feature largely absent in Africa's post-colonial history.

Yet social media is a 'double-edged sword', enabling publics to press governments more effectively, while at the same time improving the capacity of regimes to crack down on opponents.[13] Social media is likely to reinforce democratic trends already apparent in a country, while, as subsequent chapters will indicate, either being relatively ineffective or open to exploitation by regimes in authoritarian settings.

* * *

Benin today is one of Africa's democratic transition success stories. Its transition from authoritarian rule occurred in 1991, just as the democratic wave was building in Africa. However, unlike other countries that could not sustain the democratic momentum, it has improved its institutions and has successfully managed the signal moment of democracy – the handover of power to opposing parties because of the outcome of a free and fair election. It has not, however, been a smooth and easy path.[14]

Early opportunity and crisis in Benin

The cluttered reception of Nicéphore Soglo's home in Cotonou is evidence of his active career, as a minister of finance, World Bank economist, president, mayor and, now, Béninois political doyen. Soglo has unwittingly spawned a personal and continental political legacy and has a son, Léhady, who is also a presidential candidate and who succeeded him as mayor of Cotonou in 2015.

Educated in Paris, Soglo served as minister of finance under his cousin, Colonel Christophe Soglo, who had, in his second coup, overthrown President Sourou-Migan Apithy in 1965 in one of Benin's frequent, if typically non-violent, putsches in the 1960s.

Despite this shaky political start, Soglo will best be remembered for leading the democratic movement in Benin, which saw the dictator Mathieu Kérékou, who had seized power in another military coup in the then Republic of Dahomey in October 1972, booted out in 1991.

Although Soglo lost to Kérékou in the 1996 election, his place in Benin's politics is assured. Not only was Benin positioned, if imperfectly given subsequent electoral shenanigans, on a democratic path, but he was successfully able to break the mould of Marxist-Leninism, and get the economy onto some sort of market footing.

Under Kérékou, the banks and petroleum industry were nationalised, although these actions only compounded the negative effects of inefficiency and a lack of investment. The political reforms of the late 1980s occurred amid shortages that had forced Benin to apply for help from the IMF, accepting severe cuts to state expenditure in the process. These cuts provoked widespread unrest, starting among students.

Although Kérékou was re-elected as president by the National Assembly in August 1989, by December of the same year Marxism-Leninism was dropped as the state ideology. A national conference held in February 1990 stripped Kérékou of most of his power. During the televised conference, Kérékou begged forgiveness for his regime, setting the stage for his later political rehabilitation. Described by his regional peers as a 'genuinely naive man', the former president apologised for 'deplorable and regrettable incidents' that occurred during his rule.

Soglo was chosen as prime minister by the conference, taking office the following month. With a new constitution agreed in a December 1990 referendum, multi-party elections were held in March 1991, and won by Soglo, making Kérékou the first mainland African president to lose power through a popular election. Benin has been rated 'free' by Freedom House every year since 1991.

'Without a democracy,' says Soglo now, 'you cannot have durable economic development. You cannot solve all problems with just one individual. The small farmers equally need a voice. Democracy and development are all about responsibility and participation, and action.' And democracy, he reminds, allows for peaceful change. 'In 1990, the banks were empty,

10 000 people had lost their jobs and the students were on the streets.' Kérékou had sought sanctuary in the San Michel church. 'Without democracy, and change,' says Soglo, 'he would have been killed.'

Naive he may have been, but Kérékou was a deft politician. Living up to his nickname as 'the chameleon', he reclaimed the presidency in the March 1996 election. Though he won the first round, Soglo's economic reforms had caused his popularity to dip, and he lost the second, though today he alleges rigging and French interference occurred.

Kérékou was re-elected for a second five-year term in March 2001, again beating Soglo in controversial circumstances. As Soglo reflects, 'Coming from a one-party to a multi-party system is difficult for a tiny country. It's a process where you learn every day.'

Benin was among the early democratisers in 1990. It liberalised when its per capita income was just $610. It was certainly not rich, thus discounting the democracy through development argument. The income of its people had scarcely grown in constant terms from $520, 30 years earlier. Rather, frustrations over the lack of progress and absence of inclusion had sparked a sudden change, led by those infused, like Soglo, with the ideas of a different generation. The end of the Cold War also undoubtedly sparked a desire to throw off the old rulers. But equally quickly, disappointed Béninois reverted to the old guard.

Mali: From star to disappointment

Mali, as noted above, has a unique place in the history of African democratisation over the last 30 years. Since it was able to overcome the initial challenges to 'free' rule, it was thought that its relatively free practices were safely institutionalised. That the democratic experiment eventually fell apart after more than a decade should serve as an important warning to those who become overly optimistic about the overthrow of a particular leader. At the same time, there are unique elements of the Malian case that must be recognised. In particular, the international community simply chose to ignore the fact that Malian institutions were not functioning well before its collapse. Far from enjoying the benefits that are usually associated with good governance, Mali, even during its democratic phase, was highly corrupt and straightforward attempts to reduce the amount of cheating in government eventually led to political reversal in the absence of the sustained institution-building that is so critical to the virtuous democratic cycle.

Mali had transitioned to democracy in 1991 after a long period of military rule. In March that year, pro-democracy rallies and strikes, known as *les événements* ('the events') or the March Revolution, led to riots and violent clashes between students and soldiers. By 26 March, thousands of soldiers had joined the movement, refusing to fire on protestors. On the same day the then Lieutenant Colonel Amadou Toumani Touré (known universally as 'ATT') announced on radio the arrest of President Moussa Traoré. A new democratic constitution, approved by a national referendum, was drafted and adopted in 1992, and activist Professor Alpha Oumar Konaré won Mali's first democratic, multi-party presidential election. Elected for a second term in 1997, Konaré retired in 2002, after which he became the first chairperson of the African Union Commission. ATT was elected as president in 2002, and again in 2007.

Mali's democratic experiment ended in a coup that allowed US-trained Captain Amadou Sanogo to take over on 22 March 2012, citing ATT's mismanagement of the Toareg rebellion as his motive for taking power. However, the military lost control of the regional capitals of Kidal, Gao and Timbuktu within ten days of toppling the government. As a result, the French armed forces launched Operation Serval in January 2013, helping to restore some order, which is now bolstered by not less than 15 000 UN uniformed personnel.

Cheick Modibo Diarra was appointed as interim prime minister of Mali on 17 April 2012. He has a notable biography, having received a master's and PhD in aerospace from Howard University in Washington, D.C. He was subsequently recruited by Caltech's Jet Propulsion Laboratory, and played a role in several NASA programmes, after which he served as a Microsoft executive.[15]

'I had three conditions under which I would accept the job of prime minister when it was offered to me a month after the coup. First, I would not remove or appoint anyone because the military did or didn't like this. Second, I would not accept interference by the military in the politics and policies of the country. And third, public money had to be beyond everybody's reach, including my own, on my watch. I said, "If you agree with these three things, I would give it a shot." They, the military, said that they would.' Three of the 24 posts in his government – the ministries for defence, internal security and territorial administration – were assigned to military officers, though the bulk of appointments were technocrats.

Despite his agreement with the military, in December 2012 soldiers arrested Cheick, forcing a terse resignation on national television just hours after he was taken to the main army camp.

Five years later Cheick was unrepentant about his role and the importance of democracy in solving Mali's multi-layered crisis. Mali was regarded as a darling of donors during this democratic phase. The toppling of Muammar Gaddafi in neighbouring Libya is commonly taken as the reason for its subsequent collapse. As Mali's President Ibrahim Boubacar Keïta observed to us in July 2017, 'We are collateral victims of the Libyan crisis.' But Cheick disagrees. 'Everyone was searching for a poster child for success of this new era,' he says, 'but they closed their eyes on many things. This is proven simply by the speed at which it collapsed. If it was as they said, the institutions would have worked. Instead they were all fake.

'I was ringing the alarm bells in Mali for a long time when living in the United States,' Cheick continues. 'During the time of the AGOA [African Growth and Opportunity Act] discussions in Washington, people were providing a description of Mali that was just incredible. I kept saying, "It is not the democracy you think it is." It was a democracy on the surface, but there was gangrene underneath due to the prevalence of corruption.' In fact, all of the significant parties in Mali entered into the government with the result that there was not a true opposition that could play the role of critic government and a large number of people were demanding largesse. Mali had elections but not the substance of democracy, a crucial distinction that was not noticed or was deliberately overlooked by many who celebrated its successes.

Cheick says that 'a lot of people got frustrated that I did not give out any more money. Even though international aid was suspended, we were able to pay government salaries on the 25th of each month, keep schools and hospitals open, and even build a few roads. This was due simply to the money we were able to save by limiting corruption.'

He believes that his success sowed the seeds of his failure, 'since this represented the end of the political careers of many politicians'. There were also geopolitical aspects, including his intention to involve Algeria and Mauritania in his peace plan, which he says earned the ire of ECOWAS.

The soldiers who removed Cheick in December 2012 accused him of 'playing a personal agenda', saying that there was 'paralysis in the executive'. The event illustrated where power lay, albeit temporarily. Sanogo, who was promoted to general as a means of keeping him happily out of government, was arrested in 2013, charged with complicity in the kidnapping and disappearance of rivals within the Malian military.

The experience has not, however, reduced Cheick's faith in democracy. 'To the contrary,' he says, 'democracy is a continuous, non-stop dialogue. It's about finding a solution. It's the best alternative around. You can't build anything sustainable and durable without democracy; at the same time, it takes sustained effort and hard work by a lot of people to build such a system.'

The lessons of Mali's fall are that it is not enough to simply observe the conduct of elections and the facade of institutions. All may sometimes look well but the institutions that are necessary for democratisation may be failing, as they were in Bamako. Certainly, Mali demonstrates how hard it is to construct democracy after collapse. It also demonstrates the difficulty of donors pouring assistance into a weak institutional framework, and of building institutions robust enough to withstand the shock of a regional trauma of the scale of the fall of Colonel Gaddafi in Libya in October 2011.

Zambia's regression

Benin has remained a 'free' state despite challenges, while Mali eventually fell out of this category because of internal and external stress. However, Zambia represents much more the African norm: a country that was not 'born free' and that has been on 'the bubble' between 'free' and 'partly free' but has never achieved a high degree of institutional freedom. In fact, Zambia is a particularly interesting case because it has had consequential elections where the ruling party lost an election. It has had two instances (Kaunda was defeated by Frederick Chiluba of the Movement for Multi-Party Democracy [MMD] in 1991 while Rupiah Banda of the MMD was defeated in the 2011 elections by Michael Sata of the Patriotic Front)[16] since the early 1990s when the ruling party was defeated in the polls and left power, supposedly a profound test of democracy.[17] However, the successor party in each case has then largely replicated the patterns of government that had previously led to dysfunction. These failures come about because of a failure to institutionalise democratic practices and good governance even when electoral contests matter.

Kenneth Kaunda served as president of Zambia from independence in 1964 to 1991. For the last 18 years of this term his United National Independence Party (UNIP) government ran the country as a 'one-party participatory democracy', limiting freedom of political choices for citizens. As V.J. Mwanga, Kaunda's minister of foreign affairs and later a key member of the MMD, which agitated for the reinstatement of multi-party democracy in 1991, remembers of these times: 'To stand for election as a local councillor you had to be a UNIP member, and even to vote in local government elections, you had to have a valid UNIP card. You had to be a card-carrying member of UNIP to stand for parliament.' As a direct result, Mwanga recalls, 'The economy was in dire straits. The nationalised mining industry was on its knees. Eighty per cent of the economy was under state control and no direct private investment was coming into the country. There were critical shortages of foreign exchange and a short- age of basic commodities such as mielie-meal, sugar, bath and washing soap, butter, cooking oil and bread. Even Fanta, Coca-Cola, Sprite and orange juice were banned,' recalled the 73-year-old in 2017, 'and replaced by local drinks called Quench and Tip Top,' given the shortages of foreign exchange needed to import the concentrate.[18]

Chaos in the mines, in particularly, cost the country dearly. The Zambian government had nationalised the mines in 1971. By the mid-1990s, the mines were costing $1 million each day simply to stay open, while produc- tion had fallen by one-third from a peak of over 700 000 tonnes in 1972. Real GDP per capita fell from $1 455 in 1976 to $1 037 by 1987, or -3.6% per year, and to $892 by 2000. A decline in the copper price after 1973 and the simultaneous rise in the oil price did not help, but Chile, which pro- duced less copper than Zambia in 1970, by comparison rapidly increased its production over these four decades. Zambia's share of global produc- tion shrank to under 5% from 14% in 1970.

As economic conditions tightened under Kaunda, the population became increasingly restless, with food riots breaking out in the cities as donors became less keen to yet again bail out Kaunda's government. The answer then became, as Mwanga reminds us, an 'overwhelming' desire for a return of the country to a multi-party system of government, 'which would recognise the role of the private sector to act as an engine for economic growth' and act as a safety valve for these pressures. Economic reforms started during a period of gradual political liberalisation begun under

Kaunda, during which time the country briefly transitioned to 'free' status in 1991. The reforms continued with varying degrees of enthusiasm during the subsequent presidencies of Chiluba (1999–2002), Levy Mwanawasa (1992–2008), Rupiah Banda (2008–11) and Michael Sata (2011–14).

However, even though the benefits of political and economic reform were considerable, and virtually immediate, still they were rolled back. The mines, for example, which had been privatised in 2000, drove forward economic growth. But the government soon tampered with the policy regime that had driven this investment, abrogating the 'development agreements' in place with mining companies and upsetting tax regime stability.

While Zambia's democracy has delivered a degree of stability absent across much of the continent, the country remains a 'partial reformer' when it comes to governance and economic policy. For example, a 2018 World Bank study found that 75% of cabinet decisions are never implemented.[19] Zambia illustrates the cost of flawed electoral processes and a government that lacks a prioritised and detailed plan for development. With Sata, who was elected against the odds in 2011, defeating the incumbent Rupiah Banda on the basis of putting 'money into people's pockets',[20] more generally identity politics rather than issues have dominated political choices made by the electorate. Electoral and subsequent policy choices are driven instead by highly personalised politics, short-term rentier needs and distribution to predominantly tribal constituencies. As a result, voting reflects regional divisions, a pattern particularly true for Edgar Chagwa Lungu, who only narrowly won his two elections in 2015 and 2016.

As the World Bank notes, it was the 1991 'founding' election that marked a fresh start of a competitive political setting, departing from the dominant setting during Kaunda's one-party rule. However, in competitive settings where public institutions are weak and personalised, access to resources is based on relationships and patronage, rather than the public holding politicians to account on issues of interest.[21] As a result, Zambians are the least likely of all southern Africans included in the Afrobarometer series of surveys to feel that they can make things better through voting and elections, even though three-quarters continue to prefer democracy.[22] A weakness in overall democratic accountability is compounded by a failure to put up and be elected on a reform plan – a fault shared both by government and by the opposition. Government is elected based on its narrow series of promises. The pressure to do so is undermined by reliance on the minerals sector for its core income; thus resource dependency blunts the reform and diversification imperative.

Though the opposition is strong numerically in terms of its support base, their tactics undermine their role. For example, their refusal to attend parliament is counter-productive even if their reasons are just. And the institutions of governance, while possessing the form of Western counterparts – composition of laws, policies, systems and structures – are functionally weak. For example, the World Bank concludes that, despite its near best-practice form and structure, Zambia's Anti-Corruption Commission has not substantially affected perceptions of public funds abuse.

Finally, public accountability is low. Decision-making is seldom transparent, and the government does not prioritise public dissemination of information on policies and outcomes. This reinforces low standards of scrutiny, and the independent media is routinely neutralised. For example, Zambia's Freedom House ratings in 2017 deteriorated 'due to the restrictive environment for the opposition in the run-up to general elections, including unequal media access for opposition candidates and the use of the Public Order Act to ban opposition rallies.'[23] This lack of democratic space had negative consequences for economic choices. Afrobarometer surveys show that a growing number of Zambians see corruption levels in the country as rising, related to pervasive impunity and weak government institutions.[24]

Conclusion: The challenge of not being 'born free'

Being 'born free' is not an option for already existing independent states. Zambia, Benin and Mali all demonstrate the difficulties of sustaining a democratic transition for those African countries that are not 'born free'. Managing the economic ruin created by the previous ruling authoritarians, cultivating a democratic opposition and building institutions are hard work.

It is hardly surprising thus that the number of 'free' states has stagnated over the last few years. Benin and Mali, which were both celebrated for their democratic achievements at different points, demonstrate clearly why only a few states have managed all the challenges that are presented by a transition from an authoritarian past. Zambia, despite having a better electoral history than other countries, has not developed mature democratic institutions and has been unable to break out of the democratic stalemate affecting so many African countries.

Contrary to the 'sudden democratic moment' that characterised these examples, Ghana's success has been the result of an assiduous and painstaking process of incrementalism over nearly two decades, with an important supportive role being played by international and local actors.

Ghana's vice president, Mahamudu Bawumia,[25] elected in December 2016 on the ticket with Nana Akufo-Addo, says that several factors ensured a smooth transition, which then 'stuck' in Ghana. Overall, Bawumia says, 'the lessons from Ghana are not a one-size-fits-all, but in generality, they are huge lessons that African countries can emulate. Leaders willing to embrace change and not circumventing term limits, a free and open media, a strong elections board, active civil society and an open space for citizenship participation are key ingredients towards democratic reforms.' Crucially, he notes, 'the two main sides of the political divide accepted democracy, and this made it difficult for the military to intervene as they had done in the past'.

Getting transitions to 'stick' is no miracle, but the result of hard work, champions and compromise.

5

The Countries in the Middle

A critical, independent and investigative press is the lifeblood of any democracy. The press must be free from state interference. It must have the economic strength to stand up to the blandishments of government officials. It must have sufficient independence from vested interests to be bold and inquiring without fear or favour. It must enjoy the protection of the constitution, so that it can protect our rights as citizens.

— Nelson Mandela

Intimidation, harassment and violence have no place in a democracy.

— Mo Ibrahim

Chapter takeaways

- The most significant movement in African democratisation has been from the 'not free' to the 'partly free' category. In 1988, 34 countries were considered 'not free' and only 15 were judged 'partly free'. In 2008, the number of 'partly free' countries outnumbered the 'not free' by 24 to 19.

- The democratic stagnation in Africa is fundamentally due to a slippage in the 'partly free' category, which now has the same number of nations (22) as those categorised as 'not free'.

- 'Partly free' countries can stagnate because the patronage that politicians and their supporters derive from corruption can outweigh the majority's preferences for development.

'Before IPS,' says Francis Simion, 39, a Malawian farmer in the village of Njovuyalema, 'I had just half the production I have today.' He is referring to the Integrated Production System (IPS) of the Limbe Leaf Tobacco Company, from which he receives seed, fertiliser and ongoing technical advice in exchange for directly contracting his produce to the company.[1]

This system has changed his life. His five hectares of maize and four of burley tobacco now bring in more than $10 000 annually. In the seven years that he has been on the programme, he has been able to build a brick home with a corrugated iron roof and buy goats, 18 head of cattle, chickens and a five-tonne truck, which he uses to move the local produce, measured in 'oxcart units', to market. He owns one of 30 cellphones among the 56 families in the village of Njovuyalema (literally, 'The elephant is tired'), an hour's drive north of Lilongwe.

The comparison with those not on the IPS is stark.

We found Charles Layimon and his family amid the dust of nearby Mankohokwe village, sitting cross-legged on a reed mat while stripping corn from cobs. Farming three hectares of mostly maize, 'with a little bit of tobacco' since he did not have the required 10c per kilogram of tobacco crop to register as a producer with the government, his crop had to be sold on the side, earning him, on a good day, perhaps a quarter of the going rate. He showed us into his sparsely thatched mud hut nearby, two tiny, dark rooms, one with a wood fire on the floor, the other where he, his wife and two children slept. Looking much older than his claimed 42 years, his was the harsh face of hopeless poverty. He owned no livestock, could not afford the $40 to buy a bicycle and stood little prospect of ever affording the $40 per term required to send his children to a state secondary school.

Two Malawians, two stories, two Malawis, two different trajectories. This situation is replicated in other villages, in other sectors, and across the whole country and, indeed, the region. Those farmers in contractual relationships with big firms are prospering, at least by Malawian standards, and those left to fend for themselves are struggling.

The advent of democracy in 1994 prompted liberalisation and change in Malawi, though not all of it for the better. Corruption and rent-seeking have accompanied political contestation because of a combination of factors: improved human rights without a corresponding improvement in institutional capacity, increased reliance on donors, the shrivelling of local industry with liberalisation and diminished protectionism, increased consumer expectations, swelling population numbers and weak governance. All of this occurred in an environment where political parties desperately needed to find funds and patronise their supporters. 'The transition was badly handled, no doubt,' says one donor. 'There was no transparency at the start, and coupled with the need to fund political parties, it set the stage for things going wrong absent the discipline and fear that [independence leader and long-serving president] Kamuzu [Banda] instilled. Opportunity made thieves.' In fact, after a few years rated 'free' in the mid-1990s, Malawi has been categorised as 'partly free' every year since 1999.

This system inevitably led to scandal. Eighteen months into her presidency, by 2013 President Joyce Banda's government was embroiled in 'cashgate'. This scandal implicated government officials in syphoning perhaps as much as $250 million from the budget.[2]

This scandal was the final straw for the donors, a number cutting off aid in response, rocking the regime and raising questions about President Banda's survival and suitability. The extent of the rot surprised her. 'I knew when I took over for sure that we needed to recover the economy,' she says. 'But what I had not realised was the extent of the theft, that we had the same people stealing, jumping from one party to another. The reason why Malawi has remained stagnant and poor is because we built up and they siphoned off, we built up, they siphoned off, and so on. We estimated that one-third of our resources have been stolen in this way.'

They might complain, but donors have been complicit in this system for a long time, not least during Bingu wa Mutharika's regime when the $140 million annual government subsidy for seeds and fertiliser (the so-called Farm Input Subsidy Programme), donor-endorsed and funded in the interests of food security, was little more than a giant political feeding scheme. As the then Reserve Bank Governor Charles Chuka observed, 'How otherwise can you explain why we get only a one per cent increase in maize output in a year despite spending this sum?'

The public sector is the principal source of wealth creation in Malawi, and private companies are dependent on state contracts for their operation. It is a systemic problem, one that must be solved not just by removing a few personalities and tinkering with governance niceties, but by implementing a whole suite of reforms – affecting governance, public spending and private sector growth – at once.

While this goes on, many suffer. In the village of Chidoti, Mrs Levison sat forlornly, staring out of the doorway of her tiny dwelling, measuring little more than two square metres. Outside, baking in the winter sun, were her mud bricks. She complained, like all of the villagers we met, that she never saw government, though she 'just wants inputs' to get her business going.

According to the IMF, Malawi is the world's second poorest country in terms of per capita income, just above the embryonic state of South Sudan. While Malawi has been very poor for a long time, the spectre of rapid, unchecked population growth demands changing a 'business as usual' approach to its politics as well as to its development. The country continues to vote along ethnic lines in its regular elections. They change little, save those who are 'eating' at the top.

Malawi is an archetypal 'partly free' country. As Freedom House notes, it holds regular elections and has undergone multiple transfers of power between political parties. But these changes had frequently less to do with a groundswell for change based on different policy proposals than a 'result of rifts among ruling elites'. Political rights and civil liberties 'are for the most part respected by the state', however, 'corruption is endemic, police brutality and arbitrary arrests are common, and discrimination and violence toward women, minority groups, and people with albinism remain problems'.[3]

Saulos Chilima has been vice president of Malawi since 2014. A latecomer to politics, he was previously head of Malawi's leading cellphone company.[4] He says that the short-termism in policy decisions and the tendency to defer to identity in making choices stem from 'two key things: first, the parties in Malawi (except for the Malawi Congress Party) suffer from [what he terms] the founder syndrome. There is idolisation and glorification of the founders such that the followers or members literally perceive such founders as demigods and "worship" them. If the leaders are not careful (as has been the case here), they fall into this trap and start believing they are what their "subjects" make them believe.'

The second factor, he notes, 'is what we call politics of poverty in Malawi'. Politicians 'take advantage of the literacy levels and abuse the citizens. They steal from the poor people, enrich themselves and start giving handouts to poor citizens for different reasons. This happens at the expense of their ability to bring about meaningful change or development in the country. Midway through their term, they realise they haven't achieved very much because all they have done is look after themselves and their cronies.

'At this point,' observes Chilima, politicians 'panic at the fear of loss of power and, lo and behold, the genesis of short-term solutions to ensure victory at the polls with the sole reason of staying in power to reap more from their activities.'

Thus, Malawi's poverty is, put differently, the result of bad policy choices, and that is the result of bad politics. Without substantive freedom and democracy, the state will not deliver what people are promised and need. Like other 'partly free' countries, Malawi faces problems of insufficient accountability and little prospect of change.

* * *

It is the countries in the middle – like Malawi, those rated 'partly free' by Freedom House – that are both the most important to understand and the most difficult to analyse. These countries are critical because nations that have at least some freedoms and where elections are potentially consequential are most likely to supply the next batch of institutionalised democracies. It is much more difficult, as the next chapter makes clear, for countries where authoritarianism is deeply entrenched to make the leap to unambiguous political freedom. At the same time, precisely because their institutions appear to be either nascent or stillborn, the 'partly free' countries are particularly difficult to evaluate. In the last decade, as noted in Chapter 3, a large number of countries have resided in this middle category, with seemingly enough resilience to prevent a profound democratic decline but not enough to overcome the hurdles that would allow them to join the 'free' countries.

While every country is different, the general problem that 'partly free' countries face is the presence of elites who, once in power, develop a vested interest in non-democratic practices that enable them to enrich themselves and their immediate followers. Elections can sometimes force these elites to leave but democratic competition by itself has generally not proved successful in removing incumbents, precisely because those in power make and enforce the rules of the game.

'Since 1990,' notes the National Intelligence Council, 'fewer than one out of six African elections produced a change in the ruling party, in large part because of incumbents' access to state resources, electoral manipulation, and often high public approval ratings. The repeal or extension of term limits has helped to further consolidate presidential control in a dozen countries since 2000.'[5] Indeed, Nic Cheeseman and Brian Klaas have found, 'Elections aren't just failing to remove unpopular autocrats from power; they can actually make it easier for dictators to maintain political control.' They note that elections allow autocrats to divide the electorate while heightening mobilisation among supporters, and that the

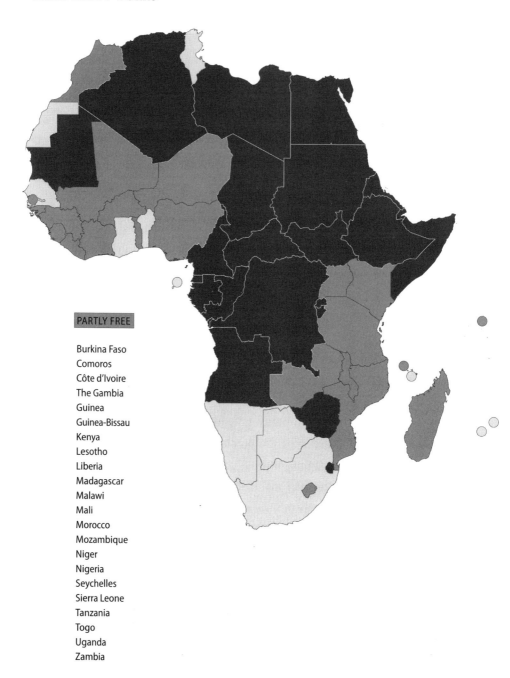

PARTLY FREE

Burkina Faso
Comoros
Côte d'Ivoire
The Gambia
Guinea
Guinea-Bissau
Kenya
Lesotho
Liberia
Madagascar
Malawi
Mali
Morocco
Mozambique
Niger
Nigeria
Seychelles
Sierra Leone
Tanzania
Togo
Uganda
Zambia

international community is often unwilling or unable to condemn even unfair elections.[6]

However, even when the incumbent is removed, the consolidation of freedom is not guaranteed. The new men (and occasionally women) who come to power may lack a genuine commitment to democracy, using elections merely as a path to power and self-enrichment. As the National Intelligence Council notes again: 'Historically, cases in which African reformers successfully pushed out autocratic leaders often failed to result in democratic transitions because the state was too weak to enforce the rule of law, the counterweights to executive power were few, and elite turnover was minimal, leaving room for new strongmen to consolidate control.'[7]

Therefore, our focus in this chapter is on what forces – be they leaders, institutions or civil society – are able to wrest control of the state from elites and convince everyone that the rules of the game will allow free competition. New leaders, even those who gain power via free elections, are often not enough because they have frequently competed not to promote freedom but instead to reward their constituents and perpetuate patrimonial politics. In many cases, even if *de jure* political power changes, *de facto* power remains with wealthy and important groups within the enduring elite – those with significant resources or high potential for violence.

This is not to downgrade the importance of elections, which remain the signal moment for any free society, as we note in Chapter 7. However, it has become clear that while elections may be necessary for political liberalisation, they are not sufficient by themselves. Strong institutions and a democratic culture are required over and above the intermittent exercise of voting.

Every country, as Tolstoy might have noted, fails in its own way, but the inability of African countries to institutionalise democracy is widespread across the continent. Tanzania, Mozambique and Kenya are examples of countries where there have been strong domestic sentiments in favour of democracy and great (if often misplaced) external optimism about each country's path. Yet, in all three cases, at times of crisis, the institutions that could have served as the protector of the populace failed. Their democratic performance, like that of so many 'partly free' countries, therefore remains unimpressive.

Tanzania: The limits of 'The Bulldozer'

Tanzania, unusually for Africa, had a transition to formal democracy that was elite-driven. In the early 1990s, founding father Julius Nyerere (who left power in 1985 but was still enormously influential until his death in 1999) and his colleagues saw what was happening in Africa and noted the displacement of some long-standing colleagues – notably Kenneth Kaunda of Zambia – who had also been young men when the winds of change first blew across Africa in the late 1950s. Fearful of a similar demise, the party that had ruled since 1977 (although its roots go back to independence), Chama Cha Mapinduzi (CCM – the 'party of the revolution'), acquiesced to the demand for formal political competition in 1992 and Tanzania initiated multi-party elections in 1994.

As many Tanzanians noted to us during a research trip in March 2018, the transition was not primarily 'demand driven'. Rather, the ruling party designed new political rules to provide something of a political opening while remaining committed to staying in power. In 1990, then President Ali Hassan Mwinyi established a commission under Chief Justice Francis Nyalali (subsequently known as the Nyalali Commission) to investigate the views of Tanzanians about political competition and to make recommendations about future structures. Tellingly, despite the Commission beginning work amid the euphoria of the fall of the Berlin Wall, 80% of the submissions it received were in favour of the continuation of one-party rule.[8] The Commission nonetheless recommended that Tanzania become a multi-party democracy, in part because it believed that most Tanzanians had known nothing but one-party rule and therefore continued to favour it.[9] Critically, the Commission concluded that 40 pieces of legislation had to be changed or repealed in order for the necessary conditions for multi-party competition to be realised.

However, the ruling party largely ignored the recommendations that would have allowed for substantive democracy. Instead, as Professor Mwesiga Baregu has noted, 'Among the many conditions recommended by the Nyalali Commission, only the removal of the party from public institutions was adopted. The rest were ignored and there was no attempt to explain why. Thus right from the beginning it would seem that the ruling party was less than fully committed to meaningful and fundamental change.'[10] Or as one opposition party leader remarked to us: '1992 was the biggest fraud ever perpetrated. Democracy was a gift to us, but it was a conditional gift. The condition was that CCM never leave power.'[11]

In fact, the CCM, when considered together with its predecessor parties (the Tanzania African National Union on the mainland and the Afro-Shirazi Party in Zanzibar), is the longest-ruling party in independent Africa. Every other party that led independence movements in the 1960s was either overthrown by military coups or displaced in the post-1989 era. The parties that led armed struggles in southern Africa (the MPLA in Angola, FRELIMO in Mozambique, ZANU in Zimbabwe, SWAPO in Namibia and the ANC in South Africa) are all still in power but they arrived later, and, given that they led armed movements and therefore had control of soldiers, their long tenures are less surprising.

A particular concern was what some in Dar es Salaam called the 'imperial presidency' because of the many powers vested in the executive. Nyerere famously said that he could have ruled as a dictator (and some believe that he did). When the Nyalali Commission recommendations were rejected, the imperial presidency was able to persevere, providing a significant power base for the CCM.

Members of the ruling party were especially committed to staying in power because control of the state was a source of self-enrichment. One newspaper editor told us that 'politics is the only source of income available to many'. A civil society activist described the CCM as 'a company of a few'. Tanzania's corruption, while hardly the most egregious in Africa, caused it to be listed as 103rd out of 180 nations by Transparency International.[12]

Tanzania was coded as 'partly free' in 1995, in part because multi-party competition had begun. In the subsequent 20 years, it was consistently accorded that status because of the ruling party's dominance on the mainland and significant electoral malfeasance on Zanzibar, including the nullification of the island's elections of 2015 and a subsequent election that was not seen as free or fair. In 2015, the government passed the Cybercrimes Act that places restrictions on social media, including supposed insults to the president, as well as allowing police to demand information from internet providers. The suppression of democracy in Zanzibar and constraints on social media led the US Millennium Challenge Corporation to suspend its partnership with Tanzania.[13]

There were new hopes when John Magufuli was elected president in 2015. Nicknamed 'The Bulldozer', he quickly excited the nation and the international community by taking unconventional steps, such as calling out Tanzania's notoriously somnolent civil servants as well as instituting prominent anti-corruption efforts.

However, demonstrating the dangers of placing too much hope on any new leader, it soon became clear that Magufuli threatened equally to 'bulldoze' the opposition. Those in Tanzania consistently report a political atmosphere that is restrictive and where everyone is afraid. Opposition party members have been threatened and attacked and bodies have started washing up on Dar es Salaam's beaches – shocking in a country that has not known political violence in decades.[14]

Magufuli has been using all of the powers that are granted to him by Tanzania's imperial presidency to accomplish this agenda.

All forms of political action that the CCM cannot control have been repressed. The media has been censored in a variety of ways. Newspaper editors report that government withdraws ads from newspapers and that, partially as a result, papers themselves practise self-censorship. One activist said simply that 'civil society has been shut down'.

In such an environment, there is widespread scepticism that elections can be free and fair. Opposition political party activists say that demonstrations have been banned outright in some cases, making it hard for them to mobilise supporters. This repression occurring well before an actual election is important to note because it places what is in many ways a binding constraint on political parties long before voting or campaigning begins, while observers tend to focus on the election period alone and may well conclude that the ballots were cast fairly.

Critically, Tanzanians told us that they did not need a unique model of democracy. They felt that the Nyalali Commission had done a good job of defining the outlines of a freer state but that its recommendations had been ignored. They were also generally happy with the form of liberal democracy that is prevalent in the West. Despite Nyerere's devotion to finding an autochthonous African version of socialism, no one suggested to us that there is a Tanzanian conception of democracy that differs radically from what currently might exist if the laws were reformed and the state operated fairly.

To date, no one in Tanzania has been able to displace the elite that has had first *de jure* (from the mid-1960s) and since 1992 *de facto* control of the political system. In particular, two forces that are often cited as threats to elite rule have been ineffective. Social media is widely available in Tanzania but the government's cybercrime laws seem to have intimidated many in the country from posting all but the most benign content. In 2018, the government began charging $900 to bloggers for a mandatory licence, an extraordinary fee in such a poor country. Even then, the permit can be revoked if a site 'causes annoyance, threatens harm or evil, encourages or incites crimes or jeopardizes national security or public health and safety'.[15]

Mange Kimambi (@mangekimambi_), a Tanzanian activist based in the US, has 1.8 million followers (as of April 2018). But her calls for protest seem to be ineffective in the face of government repression. She had urged her legions of followers to stage a dramatic mass protest on 26 April 2018, but it attracted only nine demonstrators, all of whom were promptly arrested.[16] Magufuli has taken note of Kimambi's posts and said, 'Some people have failed to engage in legitimate politics; they would like to see street protests everyday … Let them demonstrate and they will see who I am.'[17] In the end, social media is susceptible to the same modes of government repression as any other form of mobilisation, especially once activists move out of the digital realm.

Second, aid providers have not been particularly strong in responding to creeping authoritarianism, despite the status of Tanzania as a donor darling for literally decades. Indeed, Tanzania is the number one recipient of several important donor countries.[18] However, except for the Millennium Challenge Corporation – which has a mandate that demands that it automatically cease operations in countries that act in violation of its principles – the donors have not reacted strongly to the deterioration of Tanzania's political climate. Few have even threatened to cut aid and we could not find any documented cases where aid had actually been reduced because of the political environment, save for a corruption scandal in 2014 (the year before Magufuli took over), which saw the temporary suspension of $490 million in funding.[19]

Magufuli's ability to play the anti-corruption card, a direct borrowing from the playbook of Paul Kagame of Rwanda, and his pledge to shake up the notoriously inefficient Tanzanian bureaucracy, have attracted donors and seemingly assuaged any concerns that they might have had about declining political freedom. As one international donor told us, Tanzania is a pleasant place for donors to reside and some seem inclined not to rock the boat with the incumbent government. As has occurred in many cases elsewhere, donors are happy to make the trade-off between fundamental political rights and short-term economic progress.

Mozambique: The party continues

Founded in 1962, the Frente de Libertação de Moçambique (FRELIMO – Mozambique Liberation Front) has been the dominant political party in Mozambique since independence in 1975. Mozambique transitioned from a 'not free' to 'partly free' country in the early 1990s. Luísa Dias Diogo, the former finance minister and, between 2004 and 2010, prime minister, tellingly recalls: 'Between 1975 and 1994 we had democracy, but only internally and in one party, FRELIMO.'[20]

By the end of the first decade of the 2000s, Mozambique was riding high. In 2012, the national currency, the metical, was the best performing in the world against the dollar, while investment poured in. Even Portuguese nationals, who had fled en masse after independence in 1975, were trickling back to the former colony in search of better prospects and to escape Europe's economic troubles.[21]

In 2015, however, things started to go badly again. The immediate cause of the crisis was the halting of aid from the IMF, the World Bank and other international mechanisms after donors found that Mozambique had failed to declare debts of more than $1 billion taken on by state-linked companies. So severe was the economic crisis that, in July 2016, the Mozambique Finance Ministry suspended the national budget because of 'adverse national and international macro-economic conditions'. Earlier, and underlining the severity of the crisis, ratings agency Moody's had downgraded Mozambique from 'a lowly B2 to a dismal B3' credit rating.[22]

The major driver of the debt crisis was continuing poor economic governance caused by profound weaknesses in central institutions. There seems to be no structural check against widespread fraud. Mozambique ranked 153rd of 180 countries in Transparency International's 2017 Corruption Perceptions Index, down from 142/176 the year before.[23] According to the Anti-Corruption Resource Centre, the prevalence of corruption is a 'concern for both the public as well as donors, who support almost half of the state's budget. Corruption manifests,' it notes, 'in various forms, including political, petty and grand corruption, embezzlement of public funds, and a deeply embedded patronage system. Checks and balances are weak, as the executive exercises strong influence over the legislative and the judiciary. Corruption also affects several sectors in the country, such as the police, public administration, the judiciary, and public financial management.'[24] As a result, a small elite intimately linked with the ruling party dominates the economy, while the rest are left to pick up the scraps. Mozambique's institutions failed to prevent a crisis. Indeed, the political economy has been structured in a manner that appeared to make such a crisis inevitable.[25]

Daviz and Lutero Simango – sons of an early FRELIMO leader – are both in politics. The founder and president of the Democratic Movement of Mozambique (MDM), Daviz has been mayor of Beira since 2003. Older brother Lutero is an MDM member of parliament. He cautions against viewing the current system in Mozambique as 'democratic'.

'Since independence until now,' reflected Lutero in February 2018, 'we have had a type of party-state dominance in the form of FRELIMO. The first constitution was a one-party version in which FRELIMO was the guardian of the state. All those who wanted to be civil servants had to hold a FRELIMO membership card. If you wanted to be an officer in the army or police, you had to be a very good communist. Things were controlled from top to bottom of the state structure.'

Today, he argues, things are still heavily weighted against the opposition. 'When Mozambique began its multi-party system, they created electoral agencies – the National Electoral Commission (CNE) and the STAE (Technical Secretariat for Electoral Administration), essentially the electoral support body, which is supposed to be subordinate to the CNE. However, it runs to the government's orders, and it is politically motivated and directed. That's where all of our problems begin.'[26]

From his perceptive, there is another challenge. 'As a result of the civil war, it is not enough to form the CNE from the various political parties. The law does not address the management of the electoral process – specifically the registration of voters – in those areas where the state does not have a strong presence. Registration in 1994 took place mostly in those areas which were under the control of the state. People in RENAMO [the official opposition, Mozambican National Resistance or Resistência Nacional Moçambicana] areas did not have an opportunity to be registered.'

Then, in 1999, RENAMO succeeded in creating an electoral coalition, posing a much greater threat to FRELIMO at the polls. Although Chissano was re-elected with 52.3% of the vote, and FRELIMO secured 133 of 250 parliamentary seats, Lutero believes that things were skewed in the government's favour. 'Counting did not take place in Nacala [province]. No one knows those results till today. It is believed that if these votes had been counted FRELIMO would not have won.'

'All of this was managed by the STAE as a state department. Following this period, there were negotiations between Chissano and [RENAMO's leader Afonso] Dhlakama. But,' he claims, although the military structures were supposed to be shared between FRELIMO and RENAMO, 'this has not happened until today.'

He says that RENAMO support fell further in the 2004 and 2009 elections won by Armando Guebuza 'due to FRELIMO's reactivation of their party machine'. As a result, by 2014 RENAMO reverted 'to its military background to force matters, which led to an agreement, again, this time between Guebuza and Dhlakama'. RENAMO 'would prefer to have a relationship with FRELIMO with the status of an official opposition, since they don't have an agenda to rule the country. The MDM' – which he describes as a centre-right, free-market party where 'state guidance' plays a part – 'is the common enemy. They believe that if they leave the MDM alone, it could be a threat, which is why they agree to put us out of the ring, out of the political battlefield.' Dhlakama's death in his Gorongosa hideout at the age of 65 in May 2018 may be a game-changer for Mozambique's politics, not least since it shifts the balance of power between RENAMO and the government.[27]

The emergence of the MDM as a third way in Mozambican politics is amplified by their victory in key cities over FRELIMO: Beira, Nampula, Quelimane and Gurúè, in which nearly a million Mozambicans reside. As a result, Lutero observes, the central government 'has closed the tap' of financial support for these cities, 'the excuse always being the economic recession.'[28]

It's a difficult position to be in. 'According to our experience, you can change everything, but if you don't change the STAE, you change nothing. STAE should stop being a state department and instead come under the electoral commission. Without this reform, we will have the same result and issues as we have experienced in 1999, 2004, 2009 and again in 2014. FRELIMO's heart is within the STAE, where they do the manipulations, and that's why they won't consider its reform.

'Our role is made more difficult by not having television and radio exposure, without which we have little opportunity to conscientise our people. The youth today are not so interested in knowing who brought independence or democracy to the country. They are interested in education, health care, their future and their welfare.' But it is impossible to get the exposure that the MDM needs to put its view across on these issues. 'We are only scheduled to get access during the elections – and then only five minutes a day. All the time they are giving a message that the opposition is upsetting the country. They successfully shift attention from their failures, like the corruption that has led to the financial crisis now,' Lutero argues, 'by putting new issues on the table all the time.'

Mozambique demonstrates clearly how democracy can stagnate in 'partly free' countries. It has had elections and certainly has adopted the rhetoric of democracy. Mozambique has also had a relatively robust opposition that could claim genuine support in the rural areas. However, the FRELIMO elite was not committed to power-sharing, not least because they would no longer be able to enjoy the fruits of political power. As a result, governance declined for years until an unexpected series of events revealed the degree of rot in basic institutions. Despite poor governance and an economic crisis, FRELIMO has managed to stay in power, demonstrating how difficult it is to dislodge even dysfunctional party-states.

Within a quarter-century, the conflation of the party and state in Africa and the rent-seeking it produces usually saw the exit of the original liberation movement from power. This has been much slower to occur in southern Africa, where the ANC remains in government in South Africa, ZANU-PF in Zimbabwe, FRELIMO in Mozambique and the MPLA in Angola. It is difficult to imagine renewal among such corporatism, where the pursuit of power and not its purpose becomes the overwhelming goal.

Kenya: Elections and power

Elections are critical to democracy and they therefore often come to reflect all of the problems in a state. 'What has happened in Kenya with its election is not unique,' says Raila Odinga of the August 2017 election, 'in the context of Africa. The state capture of the electoral institution was followed by the judiciary,' observed the former prime minister in January 2018, 'and the security agencies, in our case the police force.' This capture arrangement has set the perfect stage for electoral autocracy on the continent, where elections are held as a ritual every four or five years, but they must be won by the incumbent at all cost. This is a threat to the process of democratisation in Africa, which started with the fall of the Berlin Wall, and competitive politics. 'Democracy in Africa,' he states, 'is under siege, which means that development is under siege.'[29]

Odinga and Uhuru Kenyatta together have a long history of contested elections. Odinga served as the prime minister for five years from 2008, a position in a power-sharing national unity government born out of the disputed 2007 election. The son of liberation icon Jaramogi Oginga Odinga, he was detained without trial for six years in the 1980s, accused of involvement in a failed coup attempt against President Daniel arap Moi.

First elected as a member of parliament in 1992, he has run four times for the presidency: 1997, 2007, 2013 and 2017. In 2007, the Kriegler report, commissioned to investigate the elections and the violent aftermath in which 1 000 died and 250 000 were displaced, found that more than a million dead names existed in the register of an election officially won by the incumbent Mwai Kibaki by just 230 000 votes.

In 2013, Odinga officially came second to Kenyatta, with 5.34 million votes (or 43.28% of the total cast), a result that he unsuccessfully appealed. The election result of 8 August 2017, which had declared Kenyatta as the winner with 54% of the votes cast to Odinga's 43%, was, however, annulled by the Supreme Court on appeal by Odinga's National Super Alliance (known as NASA) finding that the election was marred by the 'illegalities and irregularities', long claimed by Odinga. The former prime minister welcomed this, saying this move signals 'an end to business as usual, not only for Kenya, but for the rest of Africa and the developing world'.

The election nullification should have been the most important democratic moment in Africa since the first non-racial elections in South Africa in 1994. It provided a stark counterpoint to trends across Africa, and the world, in favour of creeping authoritarianism.

While donors had spent millions of dollars on an elaborate set of technologies to transmit local election results to the national counting headquarters, the electoral commission could not, after the fact, document the vote and it appears that at least some had figured out how to circumvent the system. That a senior election official had been kidnapped, tortured and murdered only a few days before the election added to the likelihood that the machines had been compromised. Good electoral technology is always important, but no one should believe that the machines by themselves guarantee a fair vote.

A subsequent fresh election ordered by the court for 26 October was won by Kenyatta when Odinga declined to participate, citing inadequate reforms to the Independent Electoral and Boundaries Commission to

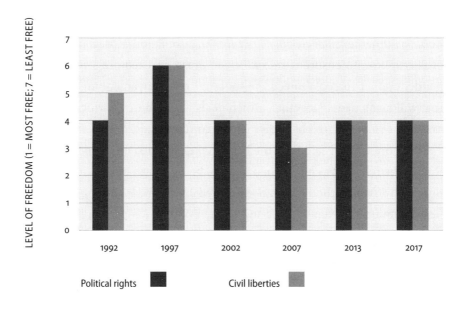

Figure 5.1: Freedom House ranking over multi-party elections in Kenya

allow a fair process. Kenyatta won 98% of the second-round vote with turnout officially at 38%, or less than half of that recorded in August.

Rather than a credible alternative to violence being opened to those in Africa who feel cheated at the election box, the electorate were let down not just once, but twice. First, there was the contradictory establishment of the people's government following the election. Subsequently, there was the personal 'handshake' deal between Kenyatta and Odinga in March 2018, which ended the impasse, without questions about the elections, however, being answered.

'My most important goal,' says Odinga of the handshake with Kenyatta, 'is unity. It is the starting point for everything: health care, education, security. By doing this, by making this agreement with Uhuru, I want to ensure that during the next election the results will be different. We need to bring these changes through dialogue to enable the elections to be free and fair. We agree,' observes the former prime minister, 'to carry out reforms, to deal with the negative impediments that make the system not work. We need to implement safeguards to prevent manipulation, to deal with issues of corruption, to ensure freedom of the press, and require a truly independent police force. We need,' he states, 'a new Kenyan culture, a system that will bring people together, which deals with ethnicity, which is based on higher values shared by the 44 ethnic communities.'[30]

The more cynical said that 'the handshake provided an opportunity for Raila to be relevant, as he was in danger of being frozen out, politically and financially'. While the deal was welcomed by many, including the business community given its lowering of the political temperature, both the conduct of the elections and the handshake represent a deeper problem in Kenya: of the elite- and ethnic-based struggles and pacts that characterise its politics, with little apparent concern for the voter and the burning issues.

The problem in Kenya is not in the main the technical and legal veracity of the elections. Nor is it about support for democracy itself. More Kenyans consider their country a democracy than before, while three-quarters say their leaders should be chosen through regular, open and honest elections.[31]

The problem, rather, is the nature of the 'it's my turn to eat' politics, and an electorate that is focused on the immediate spoils.

In Kenya, too, many politicians are focused on winning power, not what they are going to do with it save the division of the spoils. While this may be politically pragmatic if crude, the problems in Kenya grow larger with increasing population numbers (from 50 million in 2018 to a projected 95 million in 2050), too low economic growth, and a cash-strapped government. Although the official unemployment level is around 25%, nine in every ten unemployed Kenyans are 35 years and below and just half of the country's working-age population has primary school level of education. Together these trends are considered a 'ticking time-bomb'.[32] The absence of meaningful development plans from either candidate highlights this problem. For example, Kenyatta's 'Big Four' development plan – with its focus on manufacturing, universal health care, affordable housing and food security – is indicative of, if nothing else, how little substance matters. It's undoubtedly clear but wholly unachievable. The government seeks to raise the share of the manufacturing sector from nine to 15% of GDP by 2022, expand food production and food supply, provide universal health coverage for all Kenyan homes and build 500 000 affordable houses. Given the target of 1.3 million manufacturing jobs by 2022, an average of 706 jobs will have to be created each day.[33]

Yet, so long as domestic leadership prefers to mobilise along ethnic lines, this will not change. A politician who is able to break this mould and focus on issues instead of identity, or at least assemble complex multi-ethnic national coalitions, may be able to change the country's direction.

Conclusion: The challenge of consolidation

It is of course not only African countries that face the challenge of democratic consolidation and slippage.

Take Venezuela where, as María Corina Machado acknowledges, the job of an opposition politician has become increasingly tough. 'I have been called a romantic and a loser,' she says. 'But this is an ethical fight, to do with values.' She adds: 'It's very tough. I could not leave the country for the last four years. I have not been able to travel in commercial aeroplanes for the last 18 months,' she admitted in February 2018, 'at the threat of the operator losing their licence.'

Venezuela is an example of how things can quickly go badly wrong, despite a massive natural resource endowment, and despite an established democratic system and institutions. The Latin American country was, *circa* 2018, the site of an entirely man-made humanitarian emergency,[34] a result of the Bolivarian Revolution, started 20 years earlier by Comandante Hugo Chávez, who, following a failed coup in 1992, eventually acquired power through the ballot box six years later, but soon learnt how to manipulate the electoral process to his advantage. Two of the top three opposition leaders, Henrique Capriles, who received 49.12% of the vote in the April 2013 election, and Leopoldo López, a prominent opposition party organiser, were by 2018 under house arrest. SUVs with darkened windows and soldiers of the SEBIN, Venezuela's Bolivarian National Intelligence Service, stand guard outside their houses. Nicolás Maduro had referred to these two politicians and Machado as 'mercenaries' and 'fascist parasites', with the government describing them as the *trilogia de mal* (trilogy of evil).[35]

While the ruling party has enjoyed unprecedented access to state resources, the opposition has been undermined by the state changing the political funding regime, ending public support for parties – except for itself, of course. Opposition attempts to find alternative sources have been made virtually impossible by government threats against the private sector. The loyalty of the masses has been bought through the distribution of a monthly box of basic foodstuffs, while the bureaucracy has increased more than three-fold to over 2.5 million civil servants during the last two decades, ensuring a band of dedicated party loyalists.

In this process, Chávez laid out a radical playbook for other aspiring authoritarian democrats. Paradoxically, while he relied on elections to acquire power and legitimise his government, with each election the country lost more of its democracy.[36]

The media has been singled out for special attention. The cases of physical violence against journalists run into the thousands. Newspapers have been firebombed, while access to television and radio is dominated by the government, which has used the threat of heavy fines to encourage auto-censorship by journalists. The government has used national stations to broadcast repetitive propaganda, including *cadenas*, the apparently endless presidential broadcasts. In his 14 years in power, Chávez spent a total of seven months and one day on his *cadenas*. Venezuela ranked 137th out of 178 countries on the 2018 World Press Freedom listing.[37]

While Machado was not formally under imprisonment, the darkened windows of the cars outside her office were a reminder of the permanent menace of the state. Speaking from her modest Frente movement head-quarters in the Caracas suburb of Chacau, she said: 'It's hard to imagine a transition that will be tougher and more complex than the one we face. We have a humanitarian crisis, an internal security crisis and an economic crisis, which is deteriorating so fast.'

By 2018, more than 80% of Venezuelans were living in poverty. In a coun-try that produced barely one-tenth of its own food, there was widespread reliance on unaffordable imports. Supermarket shelves were pitifully bare. It is little surprise that Venezuela ranked top on Bloomberg's Misery Index for five straight years in a row from 2013.[38]

It has been a steep fall. Once the wealthiest country in Latin America, boasting a per capita income more than double the regional average up until the mid-1980s, Venezuela's fantastic store of natural resources includes the world's largest reserves of oil, and significant deposits of gold, coltan, copper, bauxite and nickel. While hyperinflation and debt defaults are not uncommon in Latin America, at the start of 2018 Venezuela was one of the few countries worldwide with a shrinking economy, and the only one with hyperinflation.

Venezuela joined Cuba in 2017 among Latin American states in Freedom House's 'not free' category. While Freedom House had found in 2009 that Venezuela was no longer an electoral democracy, it still maintained its 'partly free' status, to which it had slipped to from 'free' in 1999 as Chávez abolished congress, dismissed the judiciary and created a parallel govern-ment of military cronies in just his first year of rule.[39] By 2017, Venezuela had become an 'unambiguously authoritarian regime'.[40]

Futures are not preordained, however. Just next door, Colombia has successfully moved from a 'virtually failed state', in the words of its for-mer defence minister, Juan Carlos Pinzón,[41] at the turn of the twenty-first century, to a country that accepted no fewer than one million Venezuelan refugees between 2016 and 2018. For all of Colombia's history of human rights abuses, these different outcomes in the two neighbouring states, says Pinzón, 'reflect different trajectories, and this in turn the strength of institutions and different political choices'.[42]

* * *

The crucial problem with achieving a transition from 'partly free' to 'free' is that there is rarely sufficient internal or external pressure to do so, even when the majority wants this outcome. As the following chapter will demonstrate, the transition from authoritarianism to democracy is often precipitated by a severe crisis or conflict, and is enabled by a credible 'referee' that has the capacity to oversee reform. It is harder to imagine how a country that is performing moderately well, and has therefore reached a stable equilibrium, might make the final leap to full democracy.

There is the temptation to play identity politics around tribe (as in Kenya) or religion (Nigeria) or race (South Africa) in such socio-economic environments, with all the dangers it involves. Looking back on her public service, Helen Zille says that her 'biggest fear' in South Africa is 'mass unemployment and kids with no skills', and 'that we cannot get the economy going to absorb these kids and give them a chance in life'. This is not a uniquely South African problem, she admits, neither is it in relating to wider challenges around the rule of law. It does 'not surprise me that we have a generation that has gone through what we have and we have a default to populism with blacks blaming whites for being poor'. It is too easy, she laments, to 'scapegoat and mobilise still around race and ethnicity'.[43]

'In the long run,' Nic Cheeseman notes, 'efforts to promote development and fight corruption will not be successful unless they strengthen the institutions of the state.'[44] Ad hoc efforts to stop corruption, such as in President Magufuli's Tanzania, may attract attention and look effective, but in their highly personalised nature they only serve to compound the problem. The aim of governance is, after all, to allow for less personal discretion, not more. And it's not a question of whether individual leaders steal that defines the political economy, even though their example can be morally important. It is about whether their actions serve to strengthen or undermine institutions and their checks and balances.

6

Beginning the March to Democracy

I have cherished the ideal of a democratic and free society in which all persons live together in harmony and with equal opportunities. It is an ideal which I hope to live for and to achieve. But if needs be, it is an ideal for which I am prepared to die.

— Nelson Mandela, *Long Walk to Freedom*

Chapter takeaways

- Twenty-two African countries are rated as 'not free'. Thirteen of these countries have been consistently authoritarian since 1988.

- If Africa's most problematic countries are going to democratise, they will need some kind of 'referee' – either internal or external – who can assure the parties that the new rules of the game will be followed, and that the next election will not be the last in the context of weak institutions and lack of trust.

- The referees have to undertake a degree of risk that few politicians can stomach.

- There are relatively few leaders who have the gravitas and personal legitimacy to serve as a domestic referee.

- Integrity of the civil service and dependency on the state are critical challenges in post-conflict democratic transitions.

Frederik Willem 'F.W.' de Klerk is, on paper, an unlikely negotiator and man to help lead South Africa into a democratic, non-racial era. Born into a conservative Afrikaner political family, his National Party lineage was impeccable. His father, Jan, became secretary of the National Party in the Transvaal province in 1948, and later rose to a cabinet post and president of the senate, becoming interim state president in 1975.

Elected as a member of parliament in 1969, F.W. de Klerk first entered the cabinet in 1978 under Prime Minister B.J. Vorster as minister of posts and telecommunications and social welfare and pensions. Under P.W. Botha, who took over as prime minister in October 1978 and as state president in 1984, he held various ministerial posts, including sports and recreation; mines, energy and environmental planning; mineral and energy affairs; internal affairs; and, from 1984 to 1989, national education and planning. From 1982 he was the Transvaal leader of the National Party, and in February 1989 was elected as the national head of the National Party.

Within six months he was state president, replacing the incapacitated Botha, who supposedly had suffered a stroke. Once installed as president, after a particularly robust meeting with Botha, De Klerk lost no time in calling for a non-racist South Africa and for negotiations about the country's future. Even those closest to him expected a more cautious, controlled style of reform. Yet, De Klerk went against the grain and delivered the peaceful transition that none of his successors had been able or willing to do, accepting huge political and military costs in the process.

The reformer within him quickly came to the surface and the political pragmatist acted immediately. 'It was fundamentally a measure,' says journalist Ray Hartley, 'of F.W.'s strength of character' that he acted contrary to his political upbringing and followed his political instincts instead.[1]

On 2 February 1990, De Klerk announced the lifting of the ban on the ANC, the Pan Africanist Congress and the South African Communist Party, releasing Mandela among other imprisoned leaders. 'The season of violence is over,' De Klerk said. 'The time for reconstruction and reconciliation has arrived.' This paved the way for open negotiations on the country's future, which had begun in secret during the Botha years.[2]

'There were two major challenges to be overcome,' De Klerk reflected in 2018 on the challenges facing him in the negotiations, 'which were in step with each other. The first was to take my power base with me and to continuously do so in a democratic way to have a mandate for what I was doing. The other was the negotiation itself, to be able to reach an agreement that could be in step with real democratic values, but which would contain sufficient safeguards against the misuse of power.' These challenges were 'overcome by taking my cabinet and top management along with me in my party. At the level of government, I was seemingly losing support, losing by-elections to the right, facing calls for an election under the old order. This is why I called the [1992] referendum.' It was through tough negotiation, the former president reminds us, 'and through give and take, that we have a very good and strong constitution.'[3]

De Klerk modestly undersells his own role, and leadership, and the relationship he was able to forge in the process with Nelson Mandela, his critical negotiating partner. Whatever the ups and downs in their fraught negotiating history, they recognised that they needed each other. But De Klerk's role also highlights the importance of accepting risk in order to initiate and guide a political transition. In pursuing the March 1992 whites-only referendum, he put his political career, and possibly that of Mandela, in jeopardy.[4] Such risks were necessary to be able to negotiate his party from power.

* * *

The 22 African countries rated in 2018 as 'not free' are the most difficult settings for democratisation. As noted in Chapter 1, 13 of these countries have been consistently authoritarian since 1988. However, there have been several countries that have moved out of the 'not free' category. Some have

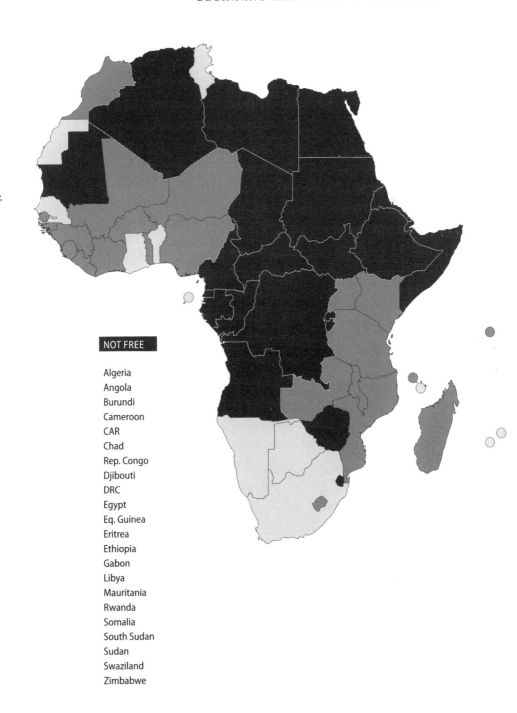

NOT FREE

Algeria
Angola
Burundi
Cameroon
CAR
Chad
Rep. Congo
Djibouti
DRC
Egypt
Eq. Guinea
Eritrea
Ethiopia
Gabon
Libya
Mauritania
Rwanda
Somalia
South Sudan
Sudan
Swaziland
Zimbabwe

done so successfully, and others, inevitably, have failed and regressed, to their old rating.

The need for a referee

Whether they have made progress on democratisation in the past or not, the countries with the lowest ratings face severe obstacles to enacting meaningful political liberalisation. While multi-party elections may be staged routinely, they do not actually pose that much of a threat to many authoritarians because holding them is an easy way to divert the attention of the international community. Over the decades of independence, a political culture has often developed that views control of the state (and the patronage thus derived) as a prize to be won through any means necessary and not to be given up by risking truly consequential elections. Countervailing institutions, such as the press and courts, are underdeveloped or controlled outright by the existing leadership. The opposition, such as might exist, is usually weak, disorganised and sometimes more interested in assuming power for material self-interest rather than to initiate a democratic order. Ethnic cleavages may have been allowed to grow unchallenged and leaders often find it easiest to mobilise constituencies around shared cultural symbols and cues rather than policies that might help the nation.

Very few, if any, of Africa's existing authoritarian regimes show the desire to begin a pacted transition, as in the case of Taiwan in the 1990s, that might result in democratisation over several decades through elite leadership. Political openings, as in Tanzania, are more likely to emerge as expedient tactics to avoid international pressure and to help quash nascent democratic stirrings in domestic politics. In environments of scarcity, the fight to control the state is so immediate that long-term thinking is discouraged. Also, African authoritarians have not based their rule on the performance legitimacy that has come to define the early industrialisers in South Korea, Taiwan and Singapore. Those leaders cultivated support by demonstrating that their countries were doing well and eventually decided, at least in the first two cases, that continued success required democratisation.

If Africa's most problematic countries are going to democratise, they will need some kind of 'referee' – either internal or external – who can assure the parties that the new rules of the game are going to be followed, that the next election will not be the last transition, and that they will be able to compete for power in the future. That kind of assurance can go a considerable way in determining whether the parties contesting power will limit themselves to democratic practices or whether, should the pursuit of power become desperate, they will seize power by force. Overcoming commitment problems is crucial to establishing a democratic regime.

The actual referee who helps enforce the rules of the game will vary depending on a country's circumstances and opportunities. In some cases, it may be an external force that has taken an interest and has adequate standing so that domestic groups find it credible. In other cases, domestic actors – say a former military leader or respected politician – may have the gravitas and legitimacy to propel the country towards a more democratic role. The crucial issue is that such a referee should exist or, if not, that local forces and external agencies should help to create one. As in South Africa, anyone who takes on this role will face substantial risk to their own political futures and, it is not an exaggeration to say, potentially to their lives.

Prospects for transition in authoritarian countries are therefore contingent on the right leaders or external forces emerging. We do not view political stagnation as inevitable but we recognise that leadership is a critical ingredient that can often not be predicted in advance. For instance, it was not obvious to many that Nigeria would succeed in its transition because the presence of military leaders who viewed it in the interest of the armed forces to leave power was not guaranteed.

Nigeria, Liberia and Burundi have profound ethnic and (in Liberia) racial divisions within their societies that have been the impetus for civil war and considerable violence. All three perform poorly across a broad range of measures of governance. However, while Nigerian democracy remains profoundly flawed, it does permit the hosting of consequential elections on a regular basis. In 2015, Nigeria witnessed, for the first time in its history, a political transition between parties when Muhammadu Buhari defeated the incumbent president, Goodluck Jonathan, and took power without violence. The transition in Nigeria from 'not free' to a 'partly free' country with elections was eventually successful because the military took it upon itself to guarantee the move towards a more liberal system. Similarly, Liberia, under the leadership of Ellen Johnson Sirleaf, has emerged from a brutal civil war and become a country that is now rated as 'partly free' and that has improved on a wide variety of governance measures. With the support of the UN and others, Liberia also enjoyed a competitive election in late 2017 when the opposition Coalition for Democratic Change, led by soccer star George Weah, defeated the United Party, led by Joseph Boakai, who had been Johnson Sirleaf's vice president for 12 years. Burundi, on the other hand, despite many such attempts, continues to replay its old dysfunctional politics because no one, internally or externally, is a credible referee for democracy.

Nigeria: The man on horseback steps aside

Distinguished-looking, with a neatly cropped white beard and a quiet manner, Abdulsalami Abubakar seems today an unlikely coup-maker. In fact, the former general ended the military's coup culture by handing over to an elected civilian administration in May 1999, when Nigeria also transitioned from 'not free' to 'partly free'. By then, Nigeria had experienced eight successful coups d'état in the first four decades of its independence.[5]

Reflecting back, Abubakar strongly 'advises against the military making a coup. It doesn't do any good to anyone. The military,' he says, in a particularly telling observation, 'are the first casualties since you usually kill each other. Then when you become a government you erode military professionalism. And you will always be watching your back. In the long run, the military have to give way to constitutional authority and come back to their primary role of maintaining and defending their country.'

It has been a long way back to the barracks for Nigeria's military. The first coup attempt, in January 1966, set the stage for what was to follow. Carried out by (mostly) Igbo army officers, it led to the deaths of the prime minister, Alhaji Sir Abubakar Tafawa Balewa, and the finance minister, Festus Okotie-Eboh, among others. Though it failed, the attempt provided the pretext for the head of the Nigerian Army, Johnson Aguiyi-Ironsi, to seize power. In the next putsch, in July 1966, Major General Yakubu Gowon succeeded Ironsi.

Gowon was in turn ousted in a palace coup in July 1975, which brought then Brigadier Murtala Mohammed to power as military head of state. Next, the abortive (so-called Dimka) coup in February 1976, in which General Mohammed was assassinated, resulted in Lieutenant General Olusegun Obasanjo taking over. Following a return to civilian rule under President Shehu Shagari in 1979, on 31 December 1983 a group of senior army officers led by Major Generals Ibrahim Babangida and Muhammadu Buhari took over, with Buhari appointed as head of state. Chief of Army Staff Babangida in turn overthrew Buhari in August 1985. Two failed coups followed in December 1985 (the 'Vatsa' attempt) and again in 1990, before the country hesitantly returned to civilian rule with the appointment of Chief Ernest Shonekan as interim president in August 1993.

Presidential elections were held on 12 June 1993, resulting in a victory for Chief Moshood Abiola. However, the elections were annulled by Babangida. As a result, Shonekan's administration lasted just three months before Sani Abacha (who had played a part in the 1983 Buhari coup) launched his own coup on 17 November 1993. Abacha's disastrous regime caused Nigeria to be downgraded to 'not free'. Following General Abacha's sudden death on 8 June 1998, General Abdulsalami Abubakar, as chief of the defence force, was sworn in as president.

Promising to hold elections, General Abubakar quickly established the Independent National Electoral Commission, which oversaw a series of local government, state, gubernatorial and National Assembly elections before the presidential vote of 27 February 1999. He, therefore, took it upon himself to be the referee that Nigeria needed. Abubakar transferred power to the elected president Olusegun Obasanjo on 29 May 1999 and retired from the army.

Abubakar was among the first members of the Nigerian armed forces who worked his way through the entire rank structure. Originally enlisting into the Nigerian Air Force, following training in West Germany, in 1966 he was seconded to the army. Commissioned as a second lieutenant into the infantry at the start of the Nigerian Civil War in 1967, he was quickly promoted. By 1978, he was the commanding officer of the Nigerian battalion in the UN force in Lebanon. Following a term as the military secretary of the army in 1986–8 and general officer commanding of the 1st Mechanised Division, between 1991 and 1993 he served as army chief of plans and policy before being appointed as chief of defence staff, the top military post, by Abacha. Due to his outstanding military career, he had considerable legitimacy throughout Nigeria.

Reflecting on why he became a democratic referee for Nigeria, Abubakar observes, 'When I took over [power], there was a lot of anti-military feeling among civilians, and this permeated into the military itself.' Far from self-interest, Abubakar noted that there were profound institutional reasons within the armed forces to ensure a transition: 'The military was never keen to make a coup. It was in this way a victim of itself. With the erosion of professionalism and discipline came a lack of training. No realistic field exercises were held. Our best leaders were not deployed in running the institutions, but were in government.'

Of critical importance was the fact that ethnic politics, which had often crippled Nigerian politics, were also degrading the armed forces: 'The military had stopped thinking about its role in a national sense. We needed to ensure that the military represented every ethnic group, not one or another, and the entire nation. As such, we needed to ensure also that the politics did not degenerate into ethnic squabbles between the northern-dominated military and southern-dominated civilian opposition. We in the military thought it necessary to checkmate this tendency by giving people the democracy they had been begging for.'

Despite several stumbling blocks, thoughtful leadership managed to eventually get Nigeria through the transition. He notes: 'First we had to ensure that we gave no party an advantage in the election. If we had put the presidential election on first, this would have determined the other results. So we had to start from the bottom up. There was also a lack of confidence. The doubting Thomases did not believe that we could achieve democratisation given our history.' The success of each of the various elections helped to address this. 'The international community also rallied around to give us support for the logistical aspects of the election.'

And so, the armed forces were out of politics. Of course, all is still not well within the Nigerian polity and many challenges remain. However, the 1999 elections did ensure that politics 'were more nationally rather than regionally focused'. Abubakar states that 'the biggest challenge that we have in Nigeria is to become a nation. We are a conglomeration of small ethnic groups amalgamated by the British. People are still thinking of their state [region] first. It is changing slowly with the emergence of a younger generation, better educated and more exposed to outsiders than we were. So we are progressing, but very slowly. Old politicians are still playing old games since they don't,' he smiles, 'want to give up power.'[6]

Liberia: The essential woman

For all of the challenges of corruption and dependency that afflict Liberia today, it is too easy to forget the long road that the country has travelled during this century. In the 1997 election, Charles Taylor campaigned on the slogan 'He killed my ma, he killed my pa, but I will vote for him'. Citizens voted for him in a landslide because they feared that he would restart the civil war if he lost.

During the 12 years (2006 to 2018) of President Ellen Johnson Sirleaf's two-term government, the economy averaged more than 7% annual growth. Per capita income rose from a low point of just $80 at the end of the second civil war in 2003 to $700, even though the population increased by nearly 50% to just under five million. Life expectancy was up from 53 to 61 years. What was once defined as a 'failed state' was now capable of taking over essential tasks. After being rated as 'not free', it has been consistently 'partly free' since 2004. In the 2017 elections to succeed Johnson Sirleaf, the opposition won, allowing Liberia to join the limited club of countries where elections had produced a peaceful transfer of power.

Johnson Sirleaf is in many ways the epitome of the referee needed for democratisation out of difficult circumstances. She campaigned for democracy for many years, gaining credibility during Liberia's worst days, and won the Nobel Peace Prize in 2011 for her efforts to rebuild the country. After leaving office in 2018 she was awarded the Ibrahim Prize for Achievement in African Leadership. In awarding the prize, the Mo Ibrahim Foundation noted: 'Since 2006, Liberia was the only country out of 54 to improve in every category and sub-category of the Ibrahim Index of African Governance. This led Liberia to move up ten places in the Index's overall ranking during this period.'[7]

President Johnson Sirleaf has a reputation as a tough-minded task-master. The whiteboard to the side of her desk identifies clear priorities, timelines and goals for government. She has focused scant resources on the things that matter. She operates out of the same, humble facility in the Ministry of Foreign Affairs as she did in 2006.

In response to the question of how Liberia managed the twin challenge of economic recovery and transition to a democratic government, she turns to the country's history. 'Let me start,' she says, 'by taking us back 12 years, to explain what the agenda items were back then.

'The first priority was to keep the peace. This was critical after two decades of war. Anything else had to be secondary, given that the record showed that there was a very high chance of post-conflict countries reverting to conflict.

'The second priority was to restore basic services to make people think once again that they were human beings, recognising that the challenges were being dealt with. And third, we had to restore the nation's reputation and creditworthiness. Liberia was a poster child of blood, death and destruction on every television around the world.'[8]

Looking back, she acknowledges there are things she might now approach differently. 'The first of these concerns capacity. We had a civil service that comprised the various warring factions, placed there for reasons of patronage. While some of them meant well, many had no qualifications. But it was difficult to get rid of them since this was their sole means of income and support for the families, with no private sector and very few NGOs. Even today,' she muses, '60% of the national budget is spent on salaries.'

'Integrity' was the next challenge. 'I made bold statements about corruption – including in my inaugural address – without realising how deep-rooted it was, and the extent to which it had become part of the culture. Even though we took some actions, it was so ingrained as a means of survival or for whatever reason, that the institutions we tried to build became a microcosm of the problem. This was worsened by the nature and the familiarity of our society, where people would expect certain things from family members.

'Perhaps we needed sociologists, or others who could help us understand the roots of the problem. Regardless, we focused on building institutions, laws and policies and improving compensation for workers and systems for remuneration, to help to remove discretion and change the incentives for corruption. Still, this aspect remains a challenge today,' she said in August 2017, 'whatever the progress we have made.'

Johnson Sirleaf believes that the issue of integrity goes hand in hand with the country's next, and ongoing, challenge – dependency. 'When we took over, many people had spent a lot of time in refugee camps.' More than 150 000 Liberians were killed in the war between 1999 and 2003. Out of a pre-war population of 2.8 million, one million had been displaced and 700 000 had fled the country. 'The manner in which they were provided with shelter and food disempowered them,' says Johnson Sirleaf. 'They got to a place where they felt entitled. But this dependency was not just concentrated at the lower end of the ladder. It quickly has become a way of life, more than the social sharing that is part of any African society. This has led to unacceptably high salaries at some levels, in part because of the demands on people to respond to the needs of others. If we did it again,' she advises, 'I would caution people "to do the hurt early".'

Johnson Sirleaf concludes that 'these main challenges – of capacity, integrity and dependency – were reflected in just about everything that we did, whether this was promoting the private sector, dealing with communities, or finding capable ways of applying rules and procedures.'

All of this related to the challenge of education – of the youth and of the public. While social media provided a tool to get the message across, 'it was too sporadic, too fragmented, too focused on day-to-day matters'. With a long-term UN mission *in situ*, she acknowledges that while external partners were 'effective in terms of providing resources to a resource-scarce nation, they were not effective in providing the opportunities for change. To get things to change, outsiders have to sometimes take account of people's priorities, and allow the locals to take the lead.'

Doing this in a democratic environment made this 'more difficult'. But any attempt to develop in a faster, authoritarian way 'could have been a trigger for conflict. We could not suppress freedom in getting things done. It was not easy to implement a democracy in such a broken society. But democracy was driven by the people's demand. It was a demand that was welcomed from my perspective. I originally wanted to do only one term.

But democracy is not linear, and the things I wanted to complete were not finished at the end of that first term.' Civil society was 'the key driver of democracy. The legislature was not that supportive of the democratic process, as they were mainly focused on retaining their own interests. My biggest surprise was quite how devilish they were, my own party included. The court system,' she says, 'really failed, too, until the last election.'

There is a need for people to understand the responsibilities that go with democratic rights. This probably has to begin,' she reflects, 'at a very early age, in the curricula of schools.

'From our side, probably there was not enough consultation with the people, and too much focus on getting things done. We needed from time to time to take a step back, to attend town hall meetings, to talk about how we go into conflict and explain how we are going to get out of it.'

Johnson Sirleaf obeyed the constitutional limit of two terms as president and elections were held to succeed her in late 2017. As a dramatic end to Johnson Sirleaf's time in office, she failed to endorse her own vice president, Joseph Boakai, who was representing her United Party and instead endorsed George Weah, who was running in the opposition Coalition for Democratic Change. Despite various court actions, Weah won in the second round and became Johnson Sirleaf's successor. A global footballing legend, 1995 FIFA World Player of the Year and recipient of the Ballon d'Or, he was 'most surprised by, wherever I go, discovering that there is no development in the slum communities. After 12 years we thought that there would be more development, not just hotels. In 170 years [of independence], from one leader to another, the place stays the same.'[9] As his predecessor notes: 'His failure to deliver what he has promised the poor could lead to disenchantment, with the youth bulge increasing every year. But the bigger challenge we have is how to change the political setting to promote democracy. This will require,' Johnson Sirleaf states, 'resetting our political party systems.'

Burundi: The endless struggle for power

Burundi's history is steeped in violence within a polity that has never had a credible referee to assure the parties that the political blood sport would end and that peaceful democratic competition was possible. As a result, while it made the transition to 'partly free' in 2003, by 2014 it was again considered 'not free'.

Even before independence, on 13 October 1961, Prince Louis Rwagasore, Burundi's prime minister, was shot and killed on the porch of the Hôtel Club du Lac Tanganyika in Bujumbura. The country's national independence hero, a member of the Tutsi royal family[10] married to a Hutu, Rwagasore was seen as someone who could bridge the divide between the two groups. He was shot by a Greek resident, Jean Kageorgis, acting apparently in cahoots with the pro-Belgian Christian Democratic Party (PDC). Belgium had allowed for the creation of political parties after 1948, out of which grew two main entities: the Union for National Progress (UPRONA) led by Rwagasore, and the PDC led by Belgian loyalists. UPRONA had won legislative elections the same month of the prince's assassination. 'It was a bit like what could have happened in South Africa if Nelson Mandela was murdered before assuming the presidency in 1994,' reflected one politician.[11] Kageorgis, allegedly paid by Belgian settlers who thought the country better under Hutu rule, was tried and executed in Bujumbura (then known as Usumbura) the following June. But the impact of his action – killing a possible referee – lasted much longer, as the country descended into a spiral of violence.

In 1965, the constitutional monarch King Mwambutsa IV appointed a Tutsi prime minister, much to the annoyance of Hutus, who comprised the majority of parliament. An attempted coup by the Hutu-dominated police was brutally put down by the army, led by Captain Michel Micombero, a Tutsi from Bururi province. Mwambutsa was eventually deposed in 1966 by his son, Prince Charles Ndizeye (who took the regal title Ntare V), but Micombero soon returned to the political fold to topple Ntare and abolish the monarchy. By 1972, violence escalated with the launch of systematic attacks by the extremist Hutu organisation Umugambwe wa'Bakozi Uburundi (Burundi Workers' Party), with the intention of exterminating all Tutsis.

Indeed, in contrast to Rwanda in 1994, it is sometimes forgotten that the mass killings of Hutus by the largely Tutsi army in Burundi in 1972 and the 1993 slaughter of Tutsis by the Hutu populace were both also genocides. In 1972, martial law was proclaimed by Micombero. Lists of Hutu targets were carefully drawn up, including the elite and those with a military background. The government claimed 15 000 were killed, while Hutu opponents put the figure at some 300 000.

Major Pierre Buyoya, also a Tutsi, staged a coup in Burundi in 1987, wresting power from Colonel Jean-Baptiste Bagaza, who had himself led a bloodless coup 11 years earlier.

Following the appointment by Buyoya of an ethnically mixed government, Melchior Ndadaye's Hutu-dominated party won the first democratic election in June 1993. But tension grew quickly between the new government and the army and its political backers, and President Ndadaye was assassinated on 21 October 1993 by Tutsi officers. Possibly as many as 300 000 Tutsi and Hutu were massacred as reprisal followed reprisal in the following months.

Following his assassination and still more violence, the next president, Cyprien Ntaryamira, also a Hutu, had the misfortune to hitch a ride with the Rwandan president, Juvénal Habyarimana, in April 1994. He was killed together with his Rwandan counterpart when their Falcon aircraft was shot down on its approach to Kigali airport, the event that sparked the ensuing Rwandan genocide in which several hundred thousand mainly Tutsi lost their lives.

After President Ntaryamira's death, Sylvestre Ntibantunganya, who was the speaker, took over as president in April 1994. After almost two years, he could not stabilise the country and, amid the Hutu rebellion attacks and the demonstrations of the Tutsi youth in the Bujumbura streets, Buyoya seized power again in a second coup d'état in 1996. The regional and international community played a key role in brokering a power-sharing agreement, known as the Arusha Accord between a Tutsi-dominated government and Hutu rebels in 2003. This led to a new constitution in 2005, and the election of a majority Hutu government under President Pierre Nkurunziza of the National Council for the Defence of Democracy–Forces for the Defence of Democracy in 2005 and again in 2010.

President Nkurunziza in 2015 violated the agreement that lay behind Burundi's transition from conflict to peace and showed that the external actors who had brokered the agreement were not credible referees. In April that year, he announced that he would run for a third term, which was followed by mass protests and a failed coup the next month. Nkurunziza then contested and won the July 2015 elections, resulting in widespread violence in which 1 200 people were killed and 400 000 displaced, the closing down of media and a political impasse. Political opponents fled the country in large numbers, accusing the regime of authoritarianism and abuse and of undermining the Arusha peace deal. Then, in a May 2018 referendum, Burundians voted overwhelmingly in favour of constitutional changes, including increasing presidential powers and extending presidential terms to seven years, effectively enabling Nkurunziza to stay on in power until 2034, like his neighbour Paul Kagame.

In reflecting on these failures in 2017, Pierre Buyoya, the African Union's regional envoy to the Sahel, notes, 'We came to democracy through a very difficult process. Following elections in 1993 the president was killed, which led to a transitional government and a long process of negotiation through the Arusha process, where we redefined democracy as one-man-one-vote with measures to accommodate the minority.'[12] He adds: 'We thought that we had defined our democracy positively for a society where we have two major ethnic groups unequally balanced. Then we had elections. [After] the first election in 2005, where

Nkurunziza was elected and governed until 2010, he was re-elected and governed again until 2015 when normally he would have no right to be a candidate again. But he refused to respect the Arusha agreement and the constitutional dispensation, saying that the first election [in 2005] did not count. Despite demonstrations against this third term and many of the population boycotting the election, he was elected again.' Nkurunziza won 69.41% of the 2.8 million votes cast. The election was marred by an extremely low turnout in the capital Bujumbura, where opposition to Nkurunziza's presidency was strongest, and where the turnout stood at 29.75% against the national average of 73.44%.[13]

'We are trying to fix the problem, now,' says the former president, 'through dialogue and mediation. But Nkurunziza no longer adheres to the term limits as provided by the Arusha agreement and the constitution. This is why he does not want dialogue. His project is to be in power for an unlimited time, and he is determined to carry it out at any cost. But there is no easy fix to this. The country is under sanction and is being boycotted by the major donors already.' There appears to be no hope of an effective external referee in Burundi: 'East Africa has tried, the African Union has tried, and the UN is *persona non grata*. Perhaps one day,' Buyoya muses, 'a free Burundi society will emerge.'

In June 2018, in a surprise move, Nkurunziza said he would step down in 2020.[14] But this commitment will depend on an external actor with sufficient power or interest to make it stick. Until then, Burundi continues to illustrate that the politics of identity and the interests of power often trump national issues and interest.

Outside of Africa, there are also examples of how referees broke political stalemates to bring about democracy. There has perhaps been no transition that has been more surprising than Taiwan, given its birth in the traumatic aftermath of the communist revolution in China and its well-earned reputation for authoritarian rule for decades. Nonetheless, Taiwan is a functioning democracy today that has also set records for prosperity.

Taiwan: The dual transition

No place epitomises Taiwan's[15] transition from authoritarian rule to democracy more than Taipei's National Chiang Kai-shek Memorial Hall.[16]

Opened in 1980 in memory of Chiang, its former president who relocated the Kuomintang (KMT) party to the island in 1949, two sets of stairs, each with 89 steps to represent Chiang's age at the time of his death in April 1975, lead to the main entrance. Inside is a large statue of the generalissimo. The hall was designed as the centrepiece of the Chiang Kai-shek Memorial Park, framed on two sides by the National Theatre and Concert Hall. It is the architecture typical of a country with reverence for an authoritarian leader.

Following the lifting of martial rule by his son and successor Chiang Ching-kuo in July 1987, the park became a favourite site for mass gatherings of the type he would certainly not have approved of. In fact, like Taiwan, Chiang's memorial has changed over time to reflect the island's preference for democracy. In 2007, then President Chen Shui-bian re-dedicated the site as 'Liberty Square'. In 2017, plans were announced to transform the hall into a centre for 'facing history, recognising agony, and respecting human rights', de-emphasising Chiang's personality cult.

Such plans are a remarkable and relatively quick repudiation of the founder's authoritarian practices, given that he lived until 1975. In comparison, the US is still tearing itself apart over monuments to Confederate leaders who fought the civil war in the 1860s.

In many ways, the democratisation of Taiwan is extraordinary. The island was ruled for many years by the KMT after they lost the mainland to the Chinese communists in 1949, even though the mainlanders were a minority in their new home. Taiwan has been seemingly waiting for the invasion from China as part of Beijing's long promised unification for almost 70 years and could easily be classified as one of the most insecure lands in the world. Indeed, by the time martial law was lifted in 1987, Taiwan had been under continuous restrictions for 38 years, the longest period of martial rule in history up to that time.

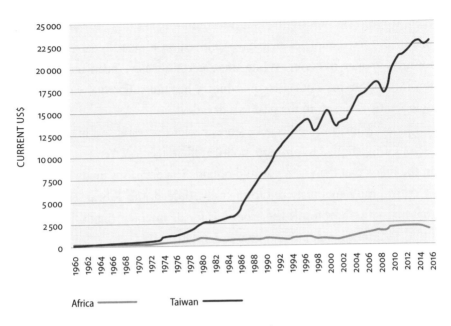

Figure 6.1: Africa and Taiwan: GDP per capita comparison

Despite these circumstances, Taiwan – as one of the original Asian Tigers – presided over an economic miracle that would by itself have been an overwhelming task for most countries. Taiwan was transformed from an ex-Japanese colony severely damaged by the Second World War to one of the leaders in global exports two generations later, with a per capita income firmly in the developed country league. It did this through rapid and consistent growth. For instance, the average income of Taiwanese citizens increased from $9 000 in 1990 to more than $22 000 a quarter-century on. By the late 2000s, the island produced 98% of the world's computer motherboards and 90% of notebook personal computers.[17] As illustrated in Figure 6.1, its per capita income has risen dramatically.[18]

Although it was never an inevitable outcome, Taiwan democratised with relatively little violence or trauma.

Until 1975, Freedom House had coded Taiwan as 'not free'. It was then considered as 'partly free' until 1996 when it was relabelled as 'free'. Since then, it has continuously retained Freedom House's highest ranking. It is one of the few countries that have enjoyed an almost linear movement towards greater freedom. While there certainly have been moments of tension and perhaps of crisis, the country has not suffered any noticeable democratic reversals in the past two decades.

Taiwan democratised because a number of domestic and international factors were aligned to promote political liberalisation. Yet, few predicted in the 1980s that democracy would obtain. The decisions made by leaders at critical moments mattered immensely. Indeed, the Taiwan case shows that no matter how fertile the ground is for democracy, the decisions that politicians take remain deeply consequential.

Housed in an old Japanese elementary school, after constitutional amendments in the 1990s that effectively did away with the National Assembly, the Legislative Yuan is today equivalent to Taiwan's parliament. As a sign of the changes, it has even been suggested that the Chiang Kai-shek Memorial Hall be converted into a new Legislative Yuan, as a potent symbol of Taiwan's democratic achievements.

Dr Chih-wei Chiu is a Democratic Progressive Party (DPP) member of the Legislative Yuan, head of the Economic Council and the Taiwan-Africa Friendship Association. He says that 'after the KMT lost the war against China, it moved to Taiwan and engaged in confrontation with various domestic parties in Taiwan. These tensions were later transferred into the pursuit of democracy.' This was encouraged by the adoption of Western thinking, he argues, by intellectuals who had travelled and studied abroad during this time. The political movement also borrowed some of the institutional tools of others, especially the US, such as the direct election of the president.

'All this translated into pressure against the KMT, which had to act to calm the situation. It took about 20 years for Taiwan to ride with the global trend,' says Chiu, 'to transform our society. Within those two decades we were able to develop political party mechanisms.'

The 'China factor' and Taiwanese nationalism played a part in the democratisation process. In 2000, 36.9% of people in Taiwan recognised themselves as Taiwanese only, 44% as both Chinese and Taiwanese, and just 12.5% as Chinese. Today these figures are 56.3%, 37.5% and 3.8%.[19] Still, while the KMT took power as a military and a minority in the late 1940s, it did have some democratic tenets that would become important. Its own ideology was conceived by Sun Yat-sen, who placed Western-style democracy at the centre of his political thought, though constitutional government would in his view come about only as the third period of national reconstruction (the first being military government; the second, political 'tutelage').

As part of its conquest of the island, the KMT introduced land reform that had the side effect of destroying a landed elite that might have been a significant barrier to democratisation. Finally, as the mainlanders were a minority on the island, the KMT eventually came to see democratisation as a way that they could try to institutionalise their own power by attempting to attract votes outside their own group. This calculation proved incorrect, but shows that political openings, even if designed to be tactical and limited in nature, can have unexpected consequences in promoting freedom.

International forces, especially starting in the 1970s, also began to propel Taiwan towards democracy. The seating of mainland China in the UN in 1971 initiated a long competition where the mainland sought to replace Taiwan as the legitimate China in every forum and capital. The recognition of the People's Republic of China by the US in 1979 made the contest with Beijing desperate for the Taiwanese. The US, especially in Congress, put considerable pressure on Taiwan to democratise. The Taiwanese were susceptible to this pressure, especially after 1979, because their continued good relations with the US, including market access, depended not on traditional diplomatic standing but on building substantial ties with American constituencies. Democracy was a way of 'branding' Taiwan so that it was different from China.

However, important decisions made by the leadership were also essential to Taiwan's democratic trajectory. Critically, in 1984, Chiang Ching-kuo, Chiang's son, chose Taiwan-born Lee Teng-hui as vice president to eventually succeed him. The decision was made in the middle of the great Taiwanese export boom, and was hardly precipitated by a domestic crisis. Soon thereafter, in 1986, Chiang pledged political reform, including a free press and lifting bans on new political parties and street protests. Emboldened, dissidents formed Taiwan's first opposition party, the DPP. A year later, martial law was lifted.

Chiang died in 1988 and Lee took power. Lee presided over the attainment of an institutionalised democracy by lifting restrictions on the press, eliminating parliamentary positions that had been frozen since the 1940s and prompting constitutional changes that eventually led him to become Taiwan's first directly elected president in 1996. In 2000, the DPP candidate for president, Chen Shui-bian, won the presidency, ending the KMT's monopoly on political power.

Taiwan's transition to democracy had certain important characteristics. It was largely a top-down affair with the leaders creating political openings that civil society would then occupy. For instance, NGOs only flourished after the democratic system was largely in place. The transition reflects decisions by leaders who could see that Taiwan needed democracy before they were forced to give up power. The Taiwanese leadership did not seem to believe that greater freedom would interfere with the ongoing economic miracle, despite worries throughout Africa that countries have to choose between freedom and prosperity. The Taiwanese instead saw democracy as building the rule of law that is critical to investor confidence and also as a way of limiting corruption. The combination of an elite commitment to democracy, a powerful common national identity, and pressure from the US avoided the need for an uprising or conflict.

It is also notable that Taiwan never had a 'constitutional moment' whereby it sought to redraw its political system with a clean sheet of paper.

The political system since 1949 largely reflected what had been in place when the KMT ruled on mainland China; indeed, parliament was essentially frozen for decades while the Taiwanese waited to retake the mainland and reinstall their legislative control. Taiwan's fraught political relationship with the mainland probably made convening a constitutional gathering impossible because it would have been perceived as a step towards independence. Taiwan's leaders made do with what they had, and changed the political system incrementally.

As one of the 'Asian Tiger' economic miracles, the relationship between Taiwan's democracy and its economy is of particular interest. Taiwan never had a true 'developmental state' as its economy was based much more on small- and medium-sized enterprises than South Korea's large *chaebol* corporations, or the similar *keiretsu* in Japan. Yet, the country chose to begin the democratisation process as the economy took off, suggesting a social consensus that democracy, rather than a heavy-handed state, was critical to growth.

It is true that growth has fallen off since the heady days of the 1990s, averaging 3.7% since the 2000s. But this does not necessarily mean that democracy caused growth to slow down. For one, mainland China was concurrently getting into its growth stride, taking away some business from Taiwan, whose entrepreneurs led the charge to move factories and jobs to the mainland, leading to a stagnation in wages among Taiwanese workers. The impact of these trends has been compounded by the attainment of middle-class status by many Taiwanese, and with it a changing set of concerns about their quality of life. These include democratic freedoms.

Indeed, Taiwan's long-term development has been driven by improvements in governance, part of which are due to democracy. As one measure, politicians have been met with the demands for public accountability that are a hallmark of democracy. Most notably, Chen Shui-bian, the first non-KMT president, and his wife Wu Shu-chen were convicted in 2009 on two bribery charges. Chen was sentenced to 19 years, reduced from a life sentence on appeal. This is a punishment of a former president that few countries could imagine. In 2013, a trial cleared Lee Teng-hui of involvement in a corruption scandal. Chen's successor as president, Ma Ying-jeou, has faced his own charges of embezzlement while he was mayor of Taipei, but was cleared just before his inauguration in May 2008.

Chiang was undoubtedly repressive, but not with the ruthlessness of Mao and the Communist Party. The island did not suffer such brutal policies as the Great Leap Forward and Cultural Revolution, which cost China as many as 30 million lives. Its political transformation has been impressive, proving the sceptics wrong that Chinese culture and democracy are incompatible. Just 2.4% of Taiwanese polled see the country as not a democracy, while nearly 60% are satisfied and 36% are dissatisfied with the way democracy works in Taiwan.[20] There is much to admire. Chiang Ching-kuo and Lee were able to take the bold steps that Deng Xiaoping, his colleagues and successors have been unable or unwilling to attempt.[21]

As evidence of the distance travelled in democratic terms over the last 20 years, downstairs from the generalissimo's statue, on the floor of Chiang's eponymous museum, a temporary exhibition observes: 'In the authoritarian period, the huge and towering mass of the hall used to be an object to which people showed great reverence, and the square represented a chessboard of uniform ranks. After democratisation, the square became a stage for a riotous profusion of protests and demonstrations.' The exhibition asks whether the Memorial Hall should be replaced. In so doing, 'the place would pass from the founder of the ROC [Republic of China] to the country, today a vibrant democracy, probably the only one of its kind in Asia.'

This democratic freedom is Taiwan's major long-term asset as it arrives at an economic and political crossroads, facing stagnation if it does not innovate, reinvent itself and diversify away from traditional IT hardware. Such efficiencies demand a quality of governance and responsiveness that are historically more likely from democratic institutions.

Conclusion: The components of continuous change

Democratic transition requires a credible referee and leaders who make the decision to embrace democracy. All of the successful cases above represent instances in which leaders have initiated democratic reforms in the presence of an effective referee, and under circumstances of necessity. And, again, as identified in Chapter 5 with the Kenya case study, all this emphasises the importance of having an overall plan for government and its purpose, and not just to acquire power, beyond the 'moment' of transition.

Leaders have to devise creative solutions in which tough and sometimes costly decisions are necessary. Some solutions stick, and some fail, while some may appear imperfect to outsiders who are not aware of the pressures, complexities, histories and dangers of individual environments. Accordingly, it is hardly surprising that so few countries have managed to permanently escape the 'not free' category.

Why have Nigeria, Liberia and South Africa shown better leadership than a post-settlement Burundi? The disheartening answer may be the luck of the draw. It is hard to see how structural forces might have determined the present situation. Certainly, at least elements of the Nigerian military saw how their continued rule was degrading the armed forces. But there have been plenty of soldiers across Africa and, for that matter, South America who were willing to tolerate the loss of war-fighting abilities in exchange for the riches of office.

Fortune also plays its part. If President Johnson Sirleaf had been assassinated at the start of her term, Liberia's history would have been quite different, just as Burundi would have had a different trajectory if Prince Rwagasore had lived. That is hardly a satisfying answer but it is perhaps a realistic one given that countries with deep authoritarian experiences have demonstrated through their history that there is no inevitable march towards democracy.

Part Three

ELECTIONS, INSIDERS AND OUTSIDERS

7

Ensuring Free and Fair Elections in Africa

In a democracy, someone who fails to get elected to office can always console himself with the thought that there was something not quite fair about it.

— Thucydides, *History of the Peloponnesian War*

For my friends, everything; for my enemies, the law.

— Oscar R. Benavides, president of Peru, 1933–9

Chapter takeaways

- Elections are an important prerequisite for democracy, but not the only indicator.

- There is a danger that outsiders support elections rather than long-term processes of democratisation, or incumbents and stability over fairness.

- Failure is not always due to the actions of the government. Oppositions need to build a credible case if and when electoral fraud has occurred, and learn from successful cases where incumbents have been removed via the ballot.

- A transparent funding regime for African elections needs to be devised.

- Good electoral technology is important, but the machines by themselves will not guarantee a fair vote.

On 11 April 2017, the Zambian government jailed the leader of the opposition, Hakainde Hichilema, on treason charges. The catalyst was a traffic incident involving rival motorcades. As a result, the Zambian Catholic Bishops' Conference described the country as, except in name, 'a dictatorship'.[1] The stage for this extreme action was, however, set earlier, with a contested election result in August 2016 and the manner in which the disputes around its legality were dealt with.

What is emerging from the Zambian and other African elections is a winning template for incumbents: close down the democratic space, run interference, misuse state resources, control the diet of information, run outrageously fake news, and, if necessary, don't let the numbers stand in the way of victory. Of course, democracy is not just about elections, and there is a danger that outsiders especially focus on this procedural aspect above all else. But it is a critical starting point for the process, and a reflection of how the government views its responsibilities to its people. As the social media wave sweeps over Africa, as it has on every other continent, it is also important to understand what can, and cannot, be accomplished by the platforms that have emerged. This chapter examines how authoritarians fixed elections in Zimbabwe and Zambia to ensure their rule. However, elections introduce fluidity into all but the most authoritarian settings and sometimes produce surprises despite the efforts of incumbents. We examine the case of Nigeria where Muhammadu Buhari was able, despite many obstacles, to defeat the incumbent president, Goodluck Jonathan, in 2015.

* * *

Elections in Zimbabwe this century have gradually created an 'autocrat's playbook', the culmination of gerrymandering, obfuscation, stalling, political manoeuvring, blatant fraud and plain old-fashioned thievery and violence.[2]

How to stay in power: The Zimbabwe election prototype

'[H]aving regard to all the circumstances, and in particular the cumulative substantial departures from international standards of free and fair elections found in Zimbabwe during the pre-election period, these elections, in our view, cannot be considered free and fair,' concluded the 27-page report on the 2002 Zimbabwean elections by South African high court judges, Dikgang Moseneke and Sisi Khampepe.[3]

The findings of what became known as the Khampepe Report were only made public in November 2014 following a Constitutional Court judgment, in which the court rejected an appeal by government against a Supreme Court finding that the documents should be released. While the authors found that the conduct of the three-day voting process, leaving aside delays in the urban areas of Harare and Chitungwiza, complied with legislative requirements and was free from violence or ballot tampering, this had to be weighed against the prevalence of pre-election intimidation, manipulation and violence. These irregularities included the deaths of 107 mainly opposition members, the amendment of the electoral laws of Zimbabwe by executive decrees in favour of the ruling party, the failure to provide final voter rolls and information on polling stations timeously to all contesting parties, the reduction of polling stations in urban areas where the opposition Movement for Democratic Change (MDC) enjoyed its greatest support, and a lack of equal or equitable access to publicly owned and funded media.

Thabo Mbeki had tasked the two judges to lead the Judicial Observer Mission to cover the 8–10 March 2002 elections and to draft the report. But their observations were never released because, according to the former South African president: 'Given its composition and mandate, we came to the firm conclusion that it was not credibly possible for the judges' mission to come to a conclusion about all major elements of the elections based on its own direct observations,' adding that 'it was not by accident that the judges' mission was directed to submit its report to the President of South Africa. That report was not meant for public distribution.'[4]

Instead, the South African president continued to endorse the result of the elections and support the view of the South African Observer Mission – one of two that had formally overseen the elections from South Africa – and its leader ambassador, Sam Motsuenyane, that the process had been 'legitimate'. In these elections, the ruling Zimbabwe African National Union-Patriotic Front's (ZANU-PF's) support plummeted from a 93% majority (in the 1996 presidential elections) to 51.9%.[5] One can only imagine what it might have been with greater openness and fairness.

A critical moment in Zimbabwe's march towards authoritarian rule and economic catastrophe was in November 1997, when, in an environment of growing frustration with the slow pace of development, the Mugabe government published a list of 1 471 white-owned farms to be expropriated,[6] even though nearly half of these farmers had purchased their land since independence. The farmers had become a juicy political target, owning nearly 40% of all land and two-thirds of the best farming areas.[7]

With one-third of listed companies dependent on the agriculture sector, the stock exchange dropped and fiscal conditions were dramatically worsened by Robert Mugabe's provision of a $400 million package of benefits to war veterans, a key political constituency. A fragile situation was worsened by Zimbabwe's participation in a costly war in the Democratic Republic of Congo that pitted the forces of Angola, Zimbabwe and the DRC against invading rebels backed by Uganda and Rwanda.

By 1997, the country had reached a tipping point, the Zimbabwe dollar collapsing by 70% on 14 November 1997, a day now commonly referred to in Zimbabwe as 'Black Friday'. The situation continued to deteriorate through 1998, during which time the Zimbabwe Congress of Trade Unions (ZCTU) grew in political strength, carrying out a number of crippling strikes, the most famous of which was a 'stayaway' held on Tuesday 10 December 1998, known as 'Red Tuesday' among Zimbabwean activists.

By the turn of the twenty-first century, living conditions among average Zimbabweans had deteriorated, with unemployment at 50%, annual inflation 60%, and real wages having fallen by a fifth since independence.[8]

Then, in February 1999, the ZCTU organised the National Working People's Convention in Harare. It was at this meeting that a broad mass of Zimbabwean activists, particularly students, middle-class professionals, the church, civic society and labour, resolved to form a political party. The MDC was formally launched on 11 September 1999 under the leadership of Gibson Sibanda and Morgan Tsvangirai, a marriage that arose out of an awareness that it was simply not possible to make trade union demands in isolation from the political process and overall concerns about human rights.

If land was the fuel that stoked an increasingly restless population, the referendum on a new constitution in February 2000 was the spark that lit the fire.

When Mugabe's draft constitution allowing land expropriation without compensation was defeated in the face of considerable opposition, led in part by the nascent MDC and its various constituent members but with the public support of the (mainly white) Commercial Farmers' Union, farm invasions began just a few days later. Realising that the farmers, like other Zimbabweans, derived strength from ownership, Mugabe took it away and dispensed the proceeds, though not the titles, to his followers. Keeping everyone beholden to the state (with all land vested in the president) solidified and tightened Mugabe's grip on power.

Over the next 17 years a total of 4 200 famers were evicted from eight million hectares of land. Income per capita, which was $1 255 in 1981, plummeted to just $541 in 2008.[9] The land reform programme was executed and engineered by the state, through a disregard for the rule of law. War veterans and the military played a key role in its execution. The conflation of interests between the government and the military made Zimbabwe a 'securocratic state', with Mugabe increasingly the nominee of an unelected elite military establishment, his presidential tenure dependent on his utility in serving military interests, the extent of his vulnerability made clear by the events of November 2017.

In the 2002 general election, fearing a victory of Morgan Tsvangirai against Robert Mugabe, the military threw its commander General Vitalis Zvinavashe into the fray. He issued a statement on the eve of the March 2002 election, and declared:[10]

> We wish to make it very clear to all Zimbabwean citizens that the security organisations will only stand in support of those political leaders that will pursue Zimbabwean values, traditions and beliefs for which thousands of lives were lost … Let it be known that the highest office in the land is a straitjacket whose occupant is expected to observe the objectives of the liberation struggle. We will therefore not accept, let alone support or salute, anyone with a different agenda that threatens the very existence of our sovereignty, our country and our people.

This was not the first or the last time that the Zimbabwean military would openly and unconstitutionally interfere with civilian politics. With the loss of popular legitimacy, Mugabe heavily relied on the military and manipulation of the state for survival. Following the March 2005 legislative elections, he attempted to extend his term until 2010, ostensibly to harmonise the various elections. This led to a mass strike in January 2007 organised under the Save Zimbabwe banner.

On 11 March 2007, the Save Zimbabwe campaign organised a peace march in the Harare township of Highfield. Several activists were shot dead and several leaders were assaulted in police custody, with Tsvangirai appearing on television channels worldwide beaten to a bloody pulp. This offered Mbeki a point of entry. An extraordinary Southern African Development Community (SADC) summit, convened on 29 March, gave him a mandate to create the dialogue for free and fair elections. This resulted in the Kariba

Constitution, so named after the place of its signature on a rickety old boat on the lake.

However, the MDC felt betrayed in the run-up to the March 2008 election, demanding that the new constitution be put in force. They realised, too, however, that Mbeki was politically weak by this time, given the Polokwane conference in December 2007, which saw him ousted as ANC president. (Mbeki resigned as South African president on 21 September 2008, and was replaced by Kgalema Motlanthe four days later.) Then, in February, Mbeki's deputy foreign affairs minister, Aziz Pahad, publicly announced that there would be an election on 29 March in spite of the lack of progress on reforms, negotiations about which he said were no longer required. Pahad's pronouncement allowed Mugabe to proclaim 29 March as the date of the 2008 election.

Despite an agreement to amend five acts – including the Public Security Order Act and Access to Information and Protection of Privacy Act – Mugabe attempted to sway things his own way through the removal, for example, of the stipulation that no police should be present within ballot stations by presidential decree. Few people gave the MDC a chance, since its own unity talks had collapsed, and it had little more than $50 000 in its bank accounts; 'just enough to buy T-shirts', as members recall.

Yet, the MDC pulled off a famous victory. From the perspective of party officials, this was down to three reasons. First, it had trained field agents, and provided for their transport and mobile phones. Second, a new requirement held that ballot boxes were no longer to be transported from the ballot stations and counted elsewhere where the results could become pregnant en route, but at the ballot stations themselves where they would then be posted outside. The MDC was able to gather these results and thereby ran 'a fairly decent' Parallel Voter Tabulation campaign, enabling it with some certainty to declare, from the Stuart Room of the Meikles Hotel, Tsvangirai as the winner on the evening of Sunday 29 March. Third, it helped that the election was not being taken seriously by the regime.

For a week it was clear that the regime was uncertain about what to do. Mugabe, it is now known, agreed to step down. But then Mbeki, in the words of the MDC, 'pulled a fast one'. He called an extraordinary SADC summit on 12 April 2008 at Lusaka's Mulungushi International Conference Centre, which declared that, since there had been no clear winner, there would be a run-off on 27 June.

Extraordinarily, the SADC summit made its decision when the results were only due on 5 May. Mbeki preferred stability over democracy, and his preferences, too, were reflective of his loyalty to a fellow liberation movement in ZANU-PF and the sensitivity of the challenge posed by a labour-based movement in the MDC.

This gambit provided the junta with the ability to carry out a pre-emptive coup, leading to massive violence and the MDC's withdrawal from the run-off, in which Mugabe subsequently won 85% of votes. Mbeki, the principal author of this crisis, then recommenced negotiations after 27 June. To facilitate this, MDC officials had to be released from prison. This resulted four months later in the signature of the so-called global political agreement on 15 September 2008 and the allocation of cabinet posts in a unity government when the new South African president, Motlanthe, chaired yet another extraordinary SADC summit in Pretoria in January 2009.

The shock of the 2008 election loss by ZANU-PF ensured that the ruling party would not make the same mistake again. In 2013, a combination of the state's continued centralised control of the media, the falsification of the 2012 population census, the gerrymandering of constituency boundaries, the party's control over food aid and agricultural inputs, the use of police and military resources in the creation of 'no-go' areas, the busing in of supporters, and the manipulation of tribal leadership together resulted in a drubbing for the opposition. This effort required substantial financial resources, estimated at $500 million.[11]

There was also a significant shift in ZANU-PF's strategy. Whereas in earlier elections the default was to beat the opposition to a pulp, it now opted for more sophisticated means, employing a foreign company to manage the digital election process. But some tried and trusted analogue methods were also employed, including having the military vote two weeks before and then again on the date of the election on 31 July 2013, deploying the extra votes as required. In addition, voters whose names did not appear on the roll were permitted to vote by presenting a voter 'slip', which was manufactured by the regime. The Electoral Commission subsequently admitted that some 305 000 voters were turned away from polls, with an additional 207 000 voters being 'assisted' in casting their ballots. There were allegedly more than 100 000 centenarian ghost voters on the electoral roll.[12]

Infamously, one incident was captured on video in Harare's affluent suburb of Mount Pleasant, in which hundreds of youngsters arrived in rural 'chicken' buses, probably from Mozambique.[13] None of them when asked could name a single street or their residences in the suburb, despite the presence of international monitors. The MDC was also prevented from operating the Parallel Voter Tabulation system, which had helped it to counter vote-rigging in 2008. And while there was little realistic possibility of ZANU-PF's victory margin of 61% to 35% being a fair reflection of the party's support, the MDC's job was undoubtably made more difficult with the political scandals that had surfaced in the media around its leader Tsvangirai.

The long history of failed government, economic collapse, party-state conflation, securocratic control and flawed elections in Zimbabwe shows how authoritarian regimes can use electoral processes to secure and reinforce their power. Even elections that are ostensibly conducted in a free and fair manner may take place in an environment of fear and intimidation, and the result may be met with violence. This is evidence that an election alone is not enough to sustain political freedom.

Election and opposition dilemmas

Zimbabwe faced a new, unexpected challenge on 14 November 2017 when military tanks appeared on the streets, and the army seized control of the single television station and all major government buildings, including parliament. This led Mugabe to resign a week later, with his long-time deputy Emmerson Mnangagwa being inaugurated as president on 23 November 2017.

These events posed a fresh challenge of legitimacy. The only way for the government to address this was through the staging of elections that would be viewed as free, fair, credible and legitimate, the implementation of the provisions of the 2013 constitution, and sweeping economic reforms to address the entwined problems of governance, growth and unemployment.

Thus, the 2018 election was a public examination as to whether Zimbabwe could resolve its challenges and claw its way back into the global economy as a stable, democratic state.

Yet, the outcome and process of the July 2018 poll raised at least as many questions as it offered answers in this regard. The official results had a two-thirds parliamentary victory for the ruling ZANU-PF, enabling it to change the constitution, while in the presidential poll, the incumbent Mnangagwa won 50.6% of votes, a suspiciously slim 0.6% margin, or 32 011 votes out of more than 4.7 million needed to gain a first-round presidential victory over the MDC's Nelson Chamisa. The results were incredible if plausible, given the low bar of expectations for a free and fair process.

On the day, the election was peaceful, although, in the words of the European Union's election observers, a 'truly level playing field was not achieved'.[14] Similarly, the joint observer mission of the US-based International Republican Institute and the National Democratic Institute said that Zimbabwe 'has not yet demonstrated that it has established a tolerant, democratic culture' permitting the opposition to be treated fairly and people to vote freely.[15]

It was not the new democratic path that many had been hoping for or that President Mnangagwa had promised before the election. The disputed outcome and its violent aftermath highlight the potential economic consequences and cost of such failings. It also illustrated how difficult it is for the opposition to operate freely, fairly and competitively.

The MDC was supposed to build a cohesive anti-government alliance in the face of an extremely determined political foe in ZANU-PF, which had enjoyed nearly four decades in power to cement its authority among state institutions and the structures of traditional, tribal leadership. The MDC was also expected to develop robust party structures along with an election machinery that would monitor and challenge the government behemoth with very little funding and scant media exposure via state-run organs. Not only did the MDC have to take on a ruthless military inseparable from ZANU-PF, but effectively also those local and foreign commercial interests seeking opportunity and profit in making deals with the ruling party. The opposition also had to develop a coherent manifesto for reform in the face of a party that has pursued its retention of raw power to the exclusion of national economic well-being and much else.

It was expected to behave peacefully, knowing that its political rival would not hesitate to take off its gloves if challenged. This reality was evident on Harare's streets following the election when the military opened fire on civilians, killing six and wounding seven times this number. And the opposition was expected to operate at all times within the electoral law in the knowledge that ZANU-PF would, based on its performance in the 2008 and 2013 elections, not be so constrained, despite the reassuring presence of greater numbers of foreign election observers.

These are near impossible tasks for an opposition believing in non-violence, constitutionalism and the rule of law, especially in a region where many liberation movements continue to rule, and where the SADC remains emasculated compared to the authority of the Economic Community of West African States.

Yet, the MDC was able to do many of these things, and against the financial odds. The final election rallies in Harare told this story and the MDC's difference from the ruling party. Unlike the concluding ZANU-PF event at the nearby National Stadium where supporters were bused and trucked in and given food, clothing and placards, MDC supporters at the open-field 'Freedom Square' mostly walked there and bought their berets and T-shirts right there. This was a stone's throw from the Rainbow Towers where khaki-clad international election observers loped around the lobby, and across from ZANU-PF's party headquarters.

The MDC's options were limited in the face of what it claimed was clear evidence of a rig. Bitter experience taught that legal challenges to African elections were likely to be a waste of time. Sure enough, the MDC's appeal to the Constitutional Court was dismissed. To gather the information to effectively challenge the outcome, the MDC would have had to serve 3 000 respondents within 48 hours of the results to be able to petition the courts within the prescribed seven-day period – an impossible task.[16] If the Zimbabwe Electoral Commission and ZANU-PF were confident of the authenticity of the results, they could, of course, have subjected the raw election data to an independent audit.

Flawed elections, however, have consequences, reminding one of Tsvangirai's comment that while ZANU-PF could rig the election, it could not rig the economy.[17]

The losers in this flawed process and the violence are once more the Zimbabwean people, who by 2018 were already twice as poor as they were at independence in 1980. Mnangagwa desperately needed a clear and cred-ible victory to turn on the taps of international funding. On Twitter he said he was 'humbled' to have won, hailing it as a 'new beginning' for the country. 'Open for business' had been his attractive mantra, recognising that the country is desperate for foreign funds to restore its infrastructure, kickstart its economy and alleviate its currency shortage, all of which is required to undo the ruin of Robert Mugabe's 37 years of ZANU-PF rule. Few investors worth their salt would commit assets where the rule of law is subservient to the rule of the military. Moreover, the violence meant it was going to be tougher for donors to lead with the funding urgently required to turn the economy around. The African observer stamp of approval is, in the circumstances, largely meaningless since that is not where the donor funds are.

Zimbabwe's 2018 event shows, yet again, that elections have to involve more than a peaceful day or two of voting and the stating of clear rules for domestic actors about the use and misuse of state resources. There needs to be verification of this on which trust can be built. There has to be a transparent code of conduct during elections for business, for the donors themselves, and for those media and other election 'consultants' intent on scratching at society's scabs through a steady infusion of fake news. There also has to be a level playing field in financial terms, not only for the parties, but for the training of activists, and voter education programmes.

The crisis in Zimbabwe did not start with the election on 30 July 2018. It started four decades earlier with ZANU's accession to power, a party that remains steadfastly a product of a bitter liberation struggle, notably in the manner in which it prosecutes the elections, of victory at any cost to the economy and, ultimately, Zimbabwe's citizens.

Lessons for outsiders and insiders: Zambia's 2016 election

Just as Hakainde Hichilema's April 2017 arrest had its roots in the contested 2016 election, this was in turn a culmination of a longer process of democratic erosion in Zambia, as was highlighted in Chapter 4.

If the 2016 election was not itself fraudulent, it certainly was conducted in a manner akin less to a democracy than a dictatorship. While international election observers worried about events on polling day, a stop-at-nothing government sought to skew the playing field well before then. In the build-up to election day, opposition campaign material was not disseminated through the media, despite major sums of money (some of it international) that were given to the state broadcaster, the Zambia National Broadcasting Corporation, to assist its election programming. This funding created an environment where only pro-government broadcasting was heard. The International Press Institute found that hindering opposition media cast a 'shadow' over Zambia's democracy.[18] While the government shut down the main opposition news source in the form of the *Post* newspaper,[19] it resorted to spreading fake news and hate propaganda via various websites, notably that of *Zambia Awakens*. This site accused the leader of the opposition inter alia of being a devil worshipper and child eater, along with alleging a conspiracy whereby the Anglo American Corporation was responsible for running the opposition campaign in an attempt to seize control of Zambia's mining assets.

From the opposition's perspective, police intimidation and violence were also far more apparent during the 2016 poll than in any previous elections in Zambia's history. On the actual day of the election, 11 August 2016, the voting process went smoothly in most areas. Afterwards, Hichilema's United Party for National Development (UPND) claimed that ballots had been thrown away, and that there had been widespread intimidation, tampered results and systematic bias in counting. The opposition alleged that the 'Gen 12' forms – those that certified the outcome of the count at every polling station with agents and representatives from all parties present signing – were withheld from UPND agents, so that they were not able to verify the results. The resulting delay, they say, enabled the Patriotic Front to fiddle with the numbers, notably in the capital, Lusaka, where nearly one in six registered voters resided. Certainly, the vote counting and the issuing of the result slowed over the weekend following the election, despite being expected much earlier – a telltale sign of the fix being in.

Despite – or perhaps *because* of all this – the Patriotic Front achieved its 50.1% winning margin by only 5 000 votes out of nearly 3.8 million cast.[20] Even if all the allegations of election malfeasance are discounted, the margin to avoid a run-off was suspiciously small, just 0.13% greater than 50%.

Before the results were made public, international observer teams found the voting and counting process, in the words of the Commonwealth report, 'credible and transparent'. The European Union Election Observation Mission said that 'voting was peaceful and generally well administered' despite being 'marred by systematic bias in the state media and restrictions on the [opposition] campaign'. There were other international missions from the Carter Center, the African Union, the Southern African Development Community, the Common Market for Eastern and Southern Africa, and the Electoral Institute for Sustainable Democracy in Africa.[21] Freedom House's subsequent downward rating of Zambia 'reflects the restrictive environment for the political opposition in the run-up to general elections', both in the media and through the use of the Public Order Act to ban opposition rallies.[22]

With their eye on preventing violence, the international community encouraged the UPND to seek legal recourse rather than take to the streets. 'Any challenges to the process at any level, from the president right down to district level, should be taken through legal means to the courts, with evidence, not to the streets,' said Janet Rogan, head of the UN resident office in Zambia, shortly after the final results had been announced.[23] Hichilema's party challenged the results in court within the prescribed seven-day period. They were then given 14 days to compile and present their case to the Constitutional Court, which ruled that the hearing would start on 2 September 2016. Thereupon the full bench (nominated by President Edgar Lungu) decided that the hearing would continue on Monday, 5 September. On the Monday, three of the five judges decided that the 14 days stipulated by the constitution for an election petition hearing had expired on 2 September and therefore threw the case out.[24]

But failure was not all due to the actions of the government. The UPND had a number of challenges, both strategic and tactical, which they could have managed better.

The first was around the difficulty in creating a party identity that extended beyond its southern Tonga leadership. The UPND's attempts at national unity largely ran aground on ethnic divisions. The Bemba comprise 21% of the population, while the Tonga 13.6%, with the remaining groups (Lozi, Ngoni, Lunda, Luvale and Kaonde) all less than 10% of the total.[25] These ethnic cleavages are deep-rooted and may be a bigger issue than one election campaign can tackle; nevertheless, the opposition failed to win the trust of a diverse range of supporters.

A significant setback occurred, undoing months of hard work to portray the UPND's vision of a united Zambia, after a private telephone call between Hichilema and one of his chiefs, in which he continuously referred to 'us' and 'them'. This conversation was tapped by Zambian intelligence and then leaked to the national media, reinforcing the perception of tribal nationalism. Efforts to combat the leak had little effect. Even when well-known Bembas (Northerners) were absorbed into the UPND, they were unable to bring the support they required. The use of videos[26] and other campaign messaging did apparently little to shift the nominal association between the UPND and the Tonga.

Attempts were also made to broaden the UPND's national appeal through the election of the former minister of defence, Geoffrey Bwalya Mwamba, known as 'GBM', as Hichilema's running mate. Not only was he a well-known Bemba figure and a political street-fighter who had delivered for President Michael Sata, but he also enjoyed deep pockets. Yet, even he did not manage to lure the Bemba vote.

The act of holding elections is by itself insufficient to sustain a democracy. Indeed, elections may even reinforce authoritarianism if they permit the subjugation of the democratic process through electoral fraud, the forms of which are often subtle and insidious. Absent the promotion of a set of clear ideas around national issues by politicians, and the support between elections from institutions of government to check and balance the executive, including an empowered and independent legal system, electoral democracy will, as Zambia shows, seldom deliver.

How to defeat an incumbent: Nigeria's 2015 election

Nigeria, despite all of its astonishing complexity, demonstrates the continuing importance and possibilities of contests for votes. In particular, Nigeria shows the role money may play in contests. Contests have begun to cost even more money given the increasing technological sophistication of campaigning. Running in the 1999 Nigerian elections, all six of them, cost the winner just $7 million. The following round, in 2003, cost no more than $9 million. Fast forward to 2015, and the opposition spent ten times this amount to win the presidential election alone, while the incumbent astonishingly spent more than $2 billion, adhering to an accepted African expenditure benchmark of a million dollars per million people.[27]

The performance of Muhammadu Buhari of the All Progressives Congress (APC) in defeating the candidate of the ruling People's Democratic Party (PDP), President Goodluck Jonathan, in 2015 showed, according to Nasir El-Rufai, who steered the Buhari campaign, that an 'entrenched, immensely rich and powerful political machine' could be defeated in an election 'with little or no violence, partisan acrimony or resort to any electoral adjudication'.

The election took place amid intense acrimony. Jonathan insisted on running for president despite the 'gentleman's agreement' of 2011, which had temporarily suspended the regional power-sharing formula of the party in his favour. He also attempted to interfere with the leadership election of the Nigeria Governors' Forum, the club of the 36 state governors of Nigeria, to the chagrin of the Forum's president, Governor Rotimi Amaechi, of the oil-rich Rivers State. Prior to the PDP convention in December 2013 that nominated Jonathan, five PDP state governors (of the Rivers, Adamawa, Kano, Kwara and Sokoto states) crossed over to the APC.

More controversially, in February 2015, former President Olusegun Obasanjo publicly left the PDP and endorsed General Buhari for the presidency. He preferred to destroy his PDP membership card than to stand by and let Jonathan use the PDP and corruption to tear Nigeria apart.[28]

To win the election against an incumbent such as President Jonathan, who had access to substantial wealth, the APC deployed the latest technologies, research and analytics. This effort included quarterly nationwide polling and biometric membership registration to ensure internal transparency and signal to the wider public that the APC would not conduct the politics of 'business as usual'. Significant resources were invested in recruiting 'national influencers', undertaking publicly visible 'consultation visits', membership mobilisation, party branding and national platform development.

These initiatives paralleled changes in the Independent National Electoral Commission (INEC). The Commission underwent significant internal reforms, removing corrupt staff, rebranding itself and publicising preparations for various by-elections. The national voters' roll was improved to remove multiple registration, while the paper-based, temporary voter's card was replaced with a machine-readable permanent voter's card. The production of more than 65 million voters' cards was a 'logistical nightmare', but was overcome, 'paradoxically after Jonathan and the PDP, sensing electoral defeat and needing more time to try to turn the tide', forced the INEC to postpone the elections by six weeks in February 2015.[29]

The INEC also introduced several other reforms to enhance electoral integrity and ease the voting process on election day. It split over-populated polling stations into sub-units of approximately 500 voters, while the security features on ballot papers were enhanced. Through these actions and regular briefings, the opposition developed greater confidence in the INEC than in previous election cycles, even though, as Governor El-Rufai notes, 'the situation remained one of sceptical optimism until the elections'.

Lessons were also learnt in the APC's loss of the election for the Ekiti governorship more than a year before the presidential election. From the APC's vantage point, this contest demonstrated that the government was willing to undermine the INEC by using the military and state security agencies to suppress votes in areas where the PDP considered itself weak.

'The army and the State Security Service (SSS),' says El-Rufai, 'were totally and unashamedly at the service of the PDP immediately before, during and after the election.' But he also notes that 'a couple of positive things came out of the Ekiti governorship race'. First, the defeated incumbent, Kayode Fayemi, 'conceded and congratulated the declared winner, notwithstanding the widespread malfeasance', in so doing setting a precedent for accepting election results. Also, the APC realised that 'unless we took extraordinary, pre-emptive measures, Jonathan and the PDP were willing and able to subvert every state institution to win'. As a result, the APC began to develop an appropriate strategy for the next gubernatorial election in Osun State, as well as for the 2015 general election. Several senior military officers would later be court-martialled and SSS personnel retired for their participation in the Ekiti electoral fraud.

The APC additionally established a National Elections Planning Committee, comprising several governors, legislators, former ministers and party leaders, with El-Rufai as the secretary. The committee conducted regular polling as it moved from state party congresses to the election of party leaders, and the primaries and national convention to elect its candidates. 'Every poll showed that we would defeat Jonathan by a margin of at least ten percentage points.'

Lacking Jonathan's financial strength, the APC also understood that it had to create the belief that it had both a private army and unlimited financial war chest. 'Relying on the unplanned outbreak of violence in the north in April 2011,' notes El-Rufai, 'we designed and carefully leaked a coherent deterrence and response plan to discourage the PDP and Jonathan from the official misconduct we witnessed in Ekiti and Osun states. This fear of a general breakdown backed by mass action proved important in persuading Jonathan and the PDP to accept the outcome of the election, and to reluctantly concede.'

The APC also mounted a well-resourced logistical operation 'to make votes count'. The APC's Elections Monitoring Centre communicated with over 200 000 trained and well-compensated polling unit agents assigned to over 150 000 voting points across the country. They could communicate by phone, SMS, and email, and via new media platforms like Facebook, Twitter, WhatsApp and BlackBerry Messenger using audio, video and photographs in order to send copies of result sheets and any other relevant information.

Finally, the APC took 'full advantage' of the improved transparency of the INEC's processes and procedures to publish as much information as possible as the election results were being announced at polling unit, ward, local government and state levels. By the end of the second day of the election, on 29 March, the APC was quite certain that it 'had won the election no matter what the PDP attempted to do'. El-Rufai continues: 'I went on national television to declare such, advising Jonathan to start writing his hand-over notes immediately.' The INEC announced the winner less than 48 hours later.

Buhari was a clear winner of the election with 53.96% of the vote to Jonathan's 44.96%.

El-Rufai highlights a number of improvements that can be made, including on campaign financing, which 'remains opaque' and is supported 'by various oligarchs and so-called political godfathers'. He believes that 'we must work towards funding political parties via capped and fully disclosed donations and annual dues payable by every registered party member'.

The governor concludes that 'four conditions are the irreducible minimums for creating a stronger and more accountable democratic order': a unified opposition, merged into a party well before an election; a credible and progressive candidate; 'honest elections that guarantee that votes count, with competent electoral commission leadership and, crucially, technologies for voter verification that drastically reduce electoral fraud'; and, finally, the 'continuous engagement of the international community, particularly in the leading stable democracies as well as in multilateral institutions, to supply a crucial external fillip to the electoral process.'

Conclusion: Living up to responsibility

Over the past quarter-century, more and more African countries have regularly held multi-party elections. Elections are not the only indicator of the state of democracy, but they are a prerequisite for democracy. Elections are critical to shaping a country's likely democratic trajectory since they help to promote participation and spur competition, and set the rules of political behaviour. As Sarah Logan notes, 'It's the failure or absence of elections that largely defines dictatorships.'[30]

The effectiveness of electoral governance – centring on the establishment of clear procedures and rules, international observation missions and, critically, the role of autonomous national election bodies – has improved overall. However, incumbents have also learnt to game the system to their advantage by restricting media coverage and civil society activities, and constraining opposition spending (while dipping into the national treasury to fund their own) along with more blatant techniques of rigging, coercion, intimidation and sometimes outright violence.

The process of improving elections is thus likely to be slow. Three main areas of reform stand out. The first is through the widespread use of sophisticated methods and technology, including Biometric Voting Registration, which can help to reduce fraud (even though it creates other problems of hacking), and Parallel Voter Tabulation, whereby official results are tracked or even pre-empted, as in the case of Nigeria, by the opposition. With few exceptions, such as the successful 2015 Buhari campaign in Nigeria, oppositions have lacked the capacity, financial or otherwise, to get ahead of incumbents and their ability to circumvent transparency and due process. Authoritarian regimes have proved quick learners in this regard.

Second, the funding transparency of political parties is a further, absolutely imperative area of reform. Political donors risk being accused of seeking political favours or, by funding oppositions, upsetting their relationship with the incumbents. A lack of a public funding regime lends itself to favouring the ruling party or the personally wealthy. The only way around this conundrum seems to be shining an even brighter light on financial flows. One means to do so is through the establishment of an independent body to which donors transparently channel funds and which openly distributes these resources. Only those who seek favours will in the circumstances choose alternative and opaque avenues.

Third, deepening democracy fundamentally depends on what African democrats, including the opposition, do for themselves. It is certainly right to focus on the many ways that incumbents try to steal elections but the weaknesses and tactical mistakes of those who seek power also have an effect on the democratic environment. Oppositions are not passive bystanders. They need to develop their own narrative, connect with voters, unify their movements, and adopt best practices from the playbook for democrats. Important steps include voter registration drives and targeted advertising based on polling outcomes, as well as the more mundane training (and funding) of polling agents, the assiduous checking of voters' rolls (especially in removing dead voters), and the mobilisation of democrats across regions.

Democrats have to work hard to win elections.

8

A Role for Outsiders?

Our message to those who would derail the democratic process is clear and unequivocal: the United States will not stand idly by when actors threaten legitimately elected governments or manipulate the fairness and integrity of democratic processes.

— President Barack Obama, 'US Strategy towards Sub-Saharan Africa', 2012

I know how it feels to lose … But you have to move on.

— John Kerry, Carter Center head of observer mission, on the 2017 Kenyan election

Chapter Takeaways

- Africa received $50.7 billion in aid in 2016, more than any other region, over one-third of the global total. Chinese aid amounted to $25 billion in 2013, and that of 'non-traditional' donors, including Russia, United Arab Emirates and Turkey, some $2.5 billion in 2015.

- Aid for democracy is small, though most donors have a democracy component.

- Donor objectives are driven by national interests that often cause promoting democratisation to be a lower priority.

- Outsiders often prefer to preserve stability and support regimes that are performing well economically or that maintain donor security interests, despite repressive policies. This leads many donors to side with undemocratic regimes.

The international community spends more than $1 billion each year retaining the United Nations Organisation Stabilisation Mission in the Democratic Republic of the Congo (or MONUSCO). It has been underway since 1999 following the removal of Mobutu Sese Seko from power two years earlier and the subsequent conclusion of a peace agreement between the regional and domestic warring parties.[1] To this bill should be added the approximately $1 billion for each of the country's two democratic elections in 2006 and 2011, and nearly $50 billion in official aid since 1999.[2]

Despite this considerable investment, the country's peace is continually challenged by incessantly violent conflict between rival militias, ethnic armies and government factions. Probably over five million people have died (no one really can say with any certainty given the conditions), with endemic violence that *The Economist* has described as 'children murdering in gangs, civilians massacred by the thousand, rape as common as petty thievery'.[3] In what is construed as the 'rape capital of the world', where abuse against women is used 'as a weapon of war', it has been estimated that 48 women are raped every hour in the Congo.[4] Despite possessing an estimated $20 trillion in mineral wealth, the country ranks 176th out of 188 countries on the UN Human Development Index.[5] The indices for misery in the Congo are apparently endless. And, unsurprisingly, the government and some of its mining partners have been at the centre of multiple corruption allegations.[6]

Elections, originally scheduled for 2016, were delayed by two years as President Joseph Kabila filibustered, in the knowledge that without changing the constitution, which he lacked the support to carry through, he could not stand for a third term. All manner of delaying tactics were employed, including preventing his main political rival, the governor of Katanga, Möise Katumbi, from returning to the country to register his candidacy. Without a shred of irony, Kabila's government has said that it could not afford the $1.8 billion for the election, while rejecting foreign aid to do so.[7] Further points of disagreement included the government's plans to use

100 000 electronic voting machines that domestic critics and international observers said would open the door to potential massive fraud.

Despite the enormous external assistance, Congo has never possessed effective and/or educated leaders committed to creating, maintaining and prioritising the governability of the country. In part, this is because the international community gave President Kabila an effective free pass in the 2006 and 2011 elections,[8] setting the stage for a wider, later crisis. Moreover, the international community failed to effectively engage in the lead-up to the end of Kabila's constitutional mandate in 2016 to ensure an effective democratic transition.

Aside from doubts about the practicality of attempting to govern a country larger than Western Europe with scant infrastructure (the difference between, for example, possessing 10.5 million and 2 800 kilometres of paved roads),[9] these election processes appeared to maintain the belief that the international community would put democracy and competitive elections above the threat of instability and that Kabila was interested in placing his people's interests over his own. Instead of cementing Kabila's popularity, the conduct of the polls divided more than they united, undermining legitimacy, entrenching patronage and bad governance, and ensuring, in a vicious cycle, that aid was badly spent on a government that cared less. A 2013 EU report, for example, noted that only €1 billion of EU aid of €1.9 billion worth of 16 aid projects into the DRC between 2003 and 2011 have 'delivered, or are likely to deliver, most of the expected results'. It added: 'Sustainability is an unrealistic prospect in most cases.'[10]

Contrary to the West's earlier bet that he would bring stability, the longer Kabila stayed on, the more likely was instability and violent conflict.

The way out of this mess is difficult, given the Congo's fictional existence (so far) as a united, governable nation. Better donor focus could, however, help, and greater discretion on what and whom they fund, but only if the overall urge to cut aid is greater than the drive to spend it. And instead of girding their loins to find ways to give more money, some honesty about aid failures would be refreshing. This transparency could include where the funds are being spent. More should go to democracy programmes, for example, rather than being consumed by support for the logistical cost of the elections themselves. In 2011, supporting contests that involved 63 000 polling sites, 11 presidential and 18 855 parliamentary candidates, representing more than 250 parties, required the use of 108 UN aircraft.[11] Foreign donors have had to organise the voting booths and pay for as many as 300 000 electoral workers and 50 000 police.[12] As Michela Wrong has cautioned, 'Thumb pads, apps and mobile phone transmission do no harm in themselves, but they cannot replace a society's generalised buy-in to the democratic process. The reason political parties rig elections so enthusiastically in many African countries is because winner-takes-all systems of government and imperial presidencies make the rewards so enormous and punish failure so severely. Now fixing that,' she notes, 'is a lot harder.'[13]

While foreign aid can distort lines of accountability by substituting for the failure of government services, it is not (by far) the villain in this picture, if a useful target. The issue is the leadership of the country and its focus on maintaining power and wealth. Too much foreign aid is on 'autopilot' with funds spent regardless of what the leadership of the country is doing/not doing. Calling that out would be useful, as would the need for donor countries to get much more proactive in calling out bad governance, corruption and incompetency.

Elections or not, the Congo will only start to work better once it has leaders who prioritise the development of the country and its people. Without that, as investors note about the country, 'foreign aid can never be anything more than plaster on a shotgun wound.'[14]

* * *

The fate of African democracies will ultimately be determined by citizens in each country, even though there are roles that outsiders can play

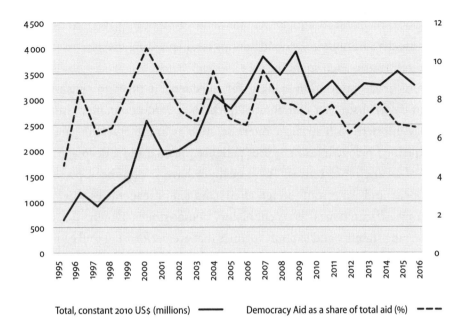

Total, constant 2010 US$ (millions) ——— Democracy Aid as a share of total aid (%) — — —

Figure 8.1: Democracy aid to sub-Saharan Africa: Development Assistance Committee and multilateral donors

in promoting democracy. The leverage of outsiders is arguably greater in Africa than elsewhere, not least because African countries are generally dependent on foreign assistance and because, across the region, leaders are closely attuned to international trends.

Africa received $50.7 billion in overseas development assistance in 2016, more than any other region and more than one-third of the global total. The top ten African recipients were Ethiopia ($4.1 billion), Nigeria ($2.5 billion), Tanzania ($2.3 billion), Kenya ($2.2 billion), DRC ($2.1 billion), Egypt ($2.1 billion), Morocco ($2 billion), Uganda ($1.8 billion), South Sudan ($1.7 billion) and Mozambique ($1.5 billion). The US was the largest individual contributing nation overall worldwide, providing $34.4 billion, with Germany at $24.7 billion and the UK just over $18 billion. Ethiopia was behind Syria ($8.9 billion) and equal to Afghanistan ($4.1 billion) in the global recipient rankings.[15] Aid for democracy among Western donors consistently amounts to around 10% of total spending, despite relatively good returns on such spending.[16]

Democracy promotion is hard for outsiders. It plays to sensitivities about colonialism that complicate efforts to reward democracy with aid. It may interfere with strategic interests, such as in the case of Uganda, as is explained below. It also requires patience, nuance and a deep appreciation of local circumstances. These qualities have seldom been present in European and American foreign affairs and aid bureaucracies when confronting African issues, as recent history demonstrates. Donors default to preserving stability and support regimes that are performing well economically, despite repressive policies or authoritarianism. This, in addition to counter-terrorism, leads many donors to side with undemocratic regimes. They err on the side of caution, and hope that development will eventually translate into greater freedom. This is seldom the case.

Donors and democracy

Western countries largely did not anticipate the wave of political liberalisation in Africa that began soon after the Berlin Wall fell. The US and its allies still viewed the continent through the prism of the Cold War and major support was therefore given to autocrats such as Mobutu Sese Seko in Zaire and Samuel Doe in Liberia, both of whose economic and political performances were woeful but who knew how to manipulate superpower rivalry. The major exception was South Africa, where the international community had long been fixated on apartheid and where donors had for decades promoted a transition to a non-racial order through rhetoric and sanctions. However, until the dramatic speech by F.W. de Klerk on 2 February 1990, when he announced the freeing of Nelson Mandela and the unbanning of the ANC and other liberation movements, the overriding assumption in Western countries was that there was little likelihood of a change of regime in Pretoria in the near future.

How to respond to the process of political liberalisation in Africa has been a persistent issue for Western countries for two decades. Their diplomacy has been constrained by three important considerations.

First, Africa is not, for the most part, a vital strategic interest for any Western power. The partial exception is France, which has traditionally seen its position as a great power being dependent on its unrivalled power in West Africa. However, the French understanding of great power interest has not, in the main – whatever President François Mitterrand's stated preferences at La Baule in June 1990 when he announced that French aid would in the future be conditional upon democratic reforms – translated into pressure for democratisation. Instead, traditional strategic interests and, more recently, counter-terrorism have dominated Paris' interests in Africa.

Second, to the extent that Western states have an interest in Africa, their objectives are multiple, driven by national interests and competing agendas. For instance, counter-terrorism efforts have risen to the top of the Western agenda, a prioritisation that African leaders are keen to exploit in order to strengthen their own security apparatuses and weaken international support for domestic opponents.

The Europeans have also come to realise that they have a profound interest in limiting inward migration given the political disruptions that anti-immigration sentiment has caused within the EU. However, this new European focus may, in fact, divert them from promoting democracy. The US government has noted that 'European interest in reducing the wave of African migration is likely to encourage some European states to bolster their support to authoritarian African leaders capable of controlling population flows within Africa'.[17]

The short-term imperative of stability may override the long-term need for economic growth and freedom as reasons for would-be migrants to stay.

Third, the West itself has been ambivalent about pushing for democracy.

Lynda Chalker was the minister of state for Overseas Development and Africa at the UK Foreign Office under the Conservative government from 1989 to 1997. 'While we always spoke about democracy in discussions with African governments, the link between aid and democracy was never written into agreements,' she recalls. From a donor perspective, 'the biggest challenge was trying to get democracy at all levels – local, regional and central government'. However, for a donor to stick to its democratic principles meant 'making greater conditionality than most governments were prepared to accept'.[18]

Similarly, Stefano Manservisi took up the appointment as director-general of the European Commission's agencies for the Directorate-General for International Cooperation and Development in May 2016. The EU provides three different sources of finance to Africa: budget support, leveraged financial instruments, and aid through both multilateral institutions and NGOs. The EU's 28 members provide some €20 billion in financial assistance to sub-Saharan Africa annually, of which €12 billion is funnelled through the EU directly. Yet, Manservisi maintains, it is very difficult, even with the leverage that the EU possesses, to work in promotion of democracy without being seen, as he notes, 'as preaching'. While there is a clear link, he admits, between democracy and development, 'the challenge is to find the means to reform democracy to make it more responsive', and to deal with the 'negative, countervailing tendencies'.[19]

Unsurprisingly, some African leaders have been quick to take advantage.

Uganda's Yoweri Museveni combined the scrapping of term limits with the promise of a return to multi-party democracy in 2005.[20] Yet, the country's third multi-party election in February 2016 was shrouded in controversy. With more than two-thirds of the electorate voting across 28 000 polling stations, incumbent President Museveni was re-elected with 61% of the vote. His rival, Kizza Besigye Kifefe, who was arrested on the day the results were announced, achieved 35%.

The 13-person Commonwealth Observer Group[21] found that the elections had 'fallen well short of meeting many of the key democratic benchmarks for the conduct of credible elections'.[22] Key problems noted included the increased prevalence of money in politics, the misuse of state resources and the competence, credibility and ability of the Electoral Commission to manage the process effectively. These problems were similar to those identified by Commonwealth groups, which had observed previous elections in the country. However, none of these previous recommendations had been substantially addressed. The Commonwealth report states: 'We have strong concerns that many of the administrative and operational processes undertaken during the electoral cycle were flawed, to the extent that the election results cannot be said to ascertain fully the true will of the people of Uganda. Such concerns also extend to the restrictions placed on the free movement of key opposition members and their supporters at all stages of the elections.'

The Commonwealth was not alone in its condemnation. The EU Observer report noted that 'voter enthusiasm for the democratic process was eclipsed by an atmosphere of intimidation and ruling party control of state resources'.[23] This is hardly surprising given that the chair of Uganda's Electoral Commission, Badru Kiggundu, broke a most basic rule of electoral neutrality in declaring that Besigye was not 'presidential material'.[24]

Yet, at the same time, outside powers – including the US and Brussels – realise that Uganda has a central role to play in the stabilisation mission in Somalia and in South Sudan. They, therefore, speak out of both sides of their mouths. The EU has funded the Somalia peace process to the tune of not less than €1 billion between 2007 and 2015, and a further €180 million annually since then.[25] This includes allowances per soldier of $822 per month.[26] As of May 2018, there were more than 6 200 Ugandan troops in the 22 126-strong African Union Mission in Somalia (AMISOM), the largest uniformed national contingent.[27]

Kampala has openly threatened the withdrawal of its troops at key moments. In 2012, for example, Amama Mbabazi, Uganda's prime minister, sent a letter to the UN advising of its withdrawal from 'all regional peace efforts' in response to leaked sections of a Security Council analysis that accused the Ugandan regime of supporting rebels in the eastern regions of the DRC. 'Why should the children of Ugandans die and we get malignment [sic] as a reward?' Mbabazi said to the parliament in Kampala.[28] In 2016, Museveni again threatened to pull his troops out of Somalia at the end of the following year, a decision that was later (predictably) rescinded.[29]

Harriett Baldwin, Britain's minister of state for Africa, highlights this tension. Support for democracy, she says, 'is a core part of the UK government's work, our values and what we stand for globally and through the Commonwealth. But spending aid is also done in countries by need, in those countries that are not democratic.'[30] The West has a particularly difficult role in this regard given the tension between values and interests.

But the bland communiqúes and delicate diplomatic evasions that are traditionally used to negotiate this difficult path may send the wrong signals and fail to secure interests in the face of naked power.

Pitfalls in democracy promotion

The association of democracy with American foreign policy became an especially important issue after the US invasion of Iraq and the development of the Bush administration's 'freedom agenda'. According to Sarah Sewall, Undersecretary of State for Civilian Security, Democracy, and Human Rights in the Obama administration, democracy promotion was seen by many countries as being a 'tool' of American foreign policy and therefore something that should be avoided.[31]

Yet, aid for democracy is still a focus of many donors, at least rhetorically. 'Democracy is important to us,' says Ulla Tørnæs, Denmark's minister for development co-operation, 'for reasons of human rights and equality. This is the Danish model; the values on which we built our society and which we want to project to the world. Denmark has a long-standing tradition of fulfilling the UN goal of 0.7% of gross national income to development assistance. We have done so since 1978 – bringing us to 40 years in a row – and we will continue to do so. We have had development co-operation in Africa for more than 50 years, and today eight out of 12 priority countries are in Africa. We have pursued targeted, consistent and principled human rights policy and promoted democracy through, for example, funding civil society, supporting the media and capacity building of accountable public institutions.'[32]

The former prime minister of Norway, Kjell Magne Bondevik, agrees. 'Democracy represents our values. It is about the respect for human dignity, that everyone has a value in society. But it is also the best framework for economic growth.' Norway spends more than 1% of its gross national income on aid, the second highest ratio in the world behind Sweden. (Denmark is fourth.) More than 60% of its annual flows of more than $4 billion are earmarked for Africa; and one-quarter of this goes to the promotion of democracy.[33]

Yet, the role of outsiders in this regard is complicated by the increasing influence of the Chinese and Russian governments, which are opposed to democratisation efforts. While statistics on how much China donates and invests in Africa are unknown, it certainly has grown quickly and become a major part of the aid landscape. Between 2000 and 2014, the US gave Africa $395 billion in overseas development assistance and it is estimated that China provided $354 billion.[34]

As a result, in contrast to the view expressed above, 'The tendency in Africa,' says the EU Commission's Manservisi, 'is trending away from democracy, towards meeting expectations of a quick fix. The rule of law is now identified with slowness, with bureaucracy. As a result, authoritarian democracy has become fashionable, shrinking democratic accountability, and yet in some cases enabling faster delivery and efficiencies. This tendency towards authoritarianism is supported by the actions of some donors since it emulates what we see in China, Turkey and other countries.'

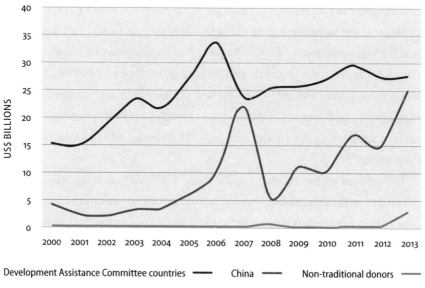

Figure 8.2: Aid flows to Africa, 2000–13

The Chinese are not leveraging their aid for the sake of democracy and freedom. Indeed, they have made their lack of concern about internal political arrangements a signature part of their approach to Africa, in part because this is attractive to African partners, and in part because this facilitates business. As with Russia, this stance is taken to reflect their internal values.[35]

New entrants who hope to have a role in Africa, including Iran and Turkey, also do not have democratisation as a priority. On the contrary, it may be a threat to their interests and way of doing business – though this issue paradoxically illustrates exactly why democracy is important to Western countries and businesses.

Even within US foreign policy, where there has been a stated commitment to promote democratisation, other priorities often dominate. In 2017, reflecting the last Obama budget, the 'Democracy, Human Rights and Governance' sector received $1.6 billion out of the $28.9 billion spent on foreign assistance, or only 5.5% of the total outlay for foreign assistance. 'Health', in contrast, received $6.6 billion (21%) while 'Peace and Security' received $6 billion (21%) and 'Humanitarian Assistance' $3.4 billion (12%).[36] US assistance to Africa is even more dramatically shaped by priorities other than democratisation. Health and humanitarian aid represent more than 80% of US aid to Africa, in good part because of President George W. Bush's large-scale programme to fight Aids, which was continued by Obama.[37]

More subtle has been the evolution of Western assistance to focus on projects that produce quantifiable results in a short period of time. Foreign assistance budgets have been pressured to make aid more accountable after numerous horror stories about waste and also by cynicism on the part of many Western taxpayers that their money is being used inappropriately. Over decades, a whole set of apparatuses, called the 'counter-bureaucracy' by Andrew Natsios, has propelled aid expenditures towards relatively short-term projects that can produce quantifiable results. The bias is, therefore, towards service delivery that can identify the number of students, patients or villagers touched as opposed to democratisation, which is inherently long term and nebulous. Natsios observes, 'One of the little understood, but most powerful and disruptive tensions in established aid agencies lies in the clash between the compliance side of aid programs – the counter-bureaucracy – and the technical, programmatic side. The essential balance', observes the former USAID director, 'between these two in development programs has now been skewed to such a degree in the US aid system (and in the World Bank as well) that the imbalance threatens program integrity.'[38]

As a result, Natsios notes that law and good governance programmes, the ones that are most central to promoting democratisation, 'are chronically underfunded at USAID, even though development theory almost universally describes rule of law and good governance as the most important factors in development'. While Natsios was writing in 2010, it is still obvious that service delivery dominates, given that health aid and humanitarian aid form the bulk of US foreign assistance to Africa. Indeed, Sewall has observed that the Obama administration was sceptical of governance and democracy promotion because 'it was never evaluated and therefore hard to justify'.

More difficult to discern is the important role that African countries will play in promoting democracy in their own region. Certainly, the days are gone when African people would accept any ruler who had physical control of the capital. In particular, African leaders have strongly pushed back against militaries that have tried to overthrow directly elected civilian governments. However, the African collective effort to promote democracy beyond this red line is still problematic. As the US government has found (and was highlighted in Chapter 5): 'Since 2007, the AU has consistently condemned flagrant violations of democratic standards, such as coups d'état, by suspending member states and in some cases imposing sanctions. However, AU officials have struggled to counter more furtive violations and have fielded election observers that often validated even the most problematic elections.'[39]

Kenya redux: The outsider's dilemma

In an ideal world, foreigners would detect the obvious signs that an election or democratisation experiment was failing and try to intervene before the crisis solidified lines of conflict and made a lasting solution improbable. In the real world of busy foreign bureaucracies for whom Africa is a very low priority, such foresight is usually sorely lacking. Sewall has noted, 'It is a continual problem to get the US bureaucracy to act in a preventative manner, before democracy collapses. It is biased against acting earlier or acting with others. This is so even though preventative action might be much less costly than dealing with actual crisis.'

Not surprisingly, outsiders often act in a clumsy manner when faced with a crisis of democracy. Certainly, that was the case of Kenya in 2007 when Raila Odinga was running against President Mwai Kibaki, a case discussed previously from the Kenyan perspective. As noted, Odinga was winning early tallies but, after several days of delay, the electoral commission proclaimed that Kibaki had won a narrow victory. There were widespread suggestions of electoral fraud. Condoleezza Rice, US secretary of state at the time, has written that fraud was so widely suspected that it 'had made the final results impossible to determine with certainty'.[40] The situation was desperate as perhaps a thousand people were killed in ethnic violence inspired by the contested election.

As the US finally began to focus on Kenya, not least because President Bush was scheduled to visit neighbouring Tanzania in a few weeks, Rice admitted, in an honesty seldom found in the memoirs of diplomats, that 'I knew that the international community had to do something but, frankly, it wasn't clear what to do'.[41] This is the precise problem when issues are left to fester until there is an explosion. Rice, former UN Secretary General Kofi Annan who was on the ground in Kenya trying to promote a reconciliation, and Western governments concluded that what Kenya needed was a government of national unity so that they could 'put the divisive elections behind them'.[42]

As a result, Kibaki, who probably lost the election, was named president and Odinga prime minister, almost certainly not what the majority of Kenyan voters wanted. This result, which did promote short-term stability and end the killings, was appealing to Western diplomats who needed to move on from low-priority Kenya. In fact, Rice's memoir is replete with mentions of the other crises she had to deal with, including higher priority conflicts in Afghanistan and Iraq where US lives and American politics were involved. Rice, obviously self-conscious about promoting a result that clearly went against the sentiments of the Kenyan people, justified the slapdash arrangement by noting, 'Sometimes young democracies need breathing space, a chance to survive a crisis, to live to fight another day, and to get it right the next time.'[43] She is firm in her belief that 'Each time the country will get closer to stable democracy.'[44]

Such a linear progression is not guaranteed, however, and certainly did not occur in Kenya. As noted in Chapter 5, the 2017 Kenyan elections were also exceptionally problematic with the Supreme Court eventually annulling the contest. The government then rigged the new round so obviously that Odinga boycotted and Uhuru Kenyatta won with an overwhelming majority, although voter participation dropped sharply as many Kenyans were obviously disgusted. Western governments nonetheless grudgingly went along with this outcome. Another power-sharing arrangement, this time between President Kenyatta and Odinga, was seen to have 'pulled Kenya back from the brink'.[45] In fact, it is highly likely that these informal arrangements, formulated in private and announced without any consultation, are in many ways an affront to the democratic ambitions of Kenyans. There is little evidence that kicking the can down the road has solved Kenya's democratic deficit, although it has probably improved prospects for short-term stability and saved lives, not an inconsequential achievement. Most importantly for foreigners, the arrangements have only taken Kenya off the immediate agenda, thereby allowing diplomats to focus on issues of greater short-term importance to them.

But the role of Africans, within and without AU member states, can be critical, as the Gambia shows.

The Gambia's search for peace, stability and justice

The Gambia, says President Adama Barrow, is on the road to recovery 'after two decades of decay, which disintegrated the social fabric of society. The political environment was dangerous, there had been a serious brain drain, and the business environment was risky as the rule of law was not respected. But,' he said, little more than a year after taking power in 2017, 'we are now engaged in institutional reform. We have released all political prisoners, decentralised powers to the ministries, and are engaged in reintegration with the international community. There is a spirit of togetherness, which is key to effectiveness.'[46]

The Gambia is a study of what happens when politics go awry. Home of the African Human Rights Charter, thus also known as the Banjul Charter, set up in 1987 and designed to 'promote and protect human rights and basic freedoms in the African continent',[47] the country was one of the few democracies in a region long defined by military regimes. That was until 1994, when Yahya Jammeh came to power via a military coup. Far from a paragon of human rights, the Gambia gained international notoriety for human rights violations. Jammeh ruled, first, as chair of the Armed Forces Provisional Ruling Council for two years and thereafter as president. Under his regime, as Freedom House notes, government opponents, independent journalists and rights activists faced intimidation, arbitrary arrest, torture and forced disappearance.

Jammeh looked set to repeat the tenure of his predecessor Sir Dawda Kairaba Jawara, who had served as the prime minister from 1962 to 1970, and then as its first president from 1970 to 1994 when Jammeh took over.

However, he was defeated, surprisingly, by Barrow in the election of November 2016. The outside challenger won the election with 43.34% of the vote. Jammeh, who received 39.6% (with a third candidate, Mama Kandeh, receiving some 17.1%), initially accepted the result, but later reneged on this, saying that he 'totally' rejected the outcome. His volte-face was condemned by the UN and the AU. Jammeh appealed his loss in the Supreme Court, and declared a state of emergency to stop Barrow, who had fled to neighbouring Senegal, from being sworn in as president. Barrow was inaugurated at the Gambian embassy in Dakar on 19 January 2017. That day an Economic Community of West African States (ECOWAS) military force led by Senegal, Nigeria and Ghana entered the Gambia to try to compel Jammeh to step down. Two days later, Jammeh was forced to leave the Gambia and go into exile in Equatorial Guinea.

On 18 February 2017, Barrow was inaugurated for a second time in the capital, Banjul. As a result, the Gambia secured one of the largest-ever improvements in its status in Freedom House's indicators in the process, registering a 21-point score increase as it moved from 'not free' to 'partly free'. Fundamental freedoms immediately improved under Barrow's government, with legislative elections held successfully in April 2017. Exiled journalists and activists returned, political prisoners were released, ministers declared their assets to an ombudsman, the press union began work on media-sector reform, and arrest warrants were issued for suspects in the 2004 murder of journalist Deyda Hydara.[48]

There are several lessons that can be garnered from the process of the Gambia's democratic success story.[49] For one, change was led by Gambians themselves, and supported by the regional community. Overall, the Gambia's undoing of Jammeh's palace coup illustrates that the key role must be played by insiders.

Social media platforms played an important role, with hashtags such as #GambiaDecides and #FreeGambia used to catalyse support. Unlike the Arab Spring, this mobilisation occurred through organised political structures, which enabled the victory of the seven-party coalition headed by Barrow.[50]

The Gambia also shows the importance of having a united regional community pushing in one direction, in this case through ECOWAS, as a critical driver of change. ECOWAS' role depended on its credibility and the leadership of the regional power, Nigeria, and goes some way to explaining why it managed to convince Jammeh to leave without a shot being fired. This posture was in stark contrast to the Intergovernmental Authority on Development's role in South Sudan or that of the Southern African Development Community (SADC) in Zimbabwe. In fact, ECOWAS has been the most effective regional economic community in promoting democratisation, in large part because its 'anchor' state – Nigeria – has had a commitment to regional democratisation. In contrast, the SADC and the

East African Community have been less successful because their respective 'anchor' states – South Africa and Kenya – have been more willing to tolerate authoritarians.[51] The Kenyan political system itself has hardly been a model of democracy, making it problematic for it to have a regional role. Other regional organisations, notably the Arab Maghreb Union and the Economic Community of Central African States, 'show minimal interest in democratisation or peacebuilding'.[52]

As a result, Freedom House has come up with a list of actions that the AU, and its members, should follow to address the democratic deficit. These include the presence of a free press as one of the key conditions necessary for free and fair elections, developing uniform standards for public safety and NGO legislation, setting clear expectations for respecting term limits, removing the immunity of leadership from prosecution on human rights issues, and including efforts to strengthen democracy and governance in economic development and integration strategies.[53]

Institutionalised African attempts at reform

The African Peer Review Mechanism (APRM) was established by African governments in 2003 as a voluntary self-assessment of countries' governance. As of October 2018, there were 37 members, while 22 countries had completed the assessment process.[54]

The head of the APRM secretariat, Eddy Maloka, has contended: 'The fact that African countries have now identified governance on their own, is an achievement ... It is now a priority for the continent.' Maloka said it must be recognised as a central node to improve governance. '[P]eople in some countries still view governance as an external imposition. And the APRM mechanism is intended as an antidote to that ... It's a self-assessment ... self-owned process ... a much better way to move the governance agenda on the continent than come here as external players ... then countries see that as interference ... as conditionality and in some cases people see that also as a regime change agenda.'[55]

However, although it started well, like other institutions, the APRM has fallen victim to a 'laundry list' approach, setting a lengthy list of governance priorities without the necessary means or will to address them. This fault has been compounded by a lack of political will 'by African leaders, especially following the exit of presidents Mbeki and Obasanjo', explains one official, who worked in the secretariat. The death in 2012 of Prime Minister Meles Zenawi of Ethiopia, though Meles refused to release his own country's report, also did not help.[56] This rudderless slump improved somewhat with the appointment of Kenya's president, Uhuru Kenyatta, as its chairperson in 2015, and Maloka as CEO in 2016.

Still, this failure of African governments – and investors – to take the APRM seriously and the lack of tough engagement around elections are indicative of a difficulty in changing domestic political dynamics, of generating leverage over the elites and their ways of doing things. As a result, the record of outsiders improving governance and democracy in Africa is poor, not least because African leaders routinely resist such 'conditionality' attached to external assistance. Donors have consequently soft-pedalled on democracy and rule-of-law interventions, preferring less controversial initiatives, such as infrastructure assistance and the development of skills. But being firmer and more outspoken on democracy is the right thing to do, for reasons of long-term economic growth and because it means taking the side of the majority of Africans.

Halfway houses to democracy

The conflicts of interest, low prioritisation of Africa, and sheer difficulty of promoting democratisation in Africa have led some to advocate a slow transition to democracy, preferring instead coalition governments as a solution, especially in fragile circumstances. The Fragile States Commission has, for example, recommended that democratic elections should be considered merely as a secondary component of good govern-ance in fragile states.[57] 'Democracy should not be an objective in itself,' says one of the report's co-authors, Paul Collier, but a means to get society out of a hole. 'This depends on two processes,' he notes, 'to an extent in paral-lel': building checks and balances on the abuse of power, which don't have to be democratic; and organising a positive agenda, in the form of a collec-tive sacrifice for a better future.[58] Collier cites the importance of building trust as an element of stability and prosperity, both among citizens and in terms of entrusting the government with their savings.

The danger in this approach, however, is that it gives a free pass on democ-ratisation issues to authoritarians in the name of stability, and essentially hands power over without challenge to the winners of civil wars. In fact, the international community need not make a choice between stability and democracy, not least since the latter is a means of engendering the very trust that is key to establishing prosperity. Instead, external actors should take their cues from what Africans are actually saying on the ground.

A particular temptation for Western governments when faced with the tension between democratisation and stability has been to promote power-sharing. These schemes are inherently non-democratic but are advocated because they may save lives by promoting stability. Such arrangements do have a role but only temporarily in creating a bridge from one type of state to another. For instance, the provision that allowed whites to elect 20% of Zimbabwe's parliament for six years, despite the fact that they amounted to only 2% of the population, did instil confidence in the country but did nothing to prevent Robert Mugabe from seizing total power once he could change the constitution in 1987 and eventually destroying the country. Similarly, South Africa's interim constitution, which mandated that the leader of the opposition be named a deputy president (De Klerk of the National Party), was helpful in the transition to non-racial rule. However, it was clear that this gambit was only short term. Indeed, De Klerk resigned before the end of his term, signifying that he did not believe that holding the office itself was critical. The opposition Democratic Alliance's rule of the City of Cape Town in South Africa also has its origins in a coalition. Just as the speaker of the regional legislature, Mark Wiley, regards 'coalition politics' as 'a little like a frail marriage, where both parties have to work very hard', the premier of the Western Cape, Helen Zille, warns against them driving 'a bad bargain. You should ask yourself "is it worthwhile sacrificing principles for power?" in putting coalitions together.'[59]

And, as is noted above, the open-ended power-sharing arrangements that have been attempted in Kenya, which are not bridges between different states but obvious ad hoc attempts to bandage over structural problems, are unlikely to work well. Given that they are profoundly non-democratic, they should therefore be viewed with great suspicion.

Reforming international observation

It would be tempting for international observers, outside governments and investors to believe that their interests are best served in fractious circumstances by doing nothing, a cliché-ridden policy choice of 'keeping your head down', 'not rocking the boat', 'letting them get on with things', and 'waiting and seeing'. The benchmark for a successful election is set very low by international observers: it is about preventing violence more than anything else, even if the books are obviously cooked. And the unwillingness of many international actors to shake the system has a strategic aspect, since other countries are unlikely to do so, and may profit from any bilateral upset.

Outsiders do have a difficult path to walk, hamstrung by the shortage of both resources and political will. Too tough and they are automatically suspected of seeking to up-end the incumbent; too quiet and they stand accused of complicity in a government cover-up. Of course they should aim, at the minimum, to do no harm, and they also have to focus on democratic conditions between the elections. Doing no harm includes realising that the presence of an observer group can have a legitimating effect on an election process. It also involves calling out those elections that are patently unfree and unfair, and ensuring that there are consequences to such malfeasance.

Even though crude ballot paper dumping, vote buying, bribery and wholesale fraud still happen, the nature of election rigging is increasingly sophisticated. The threshold for the international community calling an election unfair (and acting on this) should thus include whether the media, including Facebook and the internet, are closed down, the prevalence of violence, the up-ending of legal processes, intimidation and arrest, the partiality of the election commission, vetting and sanctioning of international observer participants, and the closing down of funding for civil society watchdogs. Remembering the cost of the erosion of election processes, the threshold for international condemnation should also avoid crude measures, notably the extent (or not) of violence, and should be consistent. If criticism is made of processes in the Gambia, Senegal and the Ivory Coast, for example, and mediators see fit to intervene, why does the same not occur elsewhere?

Criticism of African elections does not amount to unfair treatment. While there are flawed elections elsewhere, and even in the US, research has found that elections in Africa are significantly *less* likely to be branded 'unfree and unfair' than elections held elsewhere that suffer the same manipulations.[60] Analysis shows that if a candidate is excluded from elections in Africa, there is a 20% lower likelihood of donor censure than in other regions. As a result, incumbents typically get away with a wide range of abuses, including such major offences as the exclusion of rival candidates.[61]

In short, bad elections should have consequences. And observers should only participate if they are willing at the outset to call the election truthfully. Outsiders have to make insiders do their job better, but it is not up to them to fund elections or to ensure that Africa gets its house in order.

Conclusion: No false choices

Former French Prime Minister Dominique de Villepin has asked: 'While we should support democracy, what should be done about those who are not democratic? Should we invade them, attempt regime change?'[62] This presents, however, a false choice.

De Villepin answers his own question in this regard: 'We have to create states which are strong and successful, and which can act as an example to others.' If human rights are important, if economic development is deemed critical, then the answer has to be in finding the means to support democracy, from ensuring that crooked election results do not pass international muster without comment, to providing support for civil society institutions and the media between elections.

It is not merely African respondents to public opinion who favour democracy. For instance, as noted in Chapter 2, in June 2018, early in his term, Ethiopia's Prime Minister Abiy Ahmed openly criticised the behaviour of the country's security and intelligence services.[63]

The pace of change in Ethiopia, from an avowed authoritarian government to a more open regime, is startling. But it should also encourage the donors to pause for thought. Ethiopia has been a donor darling, just as Rwanda is, and Uganda was in an earlier age. The routine and obvious authoritarianism of these governments had been excused away by many donors on the basis of 'strategic interests' or impressive performance in achieving the Millennium Development Goals and now the Sustainable Development Goals.[64] Aid, in other words, continued to flow regardless of the nature of the regime because the donors needed 'success', defined in terms of technical metrics, not politics.

In the same vein, in 2017 the Danish government decided to shut its diplomatic mission to Mozambique, historically one of the most important African development aid partners of Scandinavian countries. They did so because of the need to focus Danish efforts and rationalise expenditure. Surprisingly, they did not do so on the grounds of the mismanagement of the economy, which included secret debt agreements by Maputo that had brought the local currency crashing down and one of the darlings of the international aid community to insolvency. The same question should be asked of those donors, as we noted in Chapter 6, who continue to operate in Tanzania, in spite of authoritarian tendencies.

Outsiders should be modest in understanding the role they play in democratisation in Africa. However, that is no excuse for not prioritising democracy and working in a clear-eyed manner to try to ensure that the democratic wishes of African citizens are realised. That will be hard given competing priorities that both Western and African governments suffer from in conducting foreign policy.

It is time for all actors to align their actions with their rhetoric that repeatedly cites the importance of democracy.

CONCLUSION

Rewiring Africa's Politics

The challenge of democracy is not just about elections. Our need is to build those institutions that protect human rights, that institutionalise the role of civil society and the media.

— Said Aidi, former Tunisian minister of employment

Democracy is not realised merely by having a machinery for registering voters and getting them to vote every four years, but also by there being a machinery for identifying the needs of those voters in between the election periods, and monitoring the realisation of those needs.

— Jerry John Rawlings, former head of state, Ghana

'I'll give you 15 camels,' said Caqil Tayib, a big grin on his face. The 'offer' by the camel trader was for the chief protocol officer of Somaliland's minister of foreign affairs. We managed to raise the price to 150, equivalent to a sum over $100 000, preserving the officer's honour amid much laughter in Hargeisa's Qudhac Dher market.[1]

Camels are a critical commodity for Somaliland, the former British Somaliland, which lies to Somalia's north.[2] They are not only used as dowry, but to settle disputes and as the main source of income, other than diaspora remittances, in the dry, dusty and hitherto diplomatically unrecognised land.

Somaliland originally achieved independence from Britain, which had ruled it since the 1880s, on 26 June 1960. The former Italian Somaliland followed suit five days later, when the two territories united to form the

Somali Republic on 1 July. A third 'Somali star', French Somalia – now Djibouti – achieved independence from Paris in 1977. The fourth and fifth purported stars of Somali-inhabited territory in Kenya and Ethiopia (the latter known as the Ogaden or, officially today, 'Region Five') never acquired independence, forestalling the ambition of a greater Somalia. Having borne the brunt of the Somali dictator Mohamed Siad Barre's violence against insurgents and dissidents, the Somali National Movement (SNM) and clan elders agreed that Somaliland should (re)declare its independence.

In the centre of the capital, Hargeisa, is the 18 May independence memorial, comprising a Mig-17 fighter bomber erected on a plinth. This commemorates the event when, having lost control of the province, Siad Barre ordered his air force, operating from the local airport, to bomb the city, which had been briefly captured by SNM fighters in May 1988, resulting in many thousands of civilian casualties. By the time of Siad Barre's fall three years later, Hargeisa was known as the 'roofless city'. Systematic bombing and looting by Siad Barre's forces had stripped it of roof sheeting and even doors and their frames.

Since then, the former British protectorate has developed a stable, democratic system of politics, merging modern and traditional elements, including an elected president and House of Representatives as well as an Upper House of Elders (*guurti*), securing the support of clan-based power structures. The commitment to democracy is evident in the staging of local elections in 2002, presidential elections in 2003, 2010 and 2017, and parliamentary elections in 2005.

Democracy helps to keep radicalism in check in this fractious country. As one (Western) government security official has noted, 'Somaliland is pretty good in terms of the necessary combination of political will, capacity and ability, and human rights to fight terrorism. In fact, it's probably the best place to operate globally in this regard.'

Somaliland's democracy was built in five major internal meetings, starting with the Grand Conference of the Northern Peoples in Burao, which was held over six weeks, and concluding with the declaration of Somaliland's independence from Somalia on 18 May 1991.

Peace conferences in Burao and, later, Bomora were managed and financed by Somalis, bringing their own food and shelter. As such, these events were bottom-up rather than top-down, unlike Somalia's, which has been top-down, driven by donors and largely taking place outside the country. Somalilanders concentrated on achieving peace, not on acquiring economic rents for delegates from the process – a trend that has continually blighted Somalia's attempts to the south, where conflict entrepreneurs have profited from both the fighting and the talking.

The last conference in Boroma in 1993 was held in the region of the then governor, Abdirahman Ahmed Ali Tuur, taking place over five months 'under the trees'. Ali explains: 'This type of dialogue was not new to us, as from time immemorial, from before the colonial period, Somalilanders had their own reconciliation process; and when government institutions failed, these traditional measures took over once more.'[3]

In 2002, Somaliland made the transition to multi-party democracy. The 2003 presidential election was won by Dahir Riyale Kahin by just 80 votes in nearly half a million against Ahmed M. Mahamoud Silanyo. The tables were turned between the two in 2010, with former SNM fighter Muse Bihi Abdi being elected in 2017 with 55% of the vote.

Critics say that Somaliland's democracy has been facilitated by the dominance of a single clan, the Isaaq, which is 'hegemonic'. This is unlike Somalia, which has to balance the competing interests and ambitions of two major clans (Darod and Hawiye) and several smaller ones. But this understates the differences between the Isaaq's sub-clans and sub-sub-clans, ignores the internal violence that accompanied the birth process, which had to be resolved, and overlooks the tremendous hard work that went into it. And as President Muse Bihi Abdi contends, it also underestimates the impact of the democratic culture of the SNM.

'For ten years,' he says from his modest offices in Hargeisa, 'the SNM was struggling for democracy, refusing the dictatorship of Siad Barre. The democracy we now have was also based on the constitution of the SNM, which was very democratic, in which there were regular elections every two years, and in which the central committee operated like a parliament.'

Bihi Abdi noted that the SNM changed its chairperson democratically five times, sometimes through a handful of votes among its 250-plus delegates. 'As Somalilanders, we have never had a political dynasty. In the SNM we changed leaders more times than most African countries have changed government in their lifetimes. At the end of the Boroma conference, we dismantled the SNM entirely. It was in its constitution to transfer power in two years after the advent of peace. There were lots of challenges to this in the SNM. But if we did not do this,' says the former colonel in Siad Barre's army who defected to the SNM, 'we would not have fulfilled our promise. We did not want to create leaders like [Uganda's Yoweri] Museveni or [Eritrea's Isaias] Afwerki, who stay a long time.'

The Somaliland example demonstrates that democracy is possible in Africa even amid significant material deprivation. The formal youth unemployment rate is 75%, while the rate of literacy is under 45%, and just 20% for women. Outside of remittances, Somaliland depends on its sale of sheep, camels and goats, though this has suffered from a Saudi import ban. Yet, Somaliland has managed not only to maintain relative peace and stability (especially compared to Somalia) but to rotate leaders on a regular basis. Much of the credit for this record is due to the determination of Somalilanders to build democratic institutions that are appropriate for their particular circumstances. The result has been the development of a tradition of democratic practices in one of the least hospitable areas of the world. And those successes have been achieved in spite of, or perhaps partially due to, the minimal involvement of foreigners who remain fixated on the idea of a unified Somalia.

* * *

More democracy, as we have seen, leads to better economic performance across Africa. We have also learnt that authoritarian 'success stories' should not be relied on, and that countries can transition from 'not free' to 'partly free' and then 'free' (or fail to do so).

It is impossible, of course, to develop an exact formula for instilling and improving democracy. Countries and circumstances vary too much. But a number of actions stand out from the foregoing analysis and case studies. These are divided between what government, opposition, insiders and outsiders should each focus on to make democracy work.

Actions for government

While democracy is more, much more than just elections, the contest for votes needs to be safeguarded as a critical democratic moment, a prerequisite, without which legitimacy will suffer. Now is no time for election apathy. If elections are simply a means for endorsing the status quo, they will be less a source of change than one of conflict. With a youthful, expectant population, it is necessary to instil faith in the electoral process, otherwise there will be temptation to seek relief through extra-judicial means. Such disappointment will likely set the stage for violence and result in a reduced capacity for governments to drive Africa's future prosperity.

Fair and free elections require money and a level playing field. As was noted in Chapter 7, the cost of winning an election is roughly one dollar per voter. Absent legislation limiting private financing (and the capacity for verification), other transparency initiatives should be investigated.

In particular, **funding transparency of political parties is imperative for the promotion of democracy**. Those who donate to political parties risk being accused of seeking political favours, or upsetting their relationship with incumbents. The only way around this conundrum will be to shine an even brighter light on financial flows. One means to do so is through the establishment of an independent body to which donors transparently channel funds and which openly distributes these resources. Only those who seek favours will in the circumstances choose alternative and opaque avenues. Elections and democracy overall will not work unless there is a cultural shift so that dissent and opposition voices are not only tolerated but protected. In too many African countries there is, beyond a weak rhetorical commitment, no acceptance of the idea of the 'loyal opposition' as vital to democracy.

African leaders must accept that they will never garner the benefits of democracy unless the existence of a loyal opposition is accepted and welcome. This may be difficult although those in power should also recognise, explicitly, that they or their followers will one day be the opposition themselves. Tolerance of dissent and accommodation of the opposition – the notion of a loyal opposition – are vital for liberal democracy to thrive, as is the need for continued debate on policies and practices. Unfortunately, in too many African countries, opposition leaders are harassed and often jailed to prevent them from contesting political power and to intimidate others. The arrest by Ugandan officials of opposition figures such as 'Bobi Wine' (the pop star Robert Kyagulanyi Ssentamu) in Uganda, Biram Dah Abeid in Mauritania and Diane Rwigara in Rwanda is repeated often across the continent.[4]

Looking beyond elections, democracies foster development because they allow for greater scrutiny of government, promote good governance by encouraging leaders to run on performance legitimacy (a key lesson from both Singapore and Taiwan), and allow the electorate to choose between competing ideas.

Therefore, **fostering the rule of law is essential for development, while freedom of speech is an essential guarantor of rights and of success.** The South African case study demonstrates dramatically that institutions that can constrain leaders and a civil society free to voice opposition and organise can, in the end, bring down even a powerful leader.

We have repeatedly noted that democracies have the ability to self-correct when poor policies are adopted. However, such abilities do not occur automatically. Mali, Mozambique, Zambia and, to a lesser extent, Benin are examples of countries that had the form of electoral democracies but not the structure of institutions that would make them work. **States must be intentional in building the necessary institutions and practices – including courts that are respected and offices that are protected from political pressure such as ombudsmen and special prosecutors who can bring pressure against incumbents**. We have repeatedly seen in the case studies that countries that fail to develop institutions will not be able to build on their electoral successes and face the real risk of political stagnation or even decline. The Tanzanian case also demonstrates that a leader who says that he wants to move the country forward dramatically is, in the end, a threat to democracy if institutional development is ignored. The Ethiopians have finally realised that the cult of the leader is not enough. It is likely that the Rwandans will eventually draw the same conclusion.

Finally, in states with authoritarian politics, such as Burundi, Liberia, Nigeria and South Africa, **there will be a need for leaders to step forward and take risks, both personal and political, to move beyond the political stalemate that has caused political stagnation**. Our chapter on the 'not free' countries demonstrates, repeatedly, that there must be some kind of fundamental disruption of the political system in order for institutions to begin to develop and for greater freedom to be exercised. Democracy is fundamentally about elites being confident enough in political systems to risk losing power via elections. Someone must show the way. We were honoured to have Ellen Johnson Sirleaf provide the Foreword to this book precisely because, as we demonstrated in our Liberia case study in Chapter 7, she was one of those (rare) politicians who are willing to take risks in order to build a nascent democracy.

The challenge in the referee model is that the leader must give way to institutionalised politics or the pattern of failed authoritarianism will simply be repeated. This was the genius of Nelson Mandela, who recognised that refusing to run for a second term, which he could have won uncontested, would be a critical endorsement of the new South African order. Similarly, Johnson Sirleaf's decision not to challenge her term limits, and in the end not even to endorse the candidate of her own party, marked an obvious transition from the essential woman to a more normal politics.

The returns for changing political systems so that the playing field is level, building institutions and breaking stalemates are high. As we demonstrated in Chapter 4 on 'free states', once real institutions are established, democracy becomes 'sticky' and authoritarian reverses are less likely. The Seychelles, while small, is compelling because it shows how a country most notorious for seemingly being the plaything of mercenaries could become committed to at least the ideal of democracy, while transforming its economy for the benefit of its citizens. Similarly, the contrast between Mali – hailed as an international success while actually not building institutions and governance practices – and Somaliland – ignored by the international community while it has done the hard work of democratisation – is striking. It is also possible to show African citizens who want democracy that works that meaningful progress can be made quickly. Accordingly, a virtuous cycle can be created where success builds upon success.

Potemkin democracies, those with the form of democracy but without the substance, can only lead to failure and, eventually, disenchantment with democracy.

Actions for the opposition

Citizens, not external actors, have to win the vote between elections. Some of the challenges are modern, others are as old as elections themselves. Leaders of opposition parties and civil society movements thus need to develop a 'democracy playbook' for elections. While much advice is routinely given on how incumbents promote democracy, very little attention is devoted to what oppositions must do. Too often, the opposition is simply seen as a victim in the face of an authoritarian government. There is, of course, no ignoring the very real sacrifices made by democrats across Africa, including by two of the authors of this book. However, in too many cases, oppositions make tactical errors in the pursuit of power that prevent them from running credible races. Certainly oppositions in Kenya, Zimbabwe and Zambia made mistakes in their campaigns. Given the inherent advantages of incumbency, and the willingness of at least some in power to stretch or break the law, oppositions must be very good. As was demonstrated in the unprecedented win by Buhari in Nigeria, smart oppositions can win even in settings that are extremely difficult.

It will thus be necessary to **be technically prepared and not rely on the seeming justice of running against the government**. We have seen that social media provides real opportunities for the opposition, especially as it lowers the cost of campaigning. However, social media is no panacea for those out of power because government can also take advantage of Facebook and Twitter and, when so motivated, can 'turn off' the internet. Media should be seen as one arrow in the quiver of the opposition but not the only one.

Beyond running good campaigns, oppositions, if they are to effect more than 'civilian coups', must actually have a vision that differentiates them. Although, as we have argued consistently, demography is the overwhelming challenge facing most countries, there is usually little debate during African elections that centres around different economic visions. Therefore, a critical challenge is for oppositions to **build a credible, well-organised party with alternative ideas**. If elections are to be consequential, the opposition must provide citizens with a good reason to vote for them, a choice that may be costly given the tendency of incumbents to erect barriers to voting for those out of power. Zambia, among other countries, proves that unless the opposition clearly differentiates itself by policy, even turnover prompted by incumbents losing will not change the nature of politics in a dysfunctional country.

There is a need, too, for democrats – within and without government – to establish a narrative that transcends the boundaries of identity. Such a vision is especially important in an era where young people face challenges of global competition for resources and employment, where they have other (digital) windows on the world outside of politics, and where the tendency may well thus be to 'opt out'.

Finally, the opposition **must also demonstrate its own democratic credentials**. The innate advantages of democracy are negated when the opposition's ambition is to simply replace the incumbents and then continue the systems of corruption and patronage that they nominally ran against. Mali and Zambia were notable for having had consequential elections but not benefiting from a surfeit of democracy because each government acted much the same as the last.

Actions for outsiders

Outsiders have a role to play, though insiders must lead and own change. The institutions that donors crave are, however, as in their own countries, to be founded on values and shared interests, and are thus a product of domestic politics. Inasmuch as they can influence outcomes, outsiders have to take care not to allow short-term stability and narrow commercial interests to trump democratic principles, since neglecting the latter usually destroys the former.

Outsiders must, as we note in Chapter 8, **take great care in monitoring and opining about elections, because they can be easily exploited by authoritarians with a well-developed playbook**.

Election monitoring is particularly difficult because of what authoritarians have learnt. Precisely because of the presence of monitors on election day, Judge Johann Kriegler, former head of the South African Independent

Electoral Commission, has said that 'only an idiot would try to steal an election on election day. It would have to happen already long before that.' While commenting on the Zimbabwe election of 2018, he specified, 'It's how you've kept the voters' roll over the years. You have complete control over the media as the ruling party; you have complete control of newsworthiness, such as the opening of schools, bridges and roads, maintenance and support systems for the elderly and the needy.'[5]

Understanding that kind of influence over an electoral system requires a presence in a country for many months, perhaps years, and a willingness not to be distracted by the inevitable drama of people lining up to vote, especially when they have been long denied that freedom. Observers face significant time and financial barriers to developing such a comprehensive perspective on elections, and, of course, the incumbents will work against them at every step.

African observers have a particular set of responsibilities and opportunities, not least because they do not have the burden of a history as colonisers and are therefore often seen as more credible. African governments that seek to further democratisation in Africa should adhere to the fundamental documents developed by the African Union, working to maintain democratic standards in regional bodies, and supporting resolutions in the UN, which align with these issues. The defence of liberal democracy should, as Chapter 8 argued, become a pillar of the foreign policies of African and not just Western governments.

All election observers must be careful in how they weigh the trade-off between democracy and their own ideas of stability. While stability is important, observers are not present to make that political assessment; rather, they are in a country simply to observe the election. Those who pull their punches may instead end up causing considerable damage by reducing confidence and undermining participation in such processes, risking opposition groups taking events into their own hands. If monitors are unprepared or unwilling to call out fraud, it is probably better that they stay at home than be complicit in polls that make a mockery of democracy.[6]

As we note from analyses of Kenya, South Africa and Zimbabwe, **governments of national unity, a stratagem that occasionally seems almost a default for outsiders who cannot judge the actual quality of elections, is a highly problematic tactic.** It robs voters of their voice and often does little more than postpone political problems rather than offering a breathing space for compromise.

Beyond elections, **donors must have a clear-eyed view that elections are a necessary but not sufficient condition for democracy. They must base their long-term judgements regarding the democratic performance of individual countries on the actual workings of democratic structures.** The cases throughout this book show there is no substitute for strong institutions. The Congo is perhaps the definitive example demonstrating that simply devoting large amounts of money and manpower in the hope that authoritarians will behave is often a waste when the underlying institutions and necessary leadership are missing. Similarly, in Mali, donors fooled themselves that a democracy was present, with the consequent loss of enormous assistance and effort.

* * *

Africans want democracy – and democracy is possible in Africa. However, it is very difficult. Although the quarter-century since the Berlin Wall fell has seen much tumult across the continent, the situation today must be seen as disappointing compared to the heady days when authoritarian regimes fell one after another or even compared to the height of the Arab Spring when the mass action of people toppled governments. Democracy, as we have repeatedly noted, is difficult because holding free and fair elections is challenging, given that the incumbent is required to supervise a process that may lead to him or her losing power. It is also necessary to create a set of institutions that will serve as a bulwark against authoritarianism.

Finally, basic freedoms must be enshrined so that democratic discourse and debate occur continually.

Africa needs democracy because no other political system will equip the countries in the region with the ability to handle the coming wave of young people. We do not believe that countries should fear the coming demographic changes because being the youngest region of the world offers terrific opportunities. However, those possibilities will only be realised if economic systems are in place to generate the necessary jobs. Democracy offers the possibility of not only coping with the wave of young people arriving in Africa's cities particularly, but also of benefiting from it. No other system offers such possibilities.

Africans must rewire their political systems not only for the benefit of the current populations, but also to triumph in the future.

Notes

All the website references in the notes below were working links when accessed during the researching and writing of this book.

Introduction

1 We include all countries in Africa in this work that are members of the United Nations, which numbers 54. This eschews the usual analytical and statistical convention to separate the countries of North and sub-Saharan Africa. While there are some systematic differences between North and sub-Saharan Africa, the quest for democracy in, especially, Egypt, Tunisia and Morocco has influenced African debates and, in turn, been affected by developments in other countries across the continent. Indeed, how the 'Arab Spring' is interpreted in the rest of the continent is a central question for us.

2 Steven Levitsky and Daniel Ziblatt, *How Democracies Die*. New York: Crown, 2018; Yascha Mounk, *The People vs. Democracy: Why Our Freedom is in Danger and How to Save It*. Harvard: Harvard University Press, 2018; David Runciman, *How Democracy Ends*. London: Profile Books, 2018; Robert Kuttner, *Can Democracy Survive Global Capitalism?* New York: W.W. Norton & Company, 2018; Timothy Snyder, *The Road to Unfreedom: Russia, Europe, America*. Toronto: Tim Duggan Books, 2018; Madeleine Albright, *Fascism: A Warning*. New York: HarperCollins Publishers, 2018; Ian Bremmer, *Us vs. Them: The Failure of Globalism*. New York: Penguin Random House, 2018; Dambisa Moyo, *Edge of Chaos: Why Democracy is Failing to Deliver Economic Growth and How to Fix It*. New York: Hachette Book Group, 2018; William A. Galston, *Anti-Pluralism: The Populist Threat to Liberal Democracy*. Yale: Yale University Press, 2018; David Cay Johnston, *It's Even Worse than You Think: What the Trump Administration is Doing to America*. New York: Simon & Schuster, 2018; Nic Cheeseman and Brian Klaas, *How to Rig an Election*. Yale: Yale University Press, 2018.

3 See https://freedomhouse.org/sites/default/files/Electoral%20Democracy%20Numbers%2C%20 FIW%201989-2013_0.pdf.

4 These unfortunates included the 60 million Chinese who were killed by Mao Zedong, the 'Great Helmsman', among these the many starved in his misnamed 'Great Leap Forward' of 1958–61, or tortured and killed in labour camps in the 1960s' Cultural Revolution. To this must be added the 40 million starved and murdered by Joseph Stalin's Soviet regime between 1929–53. Pol Pot's Khmer Rouge 'eliminated' around two million in Cambodia, while as many as 3.6 million are calculated to have died in the wars in Vietnam between 1954 and the fall of the South in 1975. Closer to home, Idi Amin's barbaric regime in Uganda cost as many as 500 000 lives before he was booted out in 1979 and Mobutu Sese Seko around 230 000 political opponents in Zaire, which had earlier seen eight million enslaved under King Leopold's colonial reign, outrageous even by the standards of the time. Mengistu Haile Mariam's Derg military dictatorship in Ethiopia resulted in

as many as 1.5 million deaths from conflict and related famine before he fled to Zimbabwe in 1991, where some 30 000 were killed by Robert Mugabe's Fifth Brigade in suppressing tribal dissent in Matabeleland in the *Gukurahundi* offensive between 1983–7. For a summary of these figures, see, for example, http://www.dailymail.co.uk/home/moslive/article-2091670/Hitler-Stalin-The-murderous-regimes-world.html.

5 Mounk, *The People vs. Democracy*, pp. 1–2.
6 See Anthony Butler at https://www.businesslive.co.za/bd/opinion/columnists/2017-03-10-anthony-butler-despite-the-hostility-jz-has-not-posed-a-threat-to-democracy/.
7 See, for example, https://www.washingtonpost.com/news/theworldpost/wp/2018/03/20/duterte/?noredirect=on&utm_term=.36c51dc0a782.
8 See https://freedomhouse.org/article/democracy-crisis-freedom-house-releases-freedom-world-2018.
9 See http://afrobarometer.org/sites/default/files/publications/Policy%20papers/ab_r6_policypaper036_do_africans_want_democracy.pdf.
10 Robert Mattes and Michael Bratton, 'Do Africans Still Want Democracy? This New Report Gives a Qualified Yes', 25 November 2016, http://afrobarometer.org/blogs/do-africans-still-want-democracy-new-report-gives-qualified-yes.
11 National Intelligence Council, 'Sub-Saharan Africa: Pitched Contests for Democratization through 2022', February 2018, p. 1, https://www.dni.gov/files/images/globalTrends/documents/GT-Africa_Democratization_ForPublishing-WithCovers.pdf.
12 Ibid, p. 247.
13 Fund for Peace, http://fundforpeace.org/fsi/data.
14 See Francis Fukuyama, *Political Order and Political Decay: From the Industrial Revolution to the Globalisation of Democracy*. London: Profile Books, 2014. See its review, too, at https://www.ft.com/content/67b8f490-4269-11e4-9818-00144feabdc0.
15 See http://www.mahathir.com/malaysia/speeches/1992/1992-10-14.php.
16 Making him the oldest currently serving state leader by age.
17 'Preventing Conflict in the Next Century', *The World in 2000*. London: Economist Publications, 1999, p. 91.
18 Greg Mills and Jeffrey Herbst, *Africa's Third Liberation: The New Search for Prosperity and Jobs*. Johannesburg: Penguin, 2012.
19 We have taken note of the extensive literature on the topic, including most recently Isobel Coleman and Terra Lawson-Remer, 'A User's Guide to Democratic Transitions', *Foreign Policy*, https://foreignpolicy.com/2013/06/18/a-users-guide-to-democratic-transitions/; Dambisa Moyo, http://foreignpolicy.com/2018/04/26/why-democracy-doesnt-deliver/; and Cheeseman and Klaas, *How to Rig an Election*. Also, for a captivating account of the contemporary democratic and other challenges faced by the West, see Bill Emmott, *The Fate of the West*. London: Economist Books, 2018.
20 The average of a country's or territory's political rights and civil liberties ratings is called the Freedom Rating, and it is this figure that determines the status of 'free' (1.0 to 2.5), 'partly free' (3.0 to 5.0) or 'not free' (5.5 to 7.0). See https://freedomhouse.org/report/methodology-freedom-world-2017.
21 Disclosure: Jeffrey Herbst is on the Freedom House Board of Trustees.

Chapter 1 Why Democracy Works

1 See http://www.withmaliceandforethought.com/pdf/seychelles.pdf.

2 Correspondence, 31 May 2018.

3 The following have had sanctions imposed on them as a result: Central African Republic and Guinea-Bissau (2003); Mauritania and Togo (2005); Mauritania, Madagascar and Guinea (2008); Côte d'Ivoire (2010); Mali and Guinea-Bissau (2012); Central African Republic, Egypt and Guinea-Bissau (2013); Burkina Faso (2015); and the Gambia (2016).

4 This is based on a research trip by Greg Mills to the Seychelles in May–June 2018. President Faure was interviewed on 1 June 2018.

5 See https://freedomhouse.org/report/freedom-world/2018/seychelles.

6 The only African country that does not hold elections at all is Eritrea. 'African Democracy: A Glass Half-Full', *The Economist*, 31 March 2012, https://www.economist.com/node/21551494.

7 Population Reference Bureau, '2017 World Population Data Sheet', http://www.prb.org/Publications/Datasheets/2017/2017-world-population-data-sheet.aspx.

8 This section is based on Greg Mills, Olusegun Obasanjo, Jeffrey Herbst and Dickie Davis, *Making Africa Work: A Handbook for Economic Success*. Johannesburg: Tafelberg, 2017, pp. 6–11. See also 'The Young Continent', *The Economist*, 12 December 2015, http://www.economist.com/news/briefing/21679781-fertilit y-rates-falling-more-slowly-anywhere-else-africa-faces-population.

9 'The World's 10 Youngest Populations are All in Africa', *World Economic Forum*, https://www.weforum.org/agenda/2016/05/the-world-s-10-youngest-countriesare-all-in-africa/.

10 IMF Regional Economic Outlook, 'Sub-Saharan Africa: Navigating Headwinds', https://www.imf.org/external/pubs/ft/reo/2015/afr/eng/pdf/sreo0415.pdf.

11 African Development Bank, OECD and UN Development Programme, *African Economic Outlook 2015*. Paris: OECD Publishing, 2015, p. xiii.

12 See the World Investment Report, http://unctad.org/en/PublicationsLibrary/wir2017_en.pdf.

13 This is defined as commodity exports constituting more than a 40% share of GDP.

14 Timothy Besley and Torsten Persson, 'Causes and Consequences of Development Clusters', *Annual Review of Economics* 6, 2014.

15 See https://freedomhouse.org/report-types/freedom-world.

16 See 'About the Index', http://www.heritage.org/index/about.

17 Heritage Foundation, '2018 Index of Economic Freedom', Chapter Two, https://www.heritage.org/index/book/chapter-2.

18 Index of Economic Freedom scores from https://www.heritage.org/index/ranking. All three of the missing countries (Libya, Somalia, South Sudan) are coded as 'not free' by Freedom House.

19 Transparency International, 'Corruption Perceptions Index 2017', https://www.transparency.org/news/feature/corruption_perceptions_index_2017.

20 See https://freedomhouse.org/blog/most-dangerous-children-and-human-rights.

21 Takaaki Masaki and Nicolas van de Walle, 'The Impact of Democracy on Economic Growth in sub-Saharan Africa, 1982–2012', WIDER Working Paper 2014/057, March 2014.

22 Joseph Siegle, Michael Weinstein and Morton Halperin, 'Why Democracies Excel', *Foreign Affairs* 83 (5), 2005, pp. 57–71. See also Morton Halperin, Joseph Siegle and Michael Weinstein, *The Democracy Advantage: How Democracies Promote Prosperity and Peace*. London: Routledge, 2010.

23 UNDP, 'Human Development Index, 2015', http://hdr.undp.org/en/composite/HDI.

24 Deemed as part of China for this purpose.

25 Jason Seawright, 'Regression-based Inference: A Case Study in Failed Causal Assessment', in Henry Brady and David Collier (eds), *Rethinking Social Inquiry: Diverse Tools, Shared Standards*. Lanham, MD: Rowman & Littlefield, 2010.

26 Interview by Greg Mills, Port Louis, 22 January 2018.

27 Disclosure: Greg Mills works for E. Oppenheimer & Son, among those characterised as 'White Monopoly Capitalists'.

28 See https://www.fin24.com/Economy/
sa-may-have-lost-r100bn-or-more-to-state-capture-gordhan-20180515.

29 See http://www.publicprotector.org/library/investigation_report/2013-14/Final%20Report%20
19%20March%202014%20.pdf.

30 See https://www.fin24.com/Economy/
van-rooyen-was-very-qualified-for-finance-job-zuma-20160222.

31 McKinsey, the global consulting firm, became both a casualty and part of the problem in the 'state capture' scandal characterising the presidency of Jacob Zuma in South Africa. In 2015, the firm signed a deal with Eskom, the state power utility, potentially worth $700 million, around 40% of which would go to a minority partner, Trillian Management Consulting, its largest ever deal in Africa. Trillian was connected to the Gupta family through an associate with whom McKinsey had earlier dealings in the South African government's $4.3 billion 2014 purchase of 1 064 locomotives, the largest South African government procurement in history. An amount of $200 million was to be paid by Chinese contractors as commission to companies linked to Salim Essa, a Gupta associate. Although McKinsey eventually pulled out of the deal with Eskom after eight months of work, even so its tab was nearly $100 million. McKinsey's appetite for such transactions appears to be related to a corporate culture that encouraged an 'aggressive push' into government consulting, along with methods of compensation that allowed 'at risk' contracts rather than a more traditional fee for service structure. See https://www.nytimes.com/2018/06/26/world/africa/
mckinsey-south-africa-eskom.html; and https://www.news24.com/SouthAfrica/News/exclusive-
transnets-new-chinese-locomotives-fail-first-test-20170123. See https://www.news24.com/
SouthAfrica/News/gupta-link-in-r647m-train-deal-20180520-2.

32 See, for example, the series of articles by 'Lily Gosam' at https://www.businesslive.co.za/rdm/
politics/2017-01-18-zuma-the-guptas-and-the-russians--the-inside-story/.

33 Private discussion, 2017.

34 See https://www.news24.com/SouthAfrica/News/full-text-mcebisi-jonas-statement-20160316.

35 See https://www.reuters.com/article/us-safrica-zuma-gordhan/south-african-ministers-affidavit-
details-490-million-in-gupta-transactions-reported-as-suspicious-idUSKBN12G0YQ.

36 See https://mg.co.za/article/2016-11-02-breaking-read-the-full-state-capture-report.

37 See https://www.news24.com/SouthAfrica/News/
save-sa-from-champion-of-corruption-zuma-pityana-20161123.

38 See https://www.news24.com/SouthAfrica/News/
some-ngos-are-security-agents-of-foreign-forces-mahlobo-20160426.

39 See https://www.reuters.com/article/us-safrica-politics-idUSKBN13N0D9.

40 For instance, see the Public Protector's 'Secure in Comfort' report about Nkandla or 'Derailed' (about Prasa – the Passenger Rail Agency of South Africa), or the revelations contained in the following: Crispian Olver, *How to Steal a City: The Battle for Nelson Mandela Bay: An Inside Account*. Johannesburg: Jonathan Ball Publishers, 2017; Pieter-Louis Myburg, *The Republic of Gupta: A Story of State Capture*. Johannesburg: Penguin Random House, 2017; Jacques Pauw, *The President's Keepers: Those Keeping Zuma in Power and Out of Prison*. Cape Town: Tafelberg, 2017; Adriaan Basson and Pieter du Toit, *Enemy of the People: How Jacob Zuma Stole South Africa and How the People Fought Back*. Johannesburg: Jonathan Ball Publishers, 2017; Ralph Mathekga, *When Zuma Goes*. Cape Town: Tafelberg, 2016; Richard Calland, *The Zuma Years: South Africa's Changing Face of Power*. Cape Town: Zebra Press, 2013; Adriaan Basson, *Zuma Exposed*. Johannesburg: Jonathan Ball Publishers, 2012; Johann van Loggerenberg and Adrian Lackay, *Rogue: The Inside Story of SARS's Elite Crime-busting Unit*. Johannesburg: Jonathan Ball Publishers, 2016.

41 See President Ramaphosa's February 2018 State of the Nation Address, for example, at https://www.dailymaverick.co.za/article/2018-02-16-sona-2018-cyril-ramaphosa-our-task-as-south-africans-is-to-seize-this-moment-of-hope-and-renewal/#.Wv5LxE0UmM8.

42 Discussion, Leeuwenhof, Cape Town, April 2018.

43 See https://www.businesslive.co.za/bd/opinion/columnists/2017-03-10-anthony-butler-despite-the-hostility-jz-has-not-posed-a-threat-to-democracy/.

44 See https://www.transparency.org/country/CHL.

45 See https://freedomhouse.org/report/freedom-world/2018/chile.

46 Ricardo Ffrench-Davis, *Reforming the Reforms in Latin America*. London: Macmillan, 2000.

47 For a detailed discussion, see Ricardo Ffrench-Davis, *Economic Reforms in Chile: From Dictatorship to Democracy*. London: Palgrave Macmillan, 2010.

48 See http://www.foreigninvestment.cl/index.php?option=com_content&view=article&id=123.

49 Ffrench-Davis and Presidents Frei and Lagos were interviewed by Greg Mills in Santiago in March 2018,

Chapter 2 The Authoritarian Myth

1 See https://www.bbc.com/news/uk-politics-45325701.

2 See https://www.bbc.com/news/world-africa-45368092.

3 See, for example, https://www.mckinsey.com/featured-insights/middle-east-and-africa/the-closest-look-yet-at-chinese-economic-engagement-in-africa.

4 See https://www.nytimes.com/2008/01/15/business/worldbusiness/15commodities.html.

5 'The World's Most Powerful Man', *The Economist*, 14 October 2017, https://www.economist.com/leaders/2017/10/14/xi-jinping-has-more-clout-than-donald-trump.-the-world-should-be-wary.

6 See http://www.bbc.com/news/world-asia-china-43453769.

7 Yuen Yuen Ang, 'Autocracy with Chinese Characteristics', *Foreign Affairs*, May/June 2018, p. 46.

8 Quoted in 'How to Save Tanzania', *The Economist*, 17 March 2018, https://www.economist.com/news/leaders/21738885-start-containing-president-john-magufuli-how-save-tanzania.

9 Kenneth D. Kaunda, *Humanism in Zambia and a Guide to its Implementation (Part II)*. Lusaka: Division of National Guidance, Government of the Republic of Zambia, 1974, pp. 9–11, http://exploringafrica.matrix.msu.edu/president-kaunda-statement/.

10 'Burundi: Ruling Party Gives President New Title of "Supreme Eternal Ruler"', *AllAfrica.com*, 12 March 2018, https://allafrica.com/stories/201803120768.html.

11 See http://www.bbc.co.uk/news/world-africa-24228425.

12 This section is based on a stint living and working in Rwanda in 2007/8, along with several subsequent research trips, the most recent being in October 2013; and four research trips to Burundi, including most recently in 2011 and 2013.

13 Pasteur Bizimungu, a Hutu who had been a civil servant under the government of Habyarimana before fleeing to join the Rwandan Patriotic Front, was appointed president. Kagame remained commander-in-chief of the army and *de facto* ruler of Rwanda. After Kagame accused Bizimungu of corruption and poor management, the president resigned in March 2000. A number of Hutu politicians, including Prime Minister Pierre-Célestin Rwigema, left the government at around the same time as Bizimungu. The latter started his own party following his resignation, but this was quickly banned for 'destabilising the country'. He was subsequently arrested, convicted of corruption and inciting ethnic violence, and imprisoned until 2007, when he was pardoned by Kagame.

14 Email exchange, Rwandan High Commissioner to South Africa, 7 May 2018.

15 Interview, Johannesburg, 5 May 2018.
16 See https://data.worldbank.org/indicator/NY.GDP.PCAP.CD?locations=ET-ZG-RW.
17 See http://www.worldbank.org/en/results/2016/07/12/
    rwanda-achieving-food-security-reducing-poverty-moving-up-the-value-chain.
18 See http://www.newtimes.co.rw/section/read/223763.
19 See https://www.telegraph.co.uk/travel/maps-and-graphics/safest-countries-in-the-world/.
20 See https://www.weforum.org/agenda/2017/05/
    how-rwanda-beats-almost-every-other-country-in-gender-equality/.
21 See http://ktpress.rw/2018/02/kagame-tasks-senior-govt-officials-on-division-as-retreat-kicks-off/.
22 Disclosure: Greg Mills was responsible for the structuring of the Rwanda Development Board in
    2007/8.
23 See http://www.doingbusiness.org/rankings.
24 See https://www.economist.com/briefing/2017/07/15/paul-kagame-feted-and-feared.
25 Paul Kagame, 'Rwanda and the New Lions of Africa', *Wall Street Journal*, 19 May 2013, http://
    online.wsj.com/news/articles/SB10001424127887324767004578485234078541160.
26 See https://www.theguardian.com/global-development/2018/jan/02/
    rwanda-scheme-saving-blood-drone.
27 See https://allafrica.com/stories/201411120139.html.
28 See https://pctechmag.com/2017/03/
    rwanda-tech-accelerator-inkomoko-bank-of-kigali-to-offer-interest-free-loans-to-startups/.
29 Cited in Laurence Binet, 'The Hunting and Killing of Rwandan Refugees in Zaire-Congo:
    1996–1997', https://www.msf-crash.org/en/publications/war-and-humanitarianism/
    hunting-and-killing-rwandan-refugees-zaire-congo-1996-1997.
30 See https://www.independent.co.uk/news/uk/politics/memos-reveal-how-andrew-mitchell-
    ignored-advice-on-rwandan-aid-8200019.html.
31 See https://www.theguardian.com/world/2012/oct/10/paul-kagame-rwanda-success-authoritarian.
32 See https://moguldom.com/125519/
    buffett-blair-back-kagame-for-third-presidential-term-in-rwanda/.
33 See https://foreignpolicy.com/2013/02/21/stand-with-rwanda/.
34 Ibid.
35 See https://www.economist.com/news/leaders/21725000-its-recovery-after-genocide-has-been-
    impressive-land-ruled-fear-can-never-be-happy.
36 Ibid.
37 See http://glpost.com/president-kagame-says-rwandan-dissidents-will-pay-price/; and https://
    mg.co.za/article/2014-01-12-sa-wont-respond-to-rwandas-comments-on-former-spy-chief.
38 See https://www.theglobeandmail.com/news/world/ruling-by-south-
    african-court-exposes-details-of-latest-rwandan-assassinationplot/
    article37417017/.
39 See http://africanarguments.org/2018/03/13/i-will-also-fight-with-you-president-kagame-rwanda-
    berater-in-chief/.
40 See https://www.express.co.uk/news/uk/966368/
    Rwanda-news-BBC-Arsenal-sponsorship-deal-Foreign-aid-row.
41 Cited at the World Economic Forum, Kigali, March 2016.
42 Interview, Addis Ababa, 9 October 2018.
43 Disclosure: Former Prime Minister Hailemariam is a member of The Brenthurst Foundation's
    Advisory Board.
44 Interview Rainbow Towers, Harare, 30 July 2018.
45 Discussion, Paris, September 2018.
46 See http://databank.worldbank.org/data/reports.aspx?source=world-development-indicators.

47 See https://www.export.gov/apex/article2?id=Ethiopia-Market-Overview; and https://agoa.info/news/article/6037-agoa-us-investments-in-ethiopia-climb-to-4-billion-in-2015.html.

48 See https://www.theguardian.com/us-news/2015/jul/27/obama-urges-ethiopia-end-crackdown-political-press-freedom.

49 See https://www.forbes.com/sites/thorhalvorssen/2012/08/22/requiem-for-a-reprobate-ethiopian-tyrant-should-not-be-lionized/#723d571c231f.

50 See https://www.aljazeera.com/news/2018/02/ethiopia-mass-protests-rooted-country-history-180219130441837.html.

51 Interview, Minister, Addis Ababa, July 2018.

52 Prime Minister Hailemariam Desalegn was interviewed in Addis Ababa twice by Greg Mills (in May 2016 and January 2018) and again in Harare in July 2018.

53 See https://www.bbc.co.uk/news/topics/cwlw3xz047jt/ethiopia.

54 The former president was interviewed by Greg Mills in Singapore in December 2013.

55 Discussion, Nairobi, 2016.

56 This section is based on a series of interviews in Singapore during 2013, 2015 and twice in 2018. See also Lee Kuan Yew, *From Third World to First: The Singapore Story: 1965–2000*. Singapore: Marshall Cavendish, 2000.

57 Interview, Singapore, 23 May 2018.

58 For a discussion of these processes, see Greg Mills, 'Lucky Goldstar and the Rockets', Brenthurst Discussion Paper 10/2018, https://www.thebrenthurstfoundation.org/article/lucky-goldstar-and-the-rockets-what-worked-in-south-korea/; and reproduced at https://www.dailymaverick.co.za/article/2018-10-12-lucky-goldstar-and-the-rockets-one-countrys-journey-from-poverty-to-prosperity/.

59 By President Duterte's own admission. See https://www.nytimes.com/2018/09/27/world/asia/rodrigo-duterte-philippines-drug-war.html. See also Greg Mills, 'Beware Big Men (or Women): The Lesson of the Philippines', Brenthurst Discussion Paper 11/2018, www.thebrenthurstfoundation.org.

Chapter 3 The State of Democracy in Africa

1 Self-immolation is not a new form of protest to Tunisia. After two brutal wars with rival Rome, the second of which famously featured Hannibal's march over the Alps with his elephants, 600 years of Carthaginian rule were ended in the third Punic War around 149 BC. Some 50 000 citizens of Carthage were taken prisoner, their buildings levelled and lands sown symbolically with salt. While he surrendered, the wife and children of the commander, Hasdrubal, committed suicide by self-immolation. Another 300 years lapsed before Carthage rose again to become the third-largest imperial city behind Rome and Alexandria.

2 Sidi Bouzid is the site of a battle between US forces and German Panzer divisions in February 1943, the start of what became known as the Battle of the Kasserine Pass.

3 This section is based on research trips to Tunisia in March and September 2013, March 2014, September 2017 and June 2018. The interviews with the minister of education and president were conducted in Tunis in September 2017. A series of round-table events involving the media, civil society, political parties, international actors, and think tanks were held in Tunis with the support of the Konrad-Adenauer-Stiftung in June 2018.

4 See http://www.reuters.com/article/us-mideast-crisis-syria-casualties/syrian-war-monitor-says-465000-killed-in-six-years-of-fighting-idUSKBN16K1Q1.

5 See https://www1.oecd.org/mena/49036903.pdf.

6 See http://www.europarl.europa.eu/RegData/etudes/ATAG/2017/608822/
   EPRS_ATA(2017)608822_EN.pdf.
7 See https://www.theatlantic.com/international/archive/2012/04/why-are-there-
   so-many-coups-west-africa/329209/; and https://www.news24.com/MyNews24/
   the-culture-of-coups-in-africa-20180409.
8 We believe that the organisation did make a mistake in briefly providing two scores for South
   Africa, one for the white population who had the benefit of the franchise during apartheid
   and another for oppressed blacks. In our analysis, we have used only the scores for the black
   population as a country cannot be judged on how it treats the most privileged. Data downloaded
   from Freedom House, 'About Freedom in the World', https://freedomhouse.org/report-types/
   freedom-world.
9 Interview, Nairobi, January 2018.
10 This argument was framed around a narrow interpretation of the Namibian constitution, on the
   grounds that since the president had first been elected by a Constituent Assembly, his first term
   did not count towards the limit.
11 Joseph Siegle, 'Why Term Limits Matter for Africa', Center for Security Studies blog, 3 July 2015.
12 'Kagame Says He is Seeking a Third Term for the Sake of Democracy', Quartz Africa,
   http://qz.com/682038/kagame-pushes-back-at-third-term-critics-but-for-the-west-its-not-just-
   about-rwanda/.
13 See https://foreignpolicy.com/2018/01/05/africas-generational-war-democracy-kenya-zimbabwe/.
14 Information in Figure 3.3 is taken from World Bank, World Development Indicators, http://
   databank.worldbank.org/data/reports.aspx?source=world-development-indicators.
15 See, for example, the comment of the Ibrahim Index of African Governance for 2017 that 'over
   the last decade (2007–2016) the African average score has improved by +1.4 score points from
   49.4 (out of 100) to 50.8, reaching in 2016 its highest score since the Ibrahim Index of African
   Governance's first data year (2000)'. See http://s.mo.ibrahim.foundation/u/2017/11/21165610/2017-
   IIAG-Report.pdf?_ga=2.94864156.1244028254.1527771767-1678098777.1527771767.
16 World Economic Forum, 'Global Competitiveness Index, 2017–18', http://reports.weforum.org/
   global-competitiveness-index-2017-2018/sub-saharan-africa. The quote only refers to countries
   in sub-Saharan Africa. Freedom House, 'Freedom in the World 2018', https://freedomhouse.org/
   report/freedom-world/freedom-world-2018.
17 Ibid.
18 There were 51 independent countries in Africa in 1988. By 1993, Eritrea and Namibia had gained
   their independence, raising the total to 53. South Sudan gained independence in 2011, bringing the
   continental total to 54.
19 Report and data found at https://freedomhouse.org/report/freedom-press/freedom-press-2017.
20 Robert I. Rotberg and Jennifer Erin Salahub, 'African Legislative Effectiveness', North-South
   Institute, October 2013, http://www.nsi-ins.ca/wp-content/uploads/2013/10/2013-African-
   Legislative-Effectiveness1.pdf.
21 See 'Methodology' for 2017 'Index of Economic Freedom', http://www.heritage.org/index/book/
   methodology.
22 Data downloaded from Heritage Foundation, 'Index of Economic Freedom, 2018', https://www.
   heritage.org/index/download.
23 Arendt Lijphart, Patterns of Democracy: Government Forms and Performance in Thirty-Six
   Countries. New Haven: Yale University Press, 2012, p. 3.
24 See https://en.wikipedia.org/wiki/House_of_Chiefs.

Chapter 4 The Challenges of Sustaining Democracy

1 For details on this history, see John Adedeji, 'The Legacy of JJ Rawlings in Ghanaian Politics, 1979–2000', *African Studies Quarterly* 5 (2), Summer 2001.

2 See Samuel P. Huntington, *The Third Wave*. Norman: University of Oklahoma Press, 1991.

3 Telephonic interview with Greg Mills, 9 September 2018.

4 Written response to questions, 27 March 2018.

5 National Intelligence Council, 'Sub-Saharan Africa: Pitched Contests for Democratization through 2022', February 2018, p. 1, https://www.dni.gov/files/images/globalTrends/documents/GT-Africa_Democratization_ForPublishing-WithCovers.pdf.

6 Douglass North, John Joseph Wallis and Barry Weingast, *Violence and Social Orders: A Conceptual Framework for Interpreting Recorded Human History*. Cambridge: Cambridge University Press, 2009.

7 See the argument made in Daron Acemoglu and James A. Robinson, *Economic Origins of Dictatorship and Democracy*, Cambridge: Cambridge University Press, 2005. See also https://scholar.harvard.edu/jrobinson/publications/economic-origins-dictatorship-and-democracy.

8 See also Douglass C. North, John Joseph Wallis, Steven B. Webb and Barry R. Weingast, 'Limited Access Orders in the Developing World: A New Approach to the Problems of Development', The World Bank Independent Evaluation Group Country Relations Division, September 2007, http://econweb.umd.edu/~wallis/MyPapers/Limted_Access_Orders_in_the_Developing_WorldWPS4359.pdf.

9 See https://www.afdb.org/fileadmin/uploads/afdb/Documents/Publications/The%20Middle%20of%20the%20Pyramid_The%20Middle%20of%20the%20Pyramid.pdf.

10 The World Bank defines low-income economies as those with a gross national income per capita of $1 005 or less in 2016; lower middle-income economies are those between $1 006 and $3 955; upper middle-income economies are those between $3 956 and $12 235; high-income economies are those with $12 236 or more. See https://datahelpdesk.worldbank.org/knowledgebase/articles/906519-world-bank-country-and-lending-groups.

11 National Intelligence Council, 'Sub-Saharan Africa: Pitched Contests for Democratization through 2022', February 2018, p. 2, https://www.dni.gov/files/images/globalTrends/documents/GT-Africa_Democratization_ForPublishing-WithCovers.pdf.

12 See https://www.theguardian.com/world/2018/sep/21/young-africa-new-wave-of-politicians-challenges-old-guard.

13 National Intelligence Council, 'Sub-Saharan Africa: Pitched Contests for Democratization through 2022', February 2018, p. 2, https://www.dni.gov/files/images/globalTrends/documents/GT-Africa_Democratization_ForPublishing-WithCovers.pdf.

14 Interview conducted by Greg Mills, Cotonou, July 2017.

15 Interview conducted by Greg Mills, Dubai, November 2017.

16 See https://en.wikipedia.org/wiki/Zambia.

17 Huntington, *The Third Wave*, p. 267.

18 This is based on an email exchange with V.J. Mwanga, 29 August 2017.

19 See https://diggers.news/local/2018/06/25/75-of-zambias-cabinet-decisions-are-never-implemented-world-bank/.

20 See https://www.ft.com/content/cc685352-5f3a-11e4-986c-00144feabdc0.

21 See, for example, Nic Cheeseman and Miles Larmer, 'Ethnopopulism in Africa: Opposition Mobilization in Diverse and Unequal Societies', *Democratization* 22 (1), 2015; and Brian Levy, *Working with the Grain: Integrating Governance and Growth in Development Strategies*. New York: Oxford University Press, 2014. This section draws on the World Bank diagnostic at http://documents.worldbank.org/curated/en/290011522954283481/pdf/Zambia-SCD-March-29-Final-04022018.pdf.

22 See, for example, 'Zambia: Round Six Data', http://www.afrobarometer.org/data/
zambiaround-6-data-2015.

23 See https://freedomhouse.org/report/freedom-world/2017/zambia.

24 See http://afrobarometer.org/publications/
ad213-zambians-see-corruption-rising-government-failing-anti-graft-fight.

25 Disclosure: Olusegun Obasanjo and Greg Mills have served as (unpaid) advisers to the
government of Nana Akufo-Addo.

Chapter 5 The Countries in the Middle

1 This is based on several visits to Malawi, including in March 2014, March 2016 and July 2017. The
interviews cited here were conducted during this time by Greg Mills and, in July 2017, by Greg
Mills and Olusegun Obasanjo.

2 Disclosure: Olusegun Obasanjo, Greg Mills and Jeffrey Herbst all acted as (unpaid) advisers to
President Joyce Banda during her term of office.

3 See https://freedomhouse.org/report/freedom-world/2017/malawi.

4 WhatsApp exchange, 6 September 2018.

5 National Intelligence Council, 'Sub-Saharan Africa: Pitched Contests for Democratization
through 2022', February 2018, p. 1, https://www.dni.gov/files/images/globalTrends/documents/
GT-Africa_Democratization_ForPublishing-WithCovers.pdf.

6 Nic Cheeseman and Brian Klaas, 'How Autocrats Rig Elections to Stay in Power –
and Get Away with It', The Conversation, 23 April 2018, https://theconversation.com/
how-autocrats-rig-elections-to-stay-in-power-and-get-away-with-it-95337.

7 National Intelligence Council, 'Sub-Saharan Africa: Pitched Contests for Democratization
through 2022', February 2018, p. 1, https://www.dni.gov/files/images/globalTrends/documents/
GT-Africa_Democratization_ForPublishing-WithCovers.pdf.

8 Mwesiga Baregu, 'State of Political Parties in Tanzania, 1999', International IDEA Conference,
'Towards Sustainable Democratic Institutions in Southern Africa', p. 62, http://archive.idea.int/
ideas_work/22_s_africa/parties/3_baregu.pdf.

9 Ibid.

10 Ibid., p. 63.

11 Interview, March 2018. We have not identified any of the people we spoke to in Tanzania because
of their fears about the political climate. In fact, one opposition party member who met with us
was arrested that evening, probably because of his political activities.

12 See https://www.transparency.org/country/TZA.

13 Millennium Challenge Corporation, 'MCC Statement on Decision of Board of Directors to
Suspend Partnership with Tanzania', 28 March 2016, https://www.mcc.gov/news-and-events/
release/stmt-032816-tanzania-partnership-suspended.

14 'Democracy under Assault: Tanzania's Rogue President', The Economist, 15 March 2018,
https://www.economist.com/news/middle-east-and-africa/21738919-strong-constitutions-
matter-tanzanias-rogue-president.

15 Abdi Latif Dahir, 'You Now Have to Pay the Government over $900 a Year to be a Blogger in
Tanzania', Quartz Africa, 10 April 2018, https://qz.com/1248762/tanzania-social-media-and-
blogging-regulations-charge-to-operate-online/?utm_source=Media+Review+for+April+11%2C+
2018&utm_campaign=Media+Review+for+April+11%2C+2018&utm_medium=email.

16 'Tanzanian Anti-Government Protests Flop as Magufuli Calls for Peace', Polity, 26 April 2018,
http://m.polity.org.za/article/tanzanian-anti-government-protests-flop-as-magufuli-calls-for-

peace-2018-04-26.

17 'Magufuli warns Tanzanians: "... demonstrate and see who I am"', *AfricaNews.com*, 10 March 2018, http://www.AfricaNews.com/2018/03/10/magufuli-warns-tanzanians-demonstrate-and-see-who-i-am.

18 Tanzania ranks the number one aid partner for Denmark and Sweden, second for Finland, and fourth for the US. See https://www.loc.gov/law/help/foreign-aid/sweden.php; 'Denmark Development Assistance Committee (DAC) Peer Review 2011', https://www.oecd.org/dac/peer-reviews/47866608.pdf; http://www.oecd.org/newsroom/finland-needs-a-plan-to-restore-flagging-development-aid.htm; and http://www.abc.net.au/news/2017-12-21/here-are-the-countries-that-get-the-most-foreign-aid-from-the-us/9278164.

19 See https://www.theguardian.com/global-development/2014/oct/13/uk-and-international-donors-suspend-tanzania-aid-after-corruption-claims.

20 Luísa Diogo was interviewed by Greg Mills in Mozambique in September 2017.

21 David Smith, 'Boom Time for Mozambique, Once the Basket Case of Africa', *The Guardian*, 27 March 2012, https://www.theguardian.com/world/2012/mar/27/mozambique-africa-energy-resources-bonanza.

22 'Mozambique is Floundering amid Corruption and Conflict', *The Economist*, 18 March 2016, http://www.economist.com/news/middle-east-and-africa/21695203-scandals-and-setbacks-gas-and-fishing-industries-darken-mood-mozambique.

23 See 'Corruption Perceptions Index 2016', *Transparency International*, https://www.transparency.org/news/feature/corruption_perceptions_index_2016; and https://www.transparency.org/news/feature/corruption_perceptions_index_2017#table.

24 'Overview of Corruption and Anti-Corruption in Mozambique', *U4 Anti-Corruption Resource Centre*, http://www.u4.no/publications/overview-of-corruption-and-anti-corruption-in-mozambique/.

25 Disclosure: Greg Mills has acted as an adviser to the Mozambique government, as the secretariat of the Presidential International Advisory Board from 2006–11 and to the Electricity Supply Commission (EDM) in 2017–18.

26 For details of the CNE and STAE, see http://www.ecfsadc.org/index.php/cne-mozambique.

27 See https://www.timeslive.co.za/news/africa/2018-05-09-renamo-leaders-death-a-game-changer-for-mozambique-peace-process/.

28 Lutero Simango was interviewed by Greg Mills in Maputo on 22 February 2018.

29 Correspondence, August 2017. This is based on an extensive interview with the former prime minister conducted by Greg Mills in Nairobi in January 2018.

30 Discussion, Nairobi, 28 March 2018.

31 See http://afrobarometer.org/press/despite-growing-satisfaction-with-democracy-many-kenyans-fear-political-violence.

32 See https://www.standardmedia.co.ke/business/article/2001274158/the-shame-of-jobless-kenyans.

33 For details on the Big Four plan, see https://www.nation.co.ke/news/politics/How-Uhuru-hopes-to-achieve-Big-Four-agenda/1064-4275586-rdf4pq/index.html.

34 For an excellent summary of the Chávez phenomenon, see Rory Carroll, *Comandante: Hugo Chávez's Venezuela*. London: Penguin, 2013.

35 This is based on fieldwork in Venezuela in November 2013 and March 2018. Unless otherwise cited, the interviews were conducted during the latter trip.

36 William Dobson, *Dictator's Learning Curve*. New York: Vintage, 2012, p. 96.

37 See https://rsf.org/en/ranking.

38 See https://www.bloomberg.com/news/articles/2018-02-14/most-miserable-economies-of-2018-stay-haunted-by-inflation-beast.

39 See https://freedomhouse.org/report/freedom-world/1999/venezuela.

40 See https://freedomhouse.org/blog/venezuela-sheds-its-democratic-fa-ade.
41 Disclosure: Juan-Carlos Pinzón is a member of The Brenthurst Foundation's Advisory Board.
42 Discussion, Paris, September 2018.
43 Interview, Leeuwenhof, Cape Town, April 2018.
44 Nic Cheeseman, 'Deconstructing the Magufuli Miracle in Tanzania,' 17 October 2016, https://
    africajournalismtheworld.com/2016/10/17/deconstructing-the-magufuli-miracle-in-tanzania/?fb_
    action_ids=10154594723621419&fb_action_types=news.publishes.

Chapter 6 Beginning the March to Democracy

1 Discussion, Johannesburg, 18 January 2018.
2 For an excellent summary of these negotiations, see Allister Sparks, *Tomorrow is Another
   Country: The Inside Story of South Africa's Negotiated Revolution.* Johannesburg: Struik, 1994,
   especially pp. 68–90 and pp. 109–19. The following section is based partly on a personal
   discussion and email exchange between Greg Mills and former president F.W. de Klerk during
   18–20 December 2013, and again an interview in Cape Town in April 2018.
3 Interview by Greg Mills, Cape Town, April 2018.
4 The referendum was won 69% to 31% in favour of the question: 'Do you support continuation of
   the reform process which the State President began on 2 February 1990 and which is aimed at a
   new Constitution through negotiation?'
5 General Abdulsalami Abubakar was interviewed in Addis Ababa in January 2018 by Greg Mills.
6 By 2018, Nigeria had enjoyed nearly 20 years of unbroken civilian government. Four key lessons
   stand out from Nigeria's transition to civilian leadership after nearly three decades of military
   rule. Critical to stability is, first, the need to ensure that there is not a winner-take-all approach.
   Even though he won 63% of the vote in 1999, Olusegun Obasanjo brought the other two parties
   into government. Second is the importance of providing a sense of delivery and justice, to
   secure support for democracy. In Obasanjo's case, the retrieval of $1.25 billion and £100 million
   in corrupt proceeds from Abacha and his accomplices and debt relief helped to cement this.
   Obasanjo also endeavoured to connect with the population through monthly addresses and
   phone-ins. It proved more difficult to tackle the corruption that was institutionalised through the
   devolution of power under Abacha to 36 states, which created multiple local patronage systems
   and resulted in a thin spread of available skills and experience. Stability was also ensured by the
   way in which Obasanjo cleaned the military, as soon as he took over in 1999, of those who had
   been involved in coups, replacing them with professional officers who had not been involved in
   coup-making or its benefits.
7 See http://mo.ibrahim.foundation/news/2018/
   ellen-johnson-sirleaf-wins-2017-ibrahim-prize-achievement-african-leadership/.
8 This is based on two interviews in Monrovia conducted by Greg Mills, in August 2017 and May
   2018.
9 President Weah was interviewed by Greg Mills, in August 2017 and May 2018.
10 In Burundi, members of the royal family were not technically classified as Tutsi, but as Ganwa,
   a class apart and above. Similarly, the military rulers – Micombero, Bagaza and Buyoya – were
   all from a sub-caste in Burundi known as Hima. So unlike in Rwanda, the spectrum of Tutsi in
   Burundi is usually broken down into these three sub-classes: Ganwa, Tutsi and Hima. President
   Buyoya was interviewed in Addis Ababa by Greg Mills in January 2018.
11 See http://www.executedtoday.com/2009/06/30/1962-georges-kageorgis-assassin/.
12 Interview, Addis Ababa, January 2018.

13 See https://www.reuters.com/article/us-burundi-election-results/
   burundis-nkurunziza-wins-presidential-vote-boycotted-by-rivals-idUSKCN0PY1TN20150724.

14 See https://www.news24.com/Africa/News/
   burundi-president-surprises-with-vow-to-step-down-in-2020-20180609.

15 Taiwan is not recognised by the UN as a member state. It is recognised as a province of the People's Republic of China.

16 This is based in part on a trip to Taiwan in January 2018 by Greg Mills and Jeffrey Herbst.

17 Shelley Rigger, *Why Taiwan Matters: Small Island, Global Powerhouse*. New York: Rowman & Littlefield, 2011, p. 41.

18 Note that this data is in current per capita income. Because the World Bank does not recognise Taiwan as separate from China, it does not possess (public) data. The National Statistic Agency of Taiwan only covers current US$ per capita. The Chile and Africa data is thus also in current US$ to provide a valid comparison.

19 See http://esc.nccu.edu.tw/course/news.php?Sn=166.

20 See http://teds.nccu.edu.tw/teds_plan/list.php?g_isn=117&g_tid=0&g_cid=8.

21 See Jonathan Fenby, *Tiger Head, Snake Tails*. New York: Simon & Schuster, 2013, p. 131.

Chapter 7 Ensuring Free and Fair Elections in Africa

1 See http://www.catholicherald.co.uk/news/2017/04/27/
   zambias-bishops-our-country-is-becoming-a-dictatorship-in-all-but-name/.

2 Disclosure: Tendai Biti was minister of finance in the coalition government from 2009–13 as a member of the Movement for Democratic Change.

3 For the timeline on the release of the report, see http://serve.mg.co.za/content/
   documents/2014/11/15/mgkhampepecasechronology.pdf.

4 See https://www.herald.co.zw/mbeki-slams-khampepe-report/.

5 See https://mg.co.za/article/2014-11-14-khampepe-zimbabwes-2002-elections-not-free-and-fair.

6 See http://www.qeh.ox.ac.uk/sites/www.odid.ox.ac.uk/files/www3_docs/qehwps144.pdf.

7 See https://www.theguardian.com/world/2010/nov/30/zimbabwe-mugabe-white-farmers.

8 See https://www.dailymaverick.co.za/
   article/2017-11-27-op-ed-mnangagwas-zimbabwe-breakout-nation/.

9 See https://data.worldbank.org/country/Zimbabwe.

10 See https://www.dailynews.co.zw/articles/2017/05/12/security-chiefs-love-tsvangirai.

11 See http://www.zimbabwesituation.com/news/
   zimsit_the-zimbabwe-2013-election-rigging-report-part-3/.

12 See 'Zimbabwe Electoral Commission: 305,000 Voters Turned Away,' *BBC*, 8 August 2013, https://
   www.bbc.com/news/world-africa-23618743; and https://www.economist.com/news/middle-east-
   and-africa/21583254-robert-mugabe-claims-another-dubious-victory-polls-stealing-vim.

13 See https://www.youtube.com/watch?v=EF26jAnMLeY.

14 On the surface, while the voting was peaceful and apparently harmonious, underneath the opposition alleged an 'industrial scale rig'. MDC claims centred on the absence of V11 result forms in as many as one-fifth of the nearly 11 000 voting stations, the removal of V11s at certain stations after being posted, the use of food aid to bribe rural voters, the worrying discrepancy between civil society parallel tabulations and the official results, and, most of all, the slowdown in the announcement of results, usually a telltale sign that the fix is in. Zimbabwe had just under 5.7 million registered for the 2018 election, and some 72% cast their vote on 30 July. The results of the presidential poll were known only at midnight on 2/3 August. Counting should not, at least in the

digital age, take longer than the voting procedure.

15 See https://www.news24.com/Africa/Zimbabwe/eu-mission-notes-flaws-in-zimbabwe-election-20180801; and https://www.news24.com/Africa/Zimbabwe/us-based-election-observers-criticises-zimbabwe-20180825.

16 See https://www.newsday.co.zw/2018/09/chamisa-lawyer-bares-all/.

17 See https://www.insiderzim.com/tsvangirai-says-zanu-pf-can-t-rig-economy/.

18 See http://www.freemedia.at/IPIMain/wp-content/uploads/2016/08/2016-IPI-AMI-Zambia-Press-Freedom-Mission-Report-Final.pdf. See also http://ccmgzambia.org/wp-content/uploads/2016/08/CCMG-Preliminary-EDay-Statement-12-Aug-2016.pdf.

19 The EU mission report, in noting the state broadcaster's bias, observed that news coverage on state radio and television 'largely excluded other parties, or only reported other parties negatively'. It also noted that 'provisions and application of the Public Order Act unreasonably restricted freedom of assembly to the benefit of the ruling party'. See http://africanarguments.org/2016/08/17/zambias-disputed-elections-on-binned-ballots-and-systematic-bias/.

20 The official margin was initially 13 000, but the figures originally announced by the Electoral Commission of Zambia for Lundazi were 8 000 higher than the numbers that were then provided on the official certificates. The electoral commission put this down to an administrative error.

21 'Zambia General Elections 2016: Observer Group Interim Statement', http://thecommonwealth.org/media/news/zambia-general-elections-2016-observer-group-interim-statement#sthash.sswQUDgc.dpuf. See also http://eeas.europa.eu/statements-eeas/2016/160816_01_en.htm.

22 See https://freedomhouse.org/report/freedom-world/2017/zambia.

23 Alexander Mutale, 'Zambian Elections: Clear, but Narrow, Win', *Financial Mail*, 19 August 2016, http://www.financialmail.co.za/features/2016/08/19/zambian-elections-clear-but-narrow-win.

24 'Zambian Court Throws Out Election Petition Case – Lungu to Hold Inauguration', *Africa News*, 5 September 2016, http://www.africanews.com/2016/09/05/zambian-court-throws-out-election-petition-case-lungu-to-hold-inauguration/.

25 See https://www.indexmundi.com/zambia/ethnic_groups.html.

26 Such as https://www.youtube.com/watch?v=2GyVrwyVEiE.

27 See Nasir Ahmad El-Rufai, 'Defeating a Determined Incumbent – The Nigerian Experience'. Paper prepared for a round table on elections hosted by the Konrad-Adenauer-Stiftung and The Brenthurst Foundation, Villa la Collina, Cadenabbia, Como, 7–9 May 2017. This section draws from this paper and the comments made at the event and its margins by Governor El-Rufai.

28 See https://www.vanguardngr.com/2015/02/tore-my-pdp-membership-card-obasanjo/.

29 These quotes are taken from Governor El-Rufai's interventions at the Como conference, May 2017.

30 See http://theconversation.com/why-elections-matter-for-democracy-in-africa-the-cases-of-kenya-and-rwanda-82013.

Chapter 8 A Role for Outsiders

1 See https://monusco.unmissions.org/en/facts-and-figures.

2 See source: https://stats.oecd.org/Index.aspx?DataSetCode=TABLE2A#.

3 See http://www.economist.com/node/18617876.

4 This was given on BBC Radio Four, 10 January 2014. See also https://www.theguardian.com/world/2011/may/12/48-women-raped-hour-congo.

5 See http://hdr.undp.org/en/composite/HDI.

6 See, for example, https://www.globalwitness.org/en/blog/mining-giants-forced-review-contracts-sanctioned-israeli-billionaire/; https://www.independent.co.uk/news/world/africa/

presidents-secret-deals-cost-congolese-35bn-6266335.html; and https://www.google.com/amp/s/amp.theguardian.com/business/2017/nov/05/what-is-glencore-who-is-dan-gertler-drc-mining.

7   See https://www.reuters.com/article/us-congo-politics/congo-says-it-rejects-foreign-aid-to-fund-elections-idUSKBN1H21XS.

8   For details on the alleged fraud in the 2001 election, see http://www.france24.com/en/20120224-democratic-republic-congo-election-legislative-kabila-carter-center; http://www.google.com/hostednews/afp/article/ALeqM5jlkk3cyN2vLEDkZp1-H5sTJU5xpw?docId=CNG.104a1c9e9c71e179b33042a465c95d6c.711; and http://www.congoplanet.com/news/1926/dr-congo-presidential-election-results-not-truthful-cardinal-monsengwo.jsp.

9   See https://www.foreignaffairs.com/articles/africa/2011-11-28/joseph-kabila-and-where-election-congo-went-wrong; and https://www.cia.gov/library/publications/the-world-factbook/fields/2085.html.

10   See https://euobserver.com/economic/121637; and https://www.theguardian.com/world/2012/nov/27/congo-british-aid-failure.

11   See https://foreignpolicy.com/2017/10/12/how-ballots-are-being-used-to-delay-the-congolese-election-africa-kabila-democratic-republic-congo/.

12   See https://reliefweb.int/report/democratic-republic-congo/dr-congo-ross-mountain-evaluates-costs-elections.

13   See https://www.spectator.co.uk/2013/04/the-technological-fix/.

14   Email exchange with former senior US government official, 11 July 2018.

15   See http://www2.compareyourcountry.org/aid-statistics?cr=625&cr1=oecd&lg=en&page=0; http://www2.compareyourcountry.org/aid-statistics?cr=302&cr1=oecd&lg=en&page=1; and http://www.oecd.org/dac/development-aid-rises-again-in-2016-but-flows-to-poorest-countries-dip.htm.

16   See, for example, Richard Joseph, 'The American Presidency and Democracy Promotion in Africa', *Brookings Op-ed*, 23 August 2012, https://www.brookings.edu/opinions/the-american-presidency-and-democracy-promotion-in-africa/.

17   National Intelligence Council, 'Sub-Saharan Africa: Pitched Contests for Democratization through 2022', February 2018, p. 1, https://www.dni.gov/files/images/globalTrends/documents/GT-Africa_Democratization_ForPublishing-WithCovers.pdf.

18   Telephonic interview, November 2017.

19   Interview, Johannesburg, 7 October 2017.

20   Joseph Siegle, 'Why Term Limits Matter for Africa', *Center for Security Studies blog*, 3 July 2015.

21   Disclosure: President Olusegun Obasanjo led this monitoring group.

22   See http://thecommonwealth.org/sites/default/files/inline/Uganda%20COG%20Report%20-%20Final%20-%20PRINT.pdf.

23   See https://www.eisa.org.za/pdf/uga2016eu.pdf.

24   See http://foreignpolicy.com/2016/04/29/how-election-monitors-are-failing-uganda/.

25   See https://eeas.europa.eu/headquarters/headquarters-homepage_en/10274/EU%20continues%20its%20support%20to%20the%20African%20Union%20Mission%20in%20Somalia%20(AMISOM).

26   See https://theglobalobservatory.org/2017/01/amisom-african-union-peacekeeping-financing/.

27   See http://amisom-au.org/frequently-asked-questions/.

28   See https://www.telegraph.co.uk/news/worldnews/africaandindianocean/uganda/9651943/Uganda-says-it-will-pull-out-of-Somalia-in-UN-row.html.

29   See https://www.voanews.com/a/uganda-reconsiders-pull-out-from-somali-mission/3404378.html.

30   Discussion, London, 3 July 2018.

31   Interview, 6 December 2017.

32   Discussion, Copenhagen Parliament, 13 June 2018.

33   Discussion, United Nations Development Programme, Oslo, 12 June 2018.

34 Lily Kuo, 'China's "Rogue Aid" isn't as Much or as Controversial as We Thought', *Quartz Africa*, 19 October 2017, https://qz.com/1104209/chinas-rogue-aid-to-africa-isnt-as-much-or-as-controversial-as-we-thought.

35 Interview, Stefano Manservisi, Johannesburg, 7 October 2017. The Development Assistance Committee countries are made up of: Australia, Austria, Belgium, Canada, Czech Republic, Denmark, Finland, France, Germany, Greece, Hungary, Iceland, Ireland, Italy, Japan, Korea, Luxembourg, the Netherlands, New Zealand, Norway, Poland, Portugal, Slovak Republic, Slovenia, Spain, Sweden, Switzerland, United Kingdom and the United States; the non-traditional donors: Kuwait, Saudi Arabia, Turkey, Russia and United Arab Emirates. There is no available World Bank or OECD data for Iran.

36 These statistics are taken from http://www.foreignassistance.gov.

37 See http://econofact.org/what-the-u-s-gains-from-its-development-aid-to-sub-saharan-africa.

38 Andrew Natsios, 'The Clash of the Counter-Bureaucracy and Development', July 2010, www.cgdev.org/content/publications/detail/1424271.

39 National Intelligence Council, 'Sub-Saharan Africa: Pitched Contests for Democratization through 2022', February 2018, p. 5, https://www.dni.gov/files/images/globalTrends/documents/GT-Africa_Democratization_ForPublishing-WithCovers.pdf.

40 Condoleezza Rice, *Democracy: Stories from the Long Road to Freedom.* New York: Hachette, 2017, p. 224.

41 Rice, *Democracy*, p. 223.

42 Rice, *Democracy*, p. 230.

43 Rice, *Democracy*, pp. 230–1.

44 Rice, *Democracy*, p. 234.

45 See John Campbell, 'Pulling Kenya Back from the Brink', *Council on Foreign Relations blog*, 14 March 2018, https://www.cfr.org/blog/pulling-kenya-back-brink.

46 These insights are based on a talk given by President Barrow and subsequent private discussion with Greg Mills at Chatham House, 18 April 2018.

47 See http://www.achpr.org/instruments/achpr/.

48 See https://freedomhouse.org/report/freedom-world/freedom-world-2018.

49 See http://theconversation.com/what-the-rest-of-africa-can-learn-from-the-gambias-transition-to-democracy-71822.

50 The same is true for Nigeria and Senegal in the 2015 and 2012 elections respectively, where a coalition of four major political parties in Nigeria led to the defeat of President Goodluck Jonathan's People's Democratic Party, and in Macky Sall's Benno Bokk Yakaar coalition victory in Senegal.

51 Gilbert Khadiagala, 'Regional Cooperation on Democratization and Conflict Management in Africa', *Carnegie Endowment for International Peace*, March 2018, pp. 1–2, https://carnegieendowment.org/2018/03/19/regional-cooperation-on-democratization-and-conflict-management-in-africa-pub-75769.

52 Ibid.

53 See https://freedomhouse.org/blog/5-governance-challenges-africa.

54 With thanks to Steven Gruzd for this information. See also African Union, 'African Peer Review Mechanism', http://www.au.int/en/organs/aprm; and https://www.tandfonline.com/doi/full/10.1080/09744053.2014.883757.

55 See http://www.aprm-au.org/ and https://www.youtube.com/watch?v=cdRAIQYWqTg.

56 Email correspondence, 28 October 2016.

57 See Paul Collier, Tim Besley and Adnan Khan, 'Escaping the Fragility Trap'. Report of the Commission on State Fragility, Growth and Development, chaired by David Cameron, Donald Kaberuka and Adnan Khan, International Growth Centre, London School of Economics and

Blavatnik School of Government, University of Oxford, 2018.

58 Interview, Oxford University, 10 May 2018.

59 Wiley and Zille were interviewed in April 2018.

60 See http://foreignpolicy.com/2013/11/27/the-curse-of-low-expectations/.

61 See http://foreignpolicy.com/2016/04/29/how-election-monitors-are-failing-uganda/.

62 Dinner discussion with Greg Mills, French ambassador's residence, Pretoria, 14 May 2018.

63 See https://www.bbc.co.uk/news/topics/cwlw3xz047jt/ethiopia.

64 We are grateful to the author Michela Wrong for this point.

Conclusion

1 This is based on several research trips to Somaliland by Greg Mills, including in January 2018 when President Muse Bihi Abdi and Foreign Minister Saad Shire were interviewed, and again in October 2018.

2 Like the Sahrawi Arab Democratic Republic (Western Sahara), the Republic of Somaliland is not recognised by the UN. Sahrawi, which is listed by the UN as a 'non-self-governing territory', is, however, recognised by the AU.

3 Discussion, Burao, Somaliland, April 2014.

4 'Being an Opposition Leader isn't a Crime', *Vanguard Africa Foundation*, 28 August 2018, http://vanguardafrica.com/africawatch/2018/8/28/being-an-opposition-leader-in-africa-isnt-a-crime.

5 'Zimbabwe Poll Results are Genuine – Judge Kriegler', *The Citizen*, 4 August 2018, https://citizen.co.za/news/news-africa/1991307/zimbabwe-poll-results-are-genuine-judge-kriegler/.

6 See https://www.reuters.com/article/us-kenya-election/kenyan-president-election-overturned-by-court-attacks-judiciary-idUSKCN1BD0ES.

Index